Early Childhood
EDUCATION
SECOND EDITION

TINA BRUCE

Hodder & Stoughton

A MEMBER ... NE GROUP

Order queries: please contact Bookpoint Ltd, 39 Milton Park, Abingdon, Oxon OX14
4TD. Telephone: (44) 01235 400414, Fax: (44) 01235 400454.
Lines are open from 9.00 - 6.00, Monday to Saturday, with a 24 hour message
answering service. Email address: orders@bookpoint.co.uk

British Library Cataloguing in Publication Data
A catalogue record for this title is available from The British Library

ISBN 0 340 70175 7

First published 1997
Impression number   11 10 9 8 7 6 5 4 3
Year   2004 2003 2002 2001 2000 1999 1998

Copyright © 1997 Tina Bruce

Typeset by Transet Limited, Coventry, England.
Printed in Great Britain for Hodder & Stoughton Educational, a division of
Hodder Headline Plc, 338 Euston Road, London NW1 3BH by Scotprint Ltd,
Musselburgh, Scotland.

CONTENTS

To Sybil Levy

The gods did not reveal, from the beginning
All things to us; in the course of time,
Through seeking, men find that which is the better.
But as for certain truth, no man has known it,
Nor will he know it; neither of the gods,
Nor yet of all things of which I speak.
And even if by chance he were to utter
The final truth, he would himself not know it;
For all is but a woven web of guesses

Xenophanes (c. 570–475 BC)

ACKNOWLEDGEMENTS

I should like to thank Tom Bruce for his quiet enthusiasm and sensitivity in taking the photographs in the book, and Jill Hodson and the staff, parents and children at James Lee Nursery School for making us so welcome.

My thanks also to the staff of Hodder and Stoughton, with whom I enjoy working, and Margy Whalley for her critical feedback. Thanks to Chris Athey, who has helped me more than I can ever say to enjoy thinking about and working with young children and their families and carers. Thanks to Wendy Clarke for typing and so much more!

I have really appreciated discussions with Hannah Bruce and Joanna Clarke for their practical thoughts and well thought through views on the importance of quality training for those working with other people's children, and Elizabeth Bevan Roberts who has the gift of causing thinking in very helpful ways.

Most of all, my thanks to Ian Bruce, as we move together from Silver towards Golden times, who is my best (critical) friend, who gives me real feedback, and who empowers me.

The author and publishers would also like to thank the following for permission to reproduce items in this book:

Open Books Publishing Ltd for the illustration on p.118 (top) taken from Goodnow, J. (1977) *Children's Drawing*; Rudolf Steiner Press for the illustrations on pages 118-120 taken from Strauss, M. (1978) *Understanding Children's Drawings*; Heinemann Educational Books Inc, New Hampshire for the illustrations on p.71 taken from Ferreiro and Teberosky (1983) *Literacy Before Schooling*.

INTRODUCTION TO THE SECOND

EDITION OF THE BOOK

It is now ten years since the first edition of *Early Childhood Education* was written at the suggestion of Marten Shipman, then Dean of the School of Education at Roehampton Institute of Higher Education. The essence of the first edition remains and is as important to me now as it was then. In that sense, nothing has changed. In the first edition, it was argued that if practice is to move on and develop, revisiting the core principles of philosophy and practice underlying education and care is an essential part of working with young children and their families. Re-reading what was written a decade ago, it still seems that the situation is as the philosopher Heraclitis said: 'You cannot put your hand in the same river twice'.

The river has continued to flow, and the socio-cultural context has moved on. The political climate has changed since 1987 and early childhood education and care in the UK has changed with it.

The second edition of this book is, like the first edition, about keeping the basic vision alive in ways which are appropriate for whatever lies ahead of us in the future. Keeping a sense of direction, and not being distracted from it, is an important part of this.

Covey (1992, p. 147) quotes Goethe in relation to this problem in his chapter on principles of management. 'Things which matter most must never be at the mercy of things which matter least.'

This book is for those involved in early childhood education either at the stage of initial training or subsequently when practitioners wish to assess and develop their contribution. It is for teachers, nursery nurses, members of the PLA (Pre-School Learning Alliance), parents and others with an interest in the field, such as health visitors, social workers and educational psychologists.

It attempts to reassert in a modern way, principles of the early childhood tradition in education and care, and to place them in the socio-cultural context of working with children today. This is not from a sentimental desire to continue in the past set by the early pioneers, but because there is an urgent need to conserve in them what is of value and articulate it in more modern, acceptable and accessible language. Recent theoretical and empirical evidence is introduced to produce a conceptual framework for today's needs.

Work with children has been embued with this tradition since the growth of formal education in the early nineteenth century. Such traditions are notoriously difficult to define and assess. Since the early childhood tradition directly explores how best to work with young children, it inevitably makes implicit assumptions about how the child is viewed – which might be as an empty vessel, as a person pre-programmed to unfold in certain ways, or a combination of both. However, these assumptions will rest on a view of a child that has been established in earlier times, when perhaps different versions of what a child might be dominated. It does not lead to the inevitable conclusion that what went before is outmoded and should therefore be thrown away, as Wood (1996) asserts. This would be to misunderstand the importance of review, revisiting and reflection, analysis and action to early childhood practitioners in a variety of settings. The poet T.S. Eliot encapsulates these elements in saying: 'We must not cease from exploration, and the end of our exploring will be to arrive where we began, and to know the place for the first time'.

During the last decade there has been a reduction in the number of people who are expert, knowledgeable and informed about working with young children and their families. However, with the dismantling of the disastrous Voucher Scheme and the implementation of the 'Early Excellence' document (1996) there is the real possibility that over the next decade the urgent task of passing on and sharing professional knowledge of education and care will move forward the work of early childhood education and care so that the UK regains its place in the vanguard, sharing expertise with other countries such as Reggio Emilia in Northern Italy, Spain, New Zealand (Mitchell, 1996), Finland, Denmark, Norway and Sweden (European Review, 1996), and others who have made children and families of the highest priority and invested in them in future minded spirit.

In early childhood education and care, we need to look to the future by building on the past. The core principles extrapolated (Bruce, 1987, first ed.) from the writings of pioneer educators, especially those of Froebel, Montessori and Steiner are, it seems, as important now, if not more so, than they were a decade ago. In the second edition they are revisited and the practical implications surrounding this will hopefully help early childhood workers of all kinds to make progress in the important work that they do with young children and their families.

In 1996, the Quality in Diversity Project directed by Vicky Hurst (Goldsmiths College) asked organisations to submit their literature defining views of a quality curriculum for young children. The team, Hurst, Burgess-Macey, and Ouvry, found in the documents, mostly submitted from the LEAs, but some also from voluntary and private sectors, the following six points.

1   The vast majority of the documents included a set of principles which would underpin the curriculum. Many used the principles set out by Bruce (1987) later taken up by the Early Years Curriculum Group (1989) (of which Bruce was a co-author). Examples would be Birmingham (1997) and Westminster (1993). These principles stressed the holistic nature of children's learning, the value of play and the significance of the adult's role.

Linda Miller (1997, p.36) similarly writes:

> *In 1987, Bruce in her book 'Early Childhood Education' attempted to tease out some of the common principles or beliefs which underlie the work of the pioneers in early childhood education. In 1989 these principles were adapted for publication by an influential group of early years researchers and practitioners known as the Early Years Curriculum Group, in order to offer guidance on good practice to early years educators, because of their concerns about implementing the new National Curriculum.*

2   In most of the documents there was an explanation of how young children think and learn. The importance of play and a play-based environment was stressed. This approach was claimed to be the best way of enabling the principles of early childhood education to be put into practice, particularly the principles relating to motivation and achievement on long-term learners.

3   There was general agreement in the documents about the crucial role of the adult. Good adult/child ratios and the need for sensitivity and warmth, knowledge of child development and access to high quality and initial in-service training were seen as contributing to a quality experience.

4   Space, indoor and outdoor, time for children to develop their interests, and organisation of resources to give access to provision were seen as necessary to support a quality curriculum.

5   Many of the documents cited ways of developing partnerships with parents and the importance of team-work among practitioners.

6   Many documents expressed how negative attitudes towards race, gender, disability and class can impede children's achievement.

Part 1 of this book looks, in Chapter 1, at different views of the child, in Chapter 2 at three pioneer educators, and in Chapter 3 at four modern thinkers. It is a theoretical section to identify and support core educational principles of early childhood education and care, and to put them into a modern context.

Part 2 covers the application of the principles through such topics as the curriculum, schemas, representation, communication and language. It looks at practice in the light of recent theory.

A synthesis of theory and practice is necessary because theory without practice is dead, while practice without theory has no direction. Theory with practice means that theory can inform practice enhanced with research evidence. Research evidence is no longer thought to be rigorous only if it is quantitative. The development of research projects using both quantitative and qualitative techniques have meant that there is a wider variety of research material to be drawn upon than a decade ago (for example the Effective Early Learning Project based at Worcester College of Higher Education under the direction of

Professor Christine Pascal). Such research projects help practitioners to see more clearly. Working with children in this way is energising, fulfilling and challenging, as well as being highly skilled.

The book finishes with four action points comprising an agenda for change which emphasises the socio-cultural context in which children develop and grow up, as well as the biological path that development takes (Dawkins, 1993, Bruce and Meggitt, 1996 p.236).

1   The need for a deeper knowledge of both child development and subject content.

2   The need to become less child-centred and more 'child-in-the-family'/community centred.

3   The need to work for better co-ordination and co-operation between existing services, resources and specialists.

4   The need for a sounder conceptual framework from which to operate and better ways of assessing and evaluating it.

These points of action will guard against stagnation and enable the contribution of the early childhood tradition to be incorporated into a continually renewed and regenerated framework.

PART 1

THE
EARLY CHILDHOOD
EDUCATION TRADITION

What it is and
where it comes from

1
■

THREE DIFFERENT VIEWS

OF THE CHILD

P eople working with young children profess a superficial consensus in their approaches, but closer inspection reveals confusion and disagreement. Some writers emphasise these while dismissing the areas of agreement (Penn, 1995, Wood, 1996). This book explores whether there can be any pattern, as well as any major areas of agreement, about how best to work with young children and their families.

First it is necessary to explore different ways of looking at the child. Until we are clear about the way we view children, we cannot begin to work with them, nor is it easy to work in partnership with other educators, carers or parents, because our assumptions about the child are crucial in influencing our practice. It would be easy to say that the only thing that matters in working with young children is a love of them, and enjoyment of them and a commitment to encouraging their maximum development. Yet it is amazing how far our gut reactions can take us and no-one denies that some situations cannot be presented verbally. However, this does not allow the possibility of sharing our thoughts about young children's development with colleagues and parents. 'Gut reactions' are difficult to articulate, yet articulation is essential if communication is considered a high priority.

In recent years, experts outside the field of early childhood education have exerted great influence on some practioners and taken control of curriculum content and even of methods. This is perhaps because early childhood workers have not been able to articulate their philosophy in action (Bruce 1991, Bruce, Findlay, Read and Scarborough, 1995). This has not been helped by the fact that few adults working with young children in the 1990s are trained for the work (Blenkin, Rose and Yue, 1996).

There are basically three main stances towards the child. One, often called the **empiricist** view, is the one that the child is an empty vessel to be filled. This derives from the philosophy of John Locke (1632–1704). At the opposite end of the spectrum is the **nativist** view that children are pre-programmed to unfold in certain directions. This is influenced by the philosopher Jean-Jacques Rousseau (1712–1778). These are combined in the third, or **interactionist** view, which is that children are partly empty vessels and partly pre-programmed, and that there is an interaction within and between the two. Immanuel Kant (1724–1804) originated this approach.

EMPIRICISM

The empiricist view implicitly subscribes to a deficit model of the child. The role of the adult is to identify missing experiences, skills, concepts and so on, to select appropriate experiences and transmit them to the child. This orientation came to the fore during the compensatory education movement of the late 1960s with Bereiter and Engelmann as clear proponents (Engelmann, 1971). This work built on the work of the psychologists Watson (1878–1958) and Skinner (1904–).

In 1925 Watson wrote:

> . . . *give me a dozen healthy infants, well-formed and my own special world to bring them up in and I will guarantee to take any one at random and train him to become any type of specialist I might select – doctor, lawyer, artist, merchant-chief and, yes, even beggarman and thief – regardless of his talents, penchants, tendencies, abilities and vocation and race of his ancestors (in Schaffer, 1996, p.20)*

This quote demonstrates how children in this approach are seen as something to be moulded into shape, and given experiences which are appropriate and necessary for them to take their place in society. Habit formation is valued and learning is broken down into meaningful sequences – for example, children are taught step-by-step to tie their shoes, hold their knives and forks correctly, sing songs which are part of their heritage, know their letters and numbers and so on. In the early childhood tradition, empiricism has always held a place.

Depending on whether we support the view of the child as passive recipient or as an active explorer of experiences, the adult's role in working with that child will completely change. In other words, there may be agreement that the child is shaped by events, situations, objects or people that he or she meets, but there is disagreement over the nature of that shaping.

NATIVISM

The nativist or biologically pre-programmed view of the child suggests that humans are biologically pre-programmed with a propensity to unfold in certain ways. Bower (1974, p.2) describes the nativist view 'that human knowledge and human skill were built into the structure of the organism'. Typical supporters of this stance would be Gesell, Erikson (a psychodynamic theorist) and more recently, Chomsky. For Gesell (1954, p.13), growth is seen as being

> . . . *laid down by intrinsic patterning prior to and independent of actual experience . . . environment predicts preliminary patterns; it determines the occasion, the intensity and the correlation of many aspects of behaviour development, but it does not engender the basic progressive behaviour development. These are determined by inherent maturational mechanisms.*

Sophie (aged one year) begins to walk when she is ready, not before, holding the armchairs and moving further and further from one to the other in the room. This view is supported by Erikson, (1963, p.11), another educationalist of the nativist tradition: 'If we only learn to let live, the plan for growth is all there'. Chomsky reasserts this stance when he claims that we have an innate propensity for language. The environment dictates the kind of language learned, but the Language Acquisition Device (LAD) is a genetic part of being a human.

Of the above two polarised views, empiricist and nativist, both the philosopher Robert Dearden (1968), and psychologist Kathy Sylva (BAECE Lecture, 1995) have suggested that the nativist stance is the dominant influence on the early childhood tradition. Certainly its influence is strong. In that tradition there remains a feeling that adults might interfere in a child's learning by intervening in the wrong way at an inappropriate moment. Some aspects of the child's world are seen as private and sacrosanct. Children need to play and develop creatively with imagination. Adults can offer help, but in this approach they should never insist upon it. They need to be highly skilled in the way they approach children.

The home area in an early years setting is often one such sacrosanct area with walls around it so children can be away from adults in a 'world of their own'. Inevitably this leads to a major emphasis on relationships with adults and peers, based on respect for the child's unfolding development. These assertions stem from the nativist influence on the early childhood tradition.

Dearden (1968) places the educators Montessori and Froebel in this category. Sylva sees Froebel as for non-interference. That either Montessori or Froebel take such an approach is challenged in later chapters of this book, which argues that both Montessori and Froebel are interactionist educators.

Inadequacies of either empiricism or nativism

Howard Gardner (1982) points out the dangers of adherence to one over-arching stance. He argues that this tends to narrow the approach to problems rather than opening up the exploration of them. In fact, the early childhood tradition is too complex for one to say that it sees the child from a dominantly empiricist or a nativist viewpoint.

Different emphases become the choice in different historic periods and in different parts of the world. Certainly the nativist view of the child has had its periods of ascendancy, especially in Europe, and empiricism has had periods of dominance, primarily in the USA. However, in reality the early childhood tradition is capable of embracing a much more complex approach than either of these two polarised approaches. It can even be argued that, by polarising the different ways of regarding children, the early childhood tradition has been held back in its development. Either/or situations are rarely helpful in advancing thinking. It will be seen in Chapters 2 and 3 that in reality the early childhood tradition has not taken extreme stances. As it develops it turns to the theories which seem to offer most support at each period.

Empiricism and nativism are two theories which ought to lead to entirely different ways of working with young children. In a sense, however, despite the great differences between them ideologically, they are often more polarised in theory than they are in practice (Bruce 1985; Bruce, Findlay, Read and Scarborough, 1995). This may well be because of the inadequacy of the theoretical support that either of these theories alone can give to the early childhood tradition. In the practical setting, people have to get on with the job in the absence of satisfactory theoretical support for their work. Both stances have, in fact, exerted strong influences over the early childhood tradition, but since in many respects they present diametrically-opposed ways of viewing the child, it is no wonder that there is a confusion and a lack of articulation about how the aims of that tradition can be reached in practice. If early childhood education is to move forward, which it needs to do, more adequate ways of viewing the child are needed which are not embedded in obsolete or incomplete theories (Athey, 1990).

INTERACTIONISM

Recently the early childhood tradition had drawn support from a view of the child which is less polarised than either empiricism or nativism. This is the interactionist view which Tom Bower (1975, p.241) summarises. He claims that development occurs as

> . . . *environmental events interacting with maturationally generated behaviours. The major causal factors in cognitive developments are behaviours interacting with other behaviours in their application to environmental events.*

In other words in this view of the child, which stems from the philosophy of Kant and later finds support in the philosophy of Popper, not only do the child's structures interact with each other, but they also alter each other. There is interaction with what is external, but there is also interaction within the child through the senses. This is a much more sophisticated view of the child.

At the present time it could also seem to be the most useful way of viewing the child. The interactionist view is supported by recent research which is social constructivist (Athey, 1990) and also supported by socio-cultural strands in the research (Rogoff, 1993) and by studies of the brain (Trevarthen, 1996; Greenfield, 1996). It places emphasis on the context in which children grow up and develop as much as the biological path of their development.

It implicitly reasserts the view of the pioneers of the early childhood tradition, that the role of the adult is critical. Adults are not seen as empiricist instructors giving out information and knowledge. Instead they are seen as the means, the mechanism by which children can develop their own strategies, initiatives and responses, and construct their own rules which enable their development.

In this approach children are not seen as nativist sole instigators of their knowledge, pre-programmed to act as they do, and held back, or helped as the case may be, by the variations in the environment and culture. They are instead supported by adults who help them to make maximum use of the environment and cultural setting.

The key to the interactionist approach in early childhood education lies in the notion of reciprocity or give and take – that is, sometimes the child leads and sometimes the adult leads. For example, work by Colwyn Trevarthen (1993), who has over many years studied proto-conversations between adults and babies, has shown the importance of give and take (reciprocity) in conversations.

Work with musicians by Trevarthen (1996) and colleagues shows how the musical rhythm of the conversation between babies and carers means that babies come in with a particular rhythm and beat with unerring accuracy when their mother talks with them. Similarly the earlier work of Gordon Wells (1983) showed how important it was that adults do not dominate in conversations between adults and children, but are involved in shared focus and exchanges of ideas and feelings. These research studies support the view of the pioneer educators. In short, the interactionist view of the child supports the main principles of the early childhood tradition which will be considered in Chapter 2, as well as matching with recent research findings.

The next chapter looks at the principles of the early childhood tradition and examines the work of three pioneers of early childhood education – Froebel, Montessori and Steiner – through the interactionist view. Using this stance, it is possible to give their thoughts considerable support theoretically, although it is necessary to update the terminology which surrounds their work.

Without doubt these thinkers have had great influence on the education of young children in the UK over the years, and the early childhood tradition has maintained a fairly steady course due to the work of an always small band of deeply committed workers continuing and developing those traditions.

With increased attention now being given to the theoretical context against which to view the assertions of the early childhood tradition, it is time to move on and develop a modern synthesis incorporating the work of the early pioneers in early childhood education and care.

It is also important to look beyond the UK, and examine the diversity in different cultures in educating and caring for young children and the variety of family and early years settings that can be found according to the culture.

However, to throw away all attempts to find universal, or core areas of agreement across humanity on the grounds that every culture is completely different (Penn, 1995; Wood, 1995), is to throw the baby out with the bath water. Differences are certainly important, but so are the areas of commonality both biologically and socio-culturally. Human diversity is not the same as fragmentation. It is important not to conclude that the richness of diversity across cultures means that it is not possible to find core principles.

The aim in this book is not to preserve a uniform, standardised or static approach to work with children from 0 to 8 years, but instead to conserve that which is found to be worthwhile and to build upon it. There seems little sense in preserving obsolete ways of looking at children, or taking only a westernised view of children, when more up-to-date research and theories may help us to re-evaluate and move forward the work begun by the early pioneers (Bruce, Findlay, Read and Scarborough, 1995). It is necessary to look across time and space to what we can learn from history and other cultures on a trans-global scale.

It is therefore important to assess the heritage of early childhood work in different cultures and in different parts of the world. The interpretation of the core principles will vary in Finland, New Zealand, South America, the USA, Indonesia or India, in both the broad sense and also in the interpretation of individual early childhood specialists who may vary in their outlook, even within a culture.

The interactionist view is a broad one within which there is inevitably a measure of debate and lack of agreement. It nevertheless gives present-day support to the early childhood tradition, both in theoretical ways and through research evidence.

Which philosopher influenced the approach	Which psychologist influenced the approach	Key ideas in the approach
EMPIRICISM John Locke (1632–1704)	Watson (1878–1958) and Skinner (1904)	The child is an empty vessel to be filled, or a lump of clay that can be moulded into shape. Habit formation is important. Learning/teaching is broken down into simple steps from a complex sequence (an accretion view of learning). Learning is seen as a hierarchy from simple to complex. Knowledge can be transmitted from one person to another e.g. teacher/parent to another child/group. There is emphasis on the influence of experience and socio-cultural aspects. The adult leads the child's learning and dominates it.

Which philosopher influenced the approach	Which psychologist influenced the approach	Key ideas in the approach
NATIVISM Rousseau 1712–1778	Gesell (1880–1961) Erikson (1902–1994) Chomsky (1928–)	The child is pre-programmed for development to unfold. This is determined by genetically pre programmed maturational mechanisms. The socio-cultural aspects influence, for example, the language a child speaks. If a child hears Chinese then the child learns to speak that language, but the mechanisms for learning language are already there. Adults observe children to monitor progress and emphasise milestones of normal development and check for readiness, such as in learning to read. The child is seen as leading his/her own learning, with the adult there as facilitator.

Which philosopher influenced the approach	Which psychologist influenced the approach	Key ideas in the approach
INTERACTIONISM Immanual Kant 1724–1804	Piaget (1896–1980) Vygotsky (1896–1934) Dunn (1939–)	This integrates empiricism and nativism. This approach recognises that there are biologically pre-programmed ideas to development, but it places just as much emphasis on the socio-cultural context in which the child grows up (the people and the material world, the culture). The context varies greatly according to the culture and the physical environment in different places, in one country or trans-globally. People are very important in this approach, both other children and adults. Sometimes the adults lead the child's learning and sometimes the child leads. It is a bit like a conversation. Different people can start conversations but the different speakers need to listen to each other and respond to what each says appropriately and relevantly.

2
■

TEN COMMON PRINCIPLES

OF THE PIONEERS:

THE BEDROCK OF THE EARLY

CHILDHOOD TRADITION

The Introduction stressed the pervasive influence, not just in the UK but trans-globally, of core principles of the early childhood tradition, and the need to understand and reflect on this heritage if today's early childhood workers are to be effective.

This chapter looks at three of the most influential pioneers in early childhood education and care in the UK, and draws out commonalities between them which form the bedrock of that common law, both in the UK and beyond. They are Friedrich Wilhelm **Froebel** (1782–1852), Maria **Montessori** (1869–1952) and Rudolf **Steiner** (1861–1925). All have an international reputation and influence. Each has influenced schools in different parts of the world which claim to use their approaches; each has training colleges where teachers learn about their ideas; but, perhaps most importantly, all have significantly influenced mainstream education in Europe and North America. All three were skilled practitioners as well as being educational theorists. Each was concerned, amongst other things, with world citizenship, respect for individual needs, poverty and the concept of community.

Other pioneer educators such as Pattie Smith Hill (USA), Margaret McMillan (UK) and Susan Isaacs (UK), each working in the Froebelian tradition, have also been influential in contributing to these common principles and traditions, but not across all the criteria mentioned above.

The work of these pioneer educators with young children and their families reveals a set of common principles which have endured and still have a useful future. The agreements, rather than the disagreements, between them have been fundamental in creating the 'early childhood tradition'. The emphasis in this book is on keeping the heritage in the spirit of conservation, not preservation and ossification, as discussed in the last chapter. The early childhood tradition embraces diversity, rather than fragmentation, standardisation and uniformity.

The early pioneers used language which is difficult to understand today, and this means that their common principles have become obscured. When differences between people are highlighted, the common ground between them is quickly lost. It is important to identify when differences of value become irreconcilable, or when values are shared but their practical interpretation is different.

The commonalities between Froebel, Montessori and Steiner has been under-emphasised by the vastly different practical interpretation of the principles in the 'demonstration' schools of each of these pioneers. Ironically, it is in mainstream schools where the principles and practices of the three have come together, but this has been largely through a process of osmosis and has often resulted in very confused practice and ill-defined principles.

The need to revisit, rework and own the core principles of practice in early childhood education and care is demonstrated by re-framing the wording of 1987 into that of 1996 (Bruce and Meggitt, 1996). In the first edition of this book (1987) the ten common principles were quoted as follows:

---

1   Childhood is seen as valid in itself, as part of life and not simply as preparation for adulthood. Thus education is seen similarly as something of the present and not just preparation and training for later.

2   The whole child is considered to be important. Health – physical and mental – is emphasised, as well as the importance of feelings and thinking and spiritual aspects.

3   Learning is not compartmentalised, for everything links.

4   Intrinsic motivation, resulting in child-initiated, self directed activity, is valued.

5   Self-discipline is emphasised.

6   There are specially receptive periods of learning at different stages of development.

7   What children can do (rather than what they cannot do) is the starting point in the child's education.

8   There is an inner life in the child which emerges especially under favourable conditions.

9   The people (both adults and children) with whom the child interacts are of central importance.

10   The child's education is seen as an interaction between the child and the environment the child is in – including, in particular, other people and knowledge itself.

© Tina Bruce 1987 (*Early Childhood Education*, first edition)

The ten bedrock principles revisited (1996) by Bruce and re-framed are as follows:

1   The best way to prepare children for their adult life is to give them what they need as children.

2   Children are whole people who have feelings, ideas and relationships with others, and who need to be physically, mentally, morally and spiritually healthy.

3   Subjects such as mathematics and art cannot be separated; young children learn in an integrated way and not in neat, tidy compartments.

4   Children learn best when they are given appropriate responsibility, allowed to make errors, decisions and choices, and respected as autonomous learners.

5   Self-discipline is emphasised. Indeed, this is the only kind of discipline worth having. Reward systems are very short-term and do not work in the long-term. Children need their efforts to be valued.

6   There are times when children are especially able to learn particular things.

7   What children can do (rather than what they cannot do) is the starting point of a child's education.

8   Imagination, creativity and all kinds of symbolic behaviour (reading, writing, drawing, dancing, music, mathematical numbers, algebra, role play and talking) develop and emerge when conditions are favourable.

9   Relationships with other people (both adults and children) are of central importance in a child's life.

10 Quality education is about three things: the child, the context in which learning takes place, and the knowledge and understanding which the child develops and learns.

© Tina Bruce (in Bruce and Meggitt, 1996, p.362–3)

In the next section of this chapter the ten common principles are taken in turn, and supported through reference to the interactionist philosophies of Froebel, Montessori and Steiner.

1   THE BEST WAY TO PREPARE CHILDREN FOR THEIR ADULT LIFE IS TO GIVE THEM WHAT THEY NEED AS CHILDREN

Froebel, Montessori and Steiner agree that childhood (0–8) is not merely a period when children are prepared and trained for adult life. It is a phase of life which is important in its own right although, as a by-product, the more richly childhood is experienced the more strongly the adult phase can be entered. The foundation stones are different in kind to the latter building material, but have an effect on the building as a whole. Giving children what they need during childhood is the best preparation for adulthood. Froebel saw the family as the most important first educator in the child's life. Joachim Liebschner (1985, p.35) points out that Froebel believed women were not only important in their role as parents, but were capable of teaching children, too. This was a revolutionary idea at that time! The school was seen as a community, where home and school came together. Froebel (1887, p. 89) said: 'Let us live with our children, let them live with us, so shall we gain through them what all of us need'.

Children and adults learn from each other, and enrich each other's lives. Children are not seen as being in need of instruction on how to achieve an all-knowing adulthood. Childhood is seen as a different state from adulthood, one which takes from and gives to the community in its own way (Bruce, Findlay, Read and Scarborough 1995, p.18).

Montessori also recognised the different nature of childhood. Again, she did not see the role of the adult as preparing children for adulthood. Childhood is a state to be protected and allowed to develop without damage in a specially prepared environment

> that protects the child from the difficult and dangerous obstacles that threaten him/her in the adult world. The shelter in the storm, the oasis in the desert, the place of spiritual rest ought to be created in the world precisely to assure the healthy development of the child (Montessori, 1975, p.13)

She argued that 'the child is a personality separate from the adult'. Children need different treatment, but not, for Montessori, in a community where adults 'live with their children' in the Froebelian sense. Montessori argued instead for a separate environment where adults do not enter the child's world – except for the trained directress who 'liberates' the child. Childhood is seen as a state with needs quite apart from adult life, existing in its own right.

For Steiner also there is no question of childhood simply preparing children for adulthood. Again, it exists as a period of life in its own right. In his philosophy, life after death is seen as another aspect of life before birth. There is therefore no question of childhood being 'preparation for life' but rather the idea of helping a newcomer to find his or her way. As children progress through the three phases of childhood, which involve, first, the 'will', then the 'heart' or feelings, and lastly the 'head', a fusion of spirit and body takes place.

However, during the first seven years, the period of 'willing', the child's newly reincarnated soul must be protected. The environment is therefore carefully planned (Wilkinson, 1980, p. 6):

> While the adult can offer a certain resistance to his environment, the child accepts it, drinks it in. Thus the whole environment of the child should be a positive, harmonious one.

Steiner, like Montessori, separated the child from the world during the first seven years and placed him/her in a carefully planned environment. They differ from Froebel who, while he also saw childhood as a stage with its own needs, distinct from adulthood, nevertheless saw the child as being in the community and the school as within that community. None of them saw childhood as simply preparation for adult life. Froebel, Montessori and Steiner all saw childhood as a part of life, with its own particular needs and requirements, which are important in their own right.

2 CHILDREN ARE WHOLE PEOPLE WHO HAVE FEELINGS, IDEAS AND RELATIONSHIPS WITH OTHERS, AND WHO NEED TO BE PHYSICALLY, MENTALLY, MORALLY AND SPIRITUALLY HEALTHY

Froebel, Montessori and Steiner all considered the development of the whole child to be of enormous importance.

Froebel saw the whole child as including the physical, spiritual, feeling and intellectual aspects of the person. Like Montessori and Steiner, he gave a great deal of thought to how the whole child could be developed through an appropriate curriculum. His notion of 'kindergarten', the garden of children, partly emphasises nature, partly community and partly family (Bruce, Findlay, Read and Scarborough, 1995).

Froebel addressed himself to the physical needs of the child through the 'forms of life', which involved the senses and first-hand experiences, to the feelings and imagination of the child through the 'forms of beauty' – music, arts and crafts, nature and mathematics. He addressed himself to the thinking of the child through the 'forms of knowledge'. The moral and spiritual pervades everything (Liebschner, 1991; 1992).

In his earlier work Froebel approached this through his 'Mother Songs' (1878), 'Gifts', 'Occupations', 'Movement Games' and the garden (1887). Every experience presented to the child was presented first as a whole. The first Gift was the soft sphere, the second Gift was the cube, cylinder and wooden sphere. The third, fourth, fifth and sixth Gifts were cubes divided in different ways comprising small wooden blocks (bricks) which could be built into a larger one. Only after being presented whole were they broken down into parts. The whole preceded the parts.

Later, Froebel moved increasingly away from a set curriculum and became more interested in the process of play in the child, which he began to see as the mediator between opposing forces, the natural and spiritual, emotion and intellect. In other words, he saw play as a means by which the child maintains the wholeness of his/her experiences (Bruce, 1989; 1991; 1996).

Play is a unifying mechanism and for this reason, it was for Froebel the most spiritual activity of the child. For him no single aspect in development was more important than any other. The whole child is the child where all aspects of development are enabled.

While Montessori believed equally strongly in the whole child, she approached the concept quite differently. She created a simple-to-complex hierarchical model. Each sense is developed separately and in isolation – (visual, aural, baric (weight) learning and so on) – through a sequence of carefully graded, simple-to-complex exercises. She considered that, as children master each step and arrive at the end of a sequence, they are then in a position to use in a general way the skills acquired:

> but, once the handicraft leading to the construction of vases has been learned (and this is part of the progress in the work learned from the direct and graduated instruction of the teacher), anyone can modify it according to the inspiration of his aesthetic tastes, and this is the artistic, individual part of the work (Montessori, 1912, p.22).

Montessori took each part of the child's development and built it to make the whole through her simple-to-complex model (Bruce, 1984). This contrasts with Froebel, who saw the whole as a network or matrix and helped the child to find order in it through an integrated approach in which play is the co-ordinating mechanism. In their different ways, both Froebel and Montessori stressed the 'whole child'.

Steiner was also concerned with the whole child. He believed that we bring various qualities with us into life. The whole child emerges as the four-fold picture of man (Steiner, 1965, p.21) involving the physical body, the life body, the soul element and individuality. Uneven development is seen as damaging.

> It is always a matter of balance in human values. An all-round harmonious development is the first aim, furtherance of special talent can come later (Wilkinson, 1980, p.16).

Steiner stressed different aspects of development at different stages, all of which contribute to the whole adult, but are important as phases in their own right. The wholeness comes from the way the spirit and body increasingly fuse. First, the spirit fuses with the limbs (the period of the 'will') which occurs in the first seven years. Then the spirit fuses with the rhythmic system – heart, chest, respiratory (the period of 'feeling') – during the years from seven to fourteen; then the spirit fuses with the 'head' (the period of thinking) from fourteen years of age. Life after death is seen as another aspect of life before birth. This all focusses on processes in the child.

Steiner was like both Froebel and Montessori in that he lay great emphasis on processes in the child. For him, moral sense, social feelings and religious attitude are influenced by the experiences offered to the child. The wholeness of the child's life is affected by nutrition (Steiner was a vegetarian) and proper rest (rest and activity need to be balanced).

Steiner considered that the whole is reflected in each of its parts. In this respect he was more like Froebel than Montessori. The whole comes first. (This is unlike Montessori's simple-to-complex hierarchical model.) Nevertheless, Froebel, Montessori and Steiner all emphasised the whole child and the whole cultural environment of the child, which is considered in the next section.

3   SUBJECTS SUCH AS ART AND MATHEMATICS CANNOT BE SEPARATED; YOUNG CHILDREN LEARN IN AN INTEGRATED WAY AND NOT IN NEAT, TIDY COMPARTMENTS

In the last section emphasis on the whole child was highlighted. In this section the wholeness of knowledge and the fact that everything connects is stressed. Nothing can be compartmentalised. Froebel (1887, p.128) believed that:

> *The school endeavours to render the scholar fully conscious of the nature and inner life of things and of himself and teach him to know the inner relations of things to one another, to the human being, scholar and living source and conscious unity of all things.*

This 'conscious unity of all things' was central to Froebel's philosophy. He saw a unity between home and school, and community and nature, and between different areas of knowledge. We saw in the last section the links between different aspects of the child's development. Froebel (1887, p.134) said:

> *Never forget that the essential business of the school is not so much to teach, but to communicate the variety and multiplicity of all things as it is to give prominence to the everlasting unity that is in all things.*

The soft ball (the first Gift) contrasts with and contradicts the wooden ball (the second Gift). In Froebel's notion of a sequence, there is not a smooth progression but slight changes in the familiar, since learning involves challenges to what is already known. This has important implications later in this book, when differences and common features in people are focussed upon. (Bruce, Findlay, Read and Scarborough, 1995)

In both the last section and in this, Froebel's approach to the whole and to unity across different aspects of the whole is stressed. Everything relates and connects. In the same way Montessori's simple-to-complex model can be applied both to her view of the whole child and links within and between knowledge. For Montessori, the links are gradually built, step by step, and a complicated world is thereby carefully made comprehensible. This is carried out through the use of didactic materials, or the carefully sequenced exercises of practical life. She isolated each sense, and developed each sense independently – baric, thermic, visual and so on – 'from the education of the senses to general notions, from general notions to abstract thought, from abstract thought to morality' (Montessori, 1912, p.4).

In the last section it became clear that Froebel began with the whole and worked towards the parts, whereas Montessori began with the simple and worked towards the complex.

The same applies to the way knowledge is not compartmentalised but linked. However, both Froebel and Montessori saw the whole, and the way different parts link, as important features in early childhood.

Steiner's notion of unity is more like Froebel's in that he wanted to help children towards the essential unity by formulating a network across different areas of knowledge and different stages of development, which would illuminate unifying concepts in different contexts. For instance, justice was explored in early education through the child's temperament balanced by activity and imitation. This is done with the help of the early years worker who is a mother-figure. Later, it is explored through the history of the Romans, and later still through the notion of justice as an idea, with the Romans as one example of a culture to be compared and analysed alongside others. For Steiner, natural science, literature, mathematics – indeed all areas of knowledge – link and (as seen in the previous section) so do the different facets of the child's development.

Both Froebel and Steiner saw links between subjects and between different aspects of the child's development as beginning with the home. Montessori reached the whole through the parts in a separate environment. Froebel did not stipulate a particular order and method in the way experiences are offered to the child – his later emphasis on play moved him steadily away from this. Later in this chapter, this idea will become important, as it leads towards an informally structured interactionist approach to early childhood. Montessori and Steiner, however, helped the child towards links within knowledge and unity within themselves through a formally structured interactionist approach, with a clearly set down curriculum. Froebel, Montessori and Steiner agreed that the whole and the linkage of the parts to the whole are equally important.

4   CHILDREN LEARN BEST WHEN THEY ARE GIVEN APPROPRIATE RESPONSIBILITY, ALLOWED TO MAKE ERRORS, DECISIONS AND CHOICES, AND RESPECTED AS AUTONOMOUS LEARNERS

Froebel, Montessori and Steiner agreed that children are self-motivating. There is no need for adults to find ways of motivating them. The difficulty lies in that adults tend to cut across the child's self-motivation because of a tendency to be too dominant.

Froebel made the distinction between play and work. Play is what children are involved in when they initiate the task, and work is what they do when they fulfil a task required by an adult. If the child is required to work rather than play, he or she follows a task presented to him by another, and does not reveal his or her own creativeness and inclinations but those of another. The skill of the adult educator is in entering the child's play, led by the initiative of the child, as a partner who shares the process. The adult may intervene sensitively (not interfere) when appropriate, so that the child is not dominated by the adult, but equally is not left to flounder.

Adults can support and extend children's play. There are moments when children do not require help and moments when they do. The skill of the adult, in Froebel's view, lies in knowing how and when to intervene. Through play, children can actively manipulate, rearrange, act on and reflect on their learning. Adults reflect through discussion, through literature, through writing and meditation. Children reflect through acting out past experiences, or preparing for them. Play helps them to grasp and try out their learning in concrete ways.

So Froebel, through his attitude to play, can be seen to value child-initiated and child-directed activity. He did not stress play as the only aspect of self-directed, self-motivated activity. He also emphasised the arts, natural science, mathematics, and all the areas of knowledge in the curriculum. He saw these as another mechanism through which children would make 'the inner outer and the outer inner'. As seen in Principles 2 and 3, processes in the child's development, and encounters with different areas of knowledge, emphasise and affect the child's ability to initiate and self-direct.

Montessori also stressed intrinsic motivation and the self-directed child-initiative which results. Her prepared environment was designed to encourage self-chosen tasks. In Montessori's approach, self-direction is encouraged by 'real' tasks, or apparatus which is based on Montessori's observation of children's natural concerns – for example, the way children love to put objects into rows or to build towers. However, Montessori did not value play. She saw it as an insult to the child: 'If I were persuaded that children need to play, I would provide the proper apparatus, but I am not so persuaded' (Kilpatrick, 1914, p.42). She felt that children search for a real life. Rather than toys, Montessori argues:

> We must give the child an environment that he can utilise by himself: and a little
> wash-stand of his own, some small chairs, a bureau with drawers he can open, objects
> of common use that he can operate, a small bed in which he can sleep at night under an
> attractive blanket he can fold and spread by himself (Montessori, 1975, p.116).

Her exercises of practical life were geared towards real household tasks. However, her rejection of play does not mean a rejection of self-direction: 'To take certain objects and to present them in a certain fashion to the child, and then to leave the child alone with them and not to interfere' (Montessori, 1949, p.253).

Her materials offered children choices of a different nature, within a prescribed sequence. For Montessori, children need a prepared environment in which the complicated world is simplified by means of a set sequence for the children to move through, with the tranquillity which develops concentration. The highest moment is the silence which attends the 'polarisation of the attention', when the child is so absorbed that he or she is not in communication with others. Self-motivation is fed most by isolating children from the world, and its height is reached by their choosing to isolate themselves within the prepared environment which was so designed that they may be enabled and free to do so (Bruce, 1976).

Steiner dealt with self-directed activity differently. During the early years, the child lives mainly in the 'will' element, where the spirit is beginning to fuse with the limbs. The teacher understands the temperament of each child. Children tends to be sanguine (calm), choleric (easily angered), phlegmatic (sluggish) and melancholic (peevish). Often they are a combination of these. The teacher helps the children to use their natural temperament for the best. Francis Edmund (1979, p.61) says of Steiner: 'His golden rule is never to go against the temperament of a child but always go with it'. In other words, the temperament or intrinsic motivation of the child is considered the self-directing force. Children need to be carefully observed in order to establish the way they are to be grouped and what help they will need in order that their intrinsic motivation can best be allowed to develop of itself. Different children require different kinds of help within the stage of their predominant will. The key to this stage is the point when the child actively wants to do things and has the urge to initiate.

The right setting for and organisation of this stage for individual temperaments are part of the promotion of intrinsic motivation which frees the child to initiate and self-regulate. By the age of fourteen, having progressed from the early stage of the 'will' through the period of the 'heart' or feelings to the period of the 'head', the young man or woman can self-direct his or her attention towards causes, reasons and explanations. These young people have the freedom to explore ideas.

Self-directed activity varies according to the different approaches. Froebel emphasised the value of play and language, actions, feelings and thoughts. Montessori emphasised the value of real tasks, and Steiner emphasised the different needs of the stages of the will, the heart and the head in relation to this. However, all three stressed self-directed, child-initiated activity as aspects of intrinsic motivation. Intrinsic motivation is fundamental to all three philosophies.

5 SELF-DISCIPLINE IS EMPHASISED. INDEED, THIS IS THE ONLY KIND OF DISCIPLINE WORTH HAVING. REWARD SYSTEMS ARE VERY SHORT-TERM AND DO NOT WORK IN THE LONG-TERM. CHILDREN NEED THEIR EFFORTS TO BE VALUED.

The development of self-discipline is closely linked with intrinsic motivation, and with the need to promote it by allowing children to initiate and self regulate tasks, activities and ideas. Self-discipline is probably one of the most important elements in life. Without it, no matter how imaginative, creative, logical, or skilful a person is, there will be no development towards the completion of the work. Froebel, Montessori and Steiner all agreed that self-discipline emerged from keeping intrinsic motivation intact.

We saw how Froebel emphasised play as a means by which the child willingly sees things through to completion. This sort of environment favours the development of self-discipline – the strong, confident self with sufficiently high self-esteem not to be distracted from fulfilling an objective, or working towards ideals. Froebel (1887, p.131) said: 'The faith and trust, the hope and anticipation with which the child enters school accomplishes everything.'

The early years worker must not destroy this, but a dialogue with and respect for the child will help self-discipline emerge – a discipline that is an inner influence rather than an external force. The partnership element of the relationship between adult and child was stressed. The adult helps the child to articulate and understand events in which he or she has participated through language, play and activities. Inner influence rather than external force is the key to the emergence of self-discipline. Froebel would shudder to see any kind of extrinsic reward.

At the centre of Froebel's approach to discipline was his belief that the child's intrinsic motivation should not be damaged. This is encouraged by his belief that humans are basically good. He rejected the notion of original sin. He said:

> . . the only and infallible remedy for counteracting any shortcoming and even
> wickedness is to find the originally good source, the originally good side of the human
> being that has been repressed, disturbed, or misled into the shortcoming, and then to
> foster, build up, and properly guide this good side. Thus the shortcoming will at last
> disappear, although it may involve a hard struggle **against habit, but not against**
> **original depravity** [Froebel's emphasis] in man (1887, pp.121–2).

In the disciplining of the child, Froebel placed emphasis on discussion between the adult and the child in bringing to light this good tendency. Discussion helps the child to analyse and reflect, to come to an understanding of the implications of actions and so to work out a solution to problems. Froebel emphasised mutual respect and a truly reciprocal partnership between child and adult is central to his philosophy. Froebel's attitude to self-discipline leads towards an informally-structured interactionist curriculum.

Montessori also asserted the importance of self-discipline. She did so by stressing the child's need for protection from the over-dominating adult, thus allowing space for self-regulation. The child who is separated from the 'over-directive, cacophonic' inputs of adults, and in tranquillity is allowed to fulfil his or her individual inner needs, is able to develop self-discipline.

> The child needs rest and a peaceful sameness in order to construct his inner life: yet,
> instead, we disturb him with our continual, brutal interruptions. We hurl a quantity of

> *disordered impressions at him that are often sustained with such rapidity that he has*
> *not time to absorb them. Then the child cries in the same way that he would if he were*
> *hungry or had eaten too much and was feeling the first signs of digestive disturbance*
> *(Montessori, 1975, p. 127).*

There are limits to self-discipline. Montessori (1912, p.87) said: 'The liberty of the child should have as its limit the collective interest'. The disciplining of the child is approached by isolating the child who transgresses. Contrary to Froebel's approach, there is no emphasis on discourse with others. The emphasis is rather on harmony through silence and watching others' self-regulating behaviour.

> *This isolation succeeds in calming the mind: from this position he could see the entire*
> *assembly of his companions, and the way in which they carried on their work was an*
> *object lesson much more efficacious than any words of the teacher could possibly have been.*

Froebel and Montessori encouraged self-discipline in different ways. Froebel stressed play and discourse with adults and other children. Montessori stressed silent absorption in the prepared environment and watching others. However, both Froebel and Montessori agreed that self-discipline was of central importance in the development of the child.

Steiner also asserted the importance of self-discipline. Like Froebel and Montessori, he saw it as emerging from allowing the child's natural willingness to learn, to initiate, to create an ability to self-regulate during development. He emphasised the need to have a broad understanding of the world which will awaken human potential. Like Froebel, he stressed the community as a powerful influence in the development of self-discipline.

In a Steiner education the aim is to help each person find his or her right place in life, to fulfil his or her destiny. Self-discipline is a part of this. In contrast to Froebel's emphasis on conversation and language, in the Steiner approach discussion is not introduced until much later. In this respect Steiner and Montessori are closer to each other. They saw the child as absorbing the environment in the early years. Discussion is not seen as a mechanism through which children begin to reflect on situations in the development of self-discipline. Steiner's children first develop, through the atmosphere created by the mother/teacher in the first seven years. Then their temperament is supported, in the middle years, by the authority of the teacher who extends them further – for example, with stories, songs and history. Only later does discussion relating to ideas and knowledge dominate the approach to self-discipline.

Froebel and Steiner emphasised the importance of the community of adults and children in the development of self-discipline. Froebel stresses the need for discourse as an aspect of this. In contrast, Montessori required a tranquil setting, free from over-dominant adults, or children who cut across the self-disciplined work of another child. Steiner and Montessori stressed the way children imitate their surroundings, and constructed prescribed environments in which to set children where they can be protected from damaging external influences.

Froebel's philosophy led to an informally structured approach to early childhood. Montessori's and Steiner's philosophies led to a formally structured approach with set procedures to deal with each step in the child's development. All three gave a high place to the need to create situations which enable the development of self-discipline.

6 THERE ARE TIMES WHEN CHILDREN ARE ESPECIALLY ABLE TO LEARN PARTICULAR THINGS

The end of the last section leads to the need for some consideration of stage theory in the philosophies of Froebel, Montessori and Steiner. Both Montessori and Steiner prescribed set procedures to deal with each stage in the child's development. In other words, stages in the child are closely linked with curriculum content and the environment in which the child is set. In Froebel's later philosophy, curriculum content and the child's environment are not prescribed.

Froebel's statement, 'At every stage be that stage', summarises his view. He designed the Gifts and Occupations to make use of each stage in development. For example, the soft sphere is the first Gift, the wooden sphere, cylinder and cube the second, while the Occupations include paper-folding, plaiting, cutting and pricking paper, and stick-laying.

The message he gave was to allow children fully to experience within the level at which they are functioning, rather than to attempt to accelerate them on to the next stage. He argued for activities which are broad, rather than narrow and designed only to reach the next step in the hierarchy of knowledge as quickly as possible. The skill of the adult lies in observing the child and, acting in the light of observations, extending at that level (Bruce, 1978; 1984; 1987).

'At every stage be that stage' was for Froebel optimised by paying attention to physical activity, aesthetic knowledge (feelings) and scientific knowledge (thought). In this way the child fully experiences each stage. This links with Froebel's view that every stage exists in its own right. Speedy acceleration towards adulthood cuts across breadth of knowledge and experience. A richly developed person is more likely to emerge if children are encouraged fully to experience the stage at which they are.

Montessori's notion of the 'sensitive period' (which she took from the Dutch biologist Hugo de Vries) is probably her most important contribution to the education of young children (Bruce, 1976; Bruce, Findlay, Read and Scarborough, 1995). Sensitive periods occur when 'an irresistible impulse urges the organism to select only certain elements in its environment, and for a definite, limited time' (Montessori, 1949). She was very specific about the way these sensitive periods should be dealt with, and here she parts company with Froebel. She lay down precisely, in what she called her scientific method, how her didactic materials, exercises of practical life, and potters' arts should be used to get the most out of such periods. They allow for the practising of maturing skills during sensitive periods and they contrast with Froebel's more open-ended approach.

Steiner also saw certain stages in development as particularly receptive and requiring certain attention – for example, at twelve years old Steiner believes it is right for children to start physics, chemistry and mechanics:

> *The time of [this] connection of spirit with the most physical material of the body is the right time for the introduction of Physics, Chemistry and Mechanics. Thus again we see how subjects are in tune with the forces of growth (Wilkinson, 1980, p.14).*

Steiner was more like Montessori in his reaction to stages of development, as he set down precisely what was appropriate in his method. Froebel was less precise about what ought to be done during sensitive periods, in terms of the exact knowledge children should meet, or experiences they should encounter. His concern was for adults to recognise stages of order though observing a child carefully, and work out their own ways of acting upon their insights. At one stage he began setting out more specific instructions, but later moved away from this more curriculum-based and adult-focussed approach to his earlier child-focussed work. This was probably because he found that adults used his gifts and occupations too narrowly (Liebschner, 1991; 1992). Montessori and Steiner prescribed specific action which left the adult with less choice.

These different views of how to build on the stages or sensitive periods led to important practical differences in approach which are still seen today. Froebel's view led to an indirectly structured approach. This relied heavily on sound initial training and later good quality in-service training for teachers studying child development and acquiring knowledge of the subject to be taught. His is an open system, with incompleteness (an unfinished state) an important ingredient for ensuring development – with great responsibility devolving upon the teacher. In contrast, Montessori and Steiner led to a more formally structured approach with a more tightly controlled programme which did not rely on constant new inputs, since it was a complete system in itself.

However, Froebel, Montessori and Steiner all believed that there are definite stages in development which require appropriate and sensitive handling. They all asserted that each stage is important in its own right and should not be accelerated, but enriched at that level instead.

7 WHAT CHILDREN CAN DO (RATHER THAN WHAT THEY CANNOT DO) IS THE STARTING POINT OF A CHILD'S EDUCATION

The idea of starting with what children can do, rather than with what they cannot do, is common to Froebel, Montessori and Steiner. Froebel's belief in this principle is encapsulated in one of his most famous remarks: 'Begin where the learner is'. For Froebel, play alerts the adult to what the child is able to do and what is needed in order both to support and, very importantly, to extend learning at that stage. He saw play as a mediating factor between the knowledge the child is acquiring, be it aesthetic or scientific, and the natural and spiritual development within the child.

Like Froebel, Montessori stressed observing children in order to see what they can do and to build on this. Her approach was based on the observations she made of children, many of them with special needs. These observations may account for the particular emphasis her method placed on action and the lack of emphasis on imagination and language. She developed didactic materials, exercises of practical life, and graded sequences to exploit what the child could do, and to help each child develop at his or her own pace in carefully spaced steps. Her three-part language lesson demonstrates her desire to build on success, rather than to emphasise weakness. At the point of failure, the sequence is stopped.

> *Then in order to teach the colours, she says, showing him the red, 'This is the red', raising her voice a little and pronouncing the word "red" slowly and clearly; then showing him the other colour, 'This is blue.' In order to make sure that the child has understood, she says to him, 'Give me the red, give me the blue.' Let us suppose that the child, following the last direction, made a mistake. The teacher does not repeat, and she does not insist: she smiles, gives the child a friendly caress, and takes away the colours (Montessori, 1912, p.109).*

In order to assess the point in the sequences at which the child has arrived, and to use the materials or sequences properly, the directress must be a proficient observer of children. Froebel and Montessori also stressed the importance of observing children and building on what they can do, in order to make the most use of each stage of development. Steiner also subscribed to this view. In the early years (up to seven years of age), the will is dominant as the child's spirit fuses with the limbs. Steiner's belief in reincarnation led him to insist that the adult needs to build on what the child brings with him or her from a previous life. To do this, the adult must observe the child and assess his or her temperament. Children should be grouped so that there is a balance of different temperaments. If the community (the whole) functions well, so can the parts. In a previous section, it became clear that the part is the reflection of the whole in Steiner's philosophy. In this way, the environment can be structured for the teacher to build on the child's strength by using what the child can do – it encourages physical activity (baking, painting, planting a garden, for example) and allows for imitation as the child absorbs his or her surroundings. The aim is to go with the child's abilities, not against them.

Froebel stressed both play and the people the child mixes with. Montessori stressed specially-designed equipment and exercises used with the guidance of a skilled adult. Steiner stressed physical activity, imitation and the temperament. However, each also emphasised what the child can do now, in the present. All three asserted the importance of building on strength because this does not damage the intrinsic motivation or developing self-discipline of the child.

Through careful observation, based on knowledge of the stages of child development, the adult can work with the child rather than against what is natural. In this way, children are more likely to be prepared to struggle and persevere when difficulties in learning are inevitably encountered. The message that Froebel, Montessori and Steiner gave is that self-esteem leads to success.

8   IMAGINATION, CREATIVITY AND ALL KINDS OF SYMBOLIC BEHAVIOUR (READING, WRITING, DRAWING, DANCING, MUSIC, MATHEMATICAL NUMBERS, ALGEBRA, ROLE PLAY AND TALKING) DEVELOP AND EMERGE WHEN CONDITIONS ARE FAVOURABLE

The inner life of the child was deeply valued by Froebel, Montessori and Steiner; it featured especially in children's imagination, creativity, symbolic functioning and language. Froebel stressed that children need help in absorbing and transforming knowledge into clear ideas, feelings and knowledge. He emphasised physical knowledge, aesthetic knowledge and scientific knowledge, and helped children to develop these through the Mother Songs (Froebel, 1878), Gifts, Occupations and Movement Games (Liebschner, 1991, 1992) and direct experience of nature (for example in gardening). He saw conversations as an important part of this process. He stressed play as an integrating mechanism (Froebel, 1887, p. 55). Children also need to share these learning experiences, and to use the knowledge they have 'processed' and 'transformed'. The activities mentioned also have this possibility. Children paint, fold paper (the Occupations), use wooden blocks (bricks), the Gifts and work in the garden. Froebel aimed 'to make the outer inner and the inner outer' through a wide range of experiences.

He stressed play, the imagination, and the ability of the mind to make the 'inner outer', to transform knowledge, 'to associate facts into principles'. He stressed the importance of images through the Mother Songs (Froebel, 1878) and through interacting with nature. He says that the child needs help in sharing his or her knowledge through using paint, clay, music, dance, drama, written work, conversation, mathematics and in many other ways. The inner life of the child is fed through imagery, imitation (in the sense of reconstruction and transformation by the child, rather than passive copying), and the child's developing ability in language and non-verbal representation (the symbolic mechanisms). (See Bruce, Findlay, Read and Scarborough, 1995.) Physical activity, language, the arts and natural sciences are all of critical importance in Froebel's approach. They feed different aspects of the transformation between inner and outer.

Montessori uses Seguin's three-period vocabulary lesson as the basis of her approach to language work. She drew on Seguin's work because he had achieved remarkable results with mentally-handicapped children, and she had also begun her work in education with mentally-disabled children (Lane, 1977). Her use of Seguin's three-period vocabulary lesson, which involved giving vocabulary which is first imitated by the child, then spontaneously produced by the child, does not emphasise the transformational aspect of the inner life of the child in the way that Froebel does. For Montessori, knowledge, as it stands, is absorbed and used. For Froebel, knowledge is absorbed, but transformed in the process and, after acquisition, stored in the imagination. For Montessori, tranquillity is the key to the inner life. She describes her lesson with the seriated cylinders.

> *These lessons may appear strange, because they are carried out in almost complete silence, while one thinks in general that a lesson signifies an oral recitation, almost a tiny lecture. The teacher never encourages this tranquillity with words, but with her own quiet sureness. Thus, we can say that our own 'tranquillity lessons' are symbolic of our method (1975, p. 137)*

The child directly absorbs what is before him or her. The seriated cylinders are copied within the child, and so the outer becomes inner. Language does not feed the inner life in the way that it does for Froebel. Imitation is copy rather than reconstruction. The child absorbs the teacher's tranquillity.

Steiner, on the other hand, like Froebel, stressed the inner life as the child transforms experiences through the imagination, but not during the initial stages of childhood. In the early years, special Steinerian fairy stories present wisdom in picture form, giving instruction and understanding of the world and developing the moral sense. Only later does the Steiner child actively transform the knowledge presented, for the emphasis is on helping the individual to fulfil his or her destiny. What is outer will be used inwardly in different ways, according to the individual's temperament. In approaching the first seven years, Steiner is in some respects closer to Montessori than to Froebel. The emphasis is on imitation as absorbing or copying, rather than Froebel's emphasis on reconstruction. Children speak, sing, model, paint, perform household duties (including gardening), absorbing what surrounds them like blotting paper. Imagination is stressed through fairy stories (wisdom in picture form), but a child is seen to drink in and absorb the environment without at first much transformation.

The child needs protection from the world outside the Steiner community (for instance the wrong colour scheme in rooms, inappropriate toys or TV), and this continues to some extent into middle childhood. In other words, the emphasis in the first two periods of life is on the outer being made inner through absorbing that which surrounds the child. It is not until the last period that independent thinking is considered to emerge and the inner transforms and uses what has been absorbed.

The inner life of the child is directly helped through graded sequences and experiences in a prepared environment by Montessori's method. Steiner also created a community where the child meets carefully selected experiences, led directly by the adult. Both offer direct formally-structured curricula. For Froebel, the curriculum was informally structured.

The adult, using the tools of the child's burgeoning symbolic processes – the imagination, language, objects, people, places, events – works informally with the child, often indirectly. The adult still controls and manipulates the situation but less tangibly.

Froebel, Montessori and Steiner all stressed the inner life of the child. Steiner and Montessori are alike in their approach to the early years of education in that they stressed children's ability to absorb into themselves their experiences of their surroundings. In the later years, Steiner and Froebel throughout the child's development emphasised the child's ability to transform experiences as they are taken in so that they fit with previous learning, or cause modification in what has previously been learnt. For all three, the inner life is one of the most important aspects of the child's development.

9   RELATIONSHIPS WITH OTHER PEOPLE (BOTH ADULTS AND CHILDREN) ARE OF CENTRAL IMPORTANCE IN A CHILD'S LIFE

Froebel saw the mother as the first educator in the child's life – a revolutionary view at a time when only men were seen as capable of teaching children. The adult is a partner in the child's learning, not a threat to it. First the adults in the family, then the teacher, help and guide the child into the wider community.

Through play, children manipulate, reflect, extend and experiment with their learning about social relationships, feelings and ideas. The adult is the child's helper, through conversation and provision of appropriate materials, the arbitrator in quarrels, and the orchestrator of the child's learning with other children and adults, objects, places and events. At different times children have different needs in terms of social interaction. Sometimes the adult leads and the child follows, sometimes the reverse.

Similarly, the child interacts with other children. At times children need to be alone, at times together. Other children are an essential part of Froebel's philosophy. They need to play together, to learn to negotiate, lead, follow, learn about the results of quarrels, to experience making music and to dance as a group.

Montessori saw adults, including parents, as a threat to the child's freedom, and so were other children. Her approach enabled the child to escape into independence, concentration and tranquillity. The educator organises the prepared environment so that the child can do things alone without help. The best social interaction means lack of conflict or argument

– it means harmony. Language, as conversation or negotiation, quarrels, imagination and social interactions are not given great emphasis except as aspects of harmony.

Steiner, like Froebel, emphasised the adult, peers and family. For Steiner, this was especially important initially, when the child absorbs the moral atmosphere projected by the family and school: 'What is of the very greatest importance is what kind of men we are, what impressions the child receives through us, whether it can imitate us' (Steiner, 1926, p. 22). Social interaction generally is greatly encouraged – for example, through emphasis on songs and imagination (the playhouse corner).

10 QUALITY EDUCATION IS ABOUT THREE THINGS: THE CHILD, THE CONTEXT IN WHICH LEARNING TAKES PLACE AND THE KNOWLEDGE AND UNDERSTANDING WHICH THE CHILD DEVELOPS AND LEARNS

The previous two principles led us to the interactionist stance of Froebel, Montessori and Steiner – in Principle 8 from the emphasis of the child and his or her inner structure, and in Principle 9 from the acknowledgement of the external environment, primarily in the form of other people.

Froebel's acknowledgement of the interaction between the inner development of the child and the environment needs some justification, because some theorists have put him in the nativist camp. The following statement by Froebel exemplifies his position:

> *Mothers know that the first smile marks an epoch in child development; for it comes, not from a self feeling only, but from a social feeling also (Liebschner, 1985, p.38).*

In other words, the smile is not simply maturational unfolding, but is encouraged by the mother's impact on the child. Liebschner (1991; 1992) a leading Froebelian scholar, says to those who

> *. . . maintain that Froebel's model of education underestimates social influences and those aspects we inherit from tradition' that '. . . such an assessment cannot be sustained at the level of his philosophy nor at the level of his educational theory nor at the level of his practices (1985, p.30).*

Froebel also stressed that education must be based on the natural stages of development. His view of development is that of the law of opposites. The wooden ball contrasts with the soft ball. New experiences challenge old ones. In this way, maturation and experience constantly interact with each other.

Montessori's view stressed the interaction between maturational processes in the child, the experiences the child has and the environment he or she is in. She describes this view in an analogy with nature:

> *Many species of palm tree, for example, are splendid in the tropical regions because the climatic conditions are favourable to their development, but many species of both animals and plants have been extinct in regions to which they are not able to adapt themselves (Montessori, 1912, p.5).*

Her prepared environment provided the best conditions for growth. The interaction is straightforwardly between maturing structure and experience. For her, people are not central. Even the directress must aim to become like the wallpaper and not interact with the child unless necessary.

Steiner's interaction operated differently. He stresses the way that the spirit and the body increasingly interact until eventually they fuse. The process begins with the limbs, then involves the body, then the head. During the first seven years, the period of the 'will', the child is involved through his or her temperament in absorbing the environment through the process of activities and imitation.

Froebel, Montessori and Steiner all emphasised the interaction between maturing structures in the child and the experiences and environments he or she encounters. For Froebel and Steiner, the people and community are as important as the physical experiences. For Montessori, the prepared environment is mainly physical and she stresses the education of the senses.

CONCLUSION

In this chapter, we have explored pioneer influences on early childhood education where there are areas of fundamental agreement. The practical interpretations of these approaches are at times fundamentally different. The impact of the philosophy of these pioneers is still felt today, and in terms of moving early childhood education forward these areas of agreement are of central importance. They help us to put into historic context recent developments and research evidence into the early childhood curriculum.

The disagreements are also of enormous importance. They help us to see how even within a strong tradition, diversity of practice emerges, especially if the ten principles are to be continually reassessed and so invigorated. One significant difference has proved crucial. Steiner and Montessori fused their educational principles with their educational methods and content. This has facilitated the practical handing down of the 'methods' through Montessori and Steiner schools. But this fairly close definition of method and content has worked against their absorption into mainstream schooling.

Froebel experimented with fusing his principles with a closely-defined method and content, but subsequently rejected this. Consequently his principles became the driving force behind what adults might do with children, but did not dictate precisely what should be done. Nowhere is this seen more clearly than in the curriculum.

Of the three approaches, Montessori's and Steiner's are found to be formally and directly structured curricula, while Froebel's is informally and indirectly structured. For all its intangibility, the informally structured curriculum has stood the test of time to a remarkable extent.

This more open-ended Froebelian interpretation of the ten principles has proved particularly receptive to the findings of later educationalists, especially those working from the interactionist standpoint. The next chapter looks at how four more recent theorists have supported the ten principles and refined their practical implementation – in short, the early childhood tradition reasserted and extended.

3

■

THE TEN PRINCIPLES IN THE

MODERN CONTEXT

In this chapter, recent theory and supporting empirical evidence demonstrate that the ten early childhood principles discussed in Chapter 2 still hold and remain crucial for the early childhood worker. Romantic language has been abandoned and the principles now find application with increased sophistication, in the light of gains in knowledge.

Four theorists, each of whose work has an international reputation, have been selected. They encapsulate in their thinking the ten early childhood principles and together form a context in which to set recent research. They are:

- Jerome **Bruner** (1915–)
- Mia **Kellmer Pringle** (1920–1983)
- Jean **Piaget** (1896–1980)
- Lev **Vygotsky** (1896–1934).

It is important to bear in mind socio-cultural influences on theorists. The theory arises out of the social context in which the theory is formulated. The culture, the people who live with and work with theorists, will have a huge impact on the way a theorist thinks and develops ideas. (Bruce, 1997a, p.89-99).

In the last chapter it was emphasised that Froebel, Montessori and Steiner, although innovative and original thinkers, were nevertheless thinking according to the influences of the historical and cultural era in which they operated. It is the mark of great thinkers that they can readjust to changing times without losing the essentials of their work. It is therefore likely that if they were to return in the next millennium they would significantly change their terminology and reflect, modify and extend their theories and practice (Moyles, 1990). Because Froebel did not set his theories in any specific method, they are more open to developments of this kind.

In this chapter although the impact of historic time remains an important consideration, the influence of the socio-cultural context is also emphasised. The context for Jerome

Bruner in the USA is an entirely different one to that of Europe, where Piaget lived. The USA and Switzerland have capitalism in common, but this contrasts with the Marxist context in which Vygotsky grew up. Not only this, but Piaget was an only child, whilst Vygotsky was one of several children in a large family. John Oates (1995) suggests that it is not surprising that Piaget discussed the actively exploring child, the active autonomous learner, whilst Vygotsky proposed that all learning develops out of social relationships.

Mia Kellmer Pringle, remembered for her pioneer work as Director of the UK National Children's Bureau in the late 1960s, lost many of her close family in Nazi concentration camps. It is understandable that she focussed on children's fundamental needs, building on the work of Maslow and Susan Isaacs.

Bruner, Kellmer Pringle, Piaget and Vygotsky each implicitly supports the early childhood tradition and aids interpretation and illumination of current research. Each of the ten early childhood principles could be supported by each of these four interactionists, but that would be a book in itself. In this chapter, a selection of the most interesting instances of support for each principle has been made on the basis of extending the principle and helping with its practical interpretation.

1   THE BEST WAY TO PREPARE CHILDREN FOR THEIR ADULT LIFE IS TO GIVE THEM WHAT THEY NEED AS CHILDREN

Bruner's thinking has moved forward since he formulated the notion of the spiral curriculum (1977). However, it remains very useful in helping educators to make links between what is appropriate and relevant to the child in the here and now and how this needs to have within it the embryo of more complex sophisticated knowledge which will be required later on. He says, 'Learning should not only take us somewhere; it should allow us later to go further more easily' (1977, p.17). A common activity presents an example of the spiral curriculum in action. Finger painting is often an activity in which young children participate in schools, day nurseries, playgroups and sometimes at home. It involves children transforming coloured powder into coloured sludge. Transformations of materials from powder to solid are later central to the study of science, particularly chemistry.

The spiral curriculum enables the early childhood educator to match the child's stage of development with the area of knowledge being taught. In other words, it is possible to teach basic chemistry to three year-olds through the activity of finger painting. Bruner states that: 'Any subject can be taught to any child at any age in some form that is honest' (1977, p ix). He asserts that if what is offered to the child does not have within it possibilities for future developments in knowledge, then it should be discarded as 'clutter'. This is a very useful way to get a good balance between what children need now and what they need later as adults. This is sometimes called 'forward feed'. He looks at early childhood education as a part of life valid in its own right, with its own particular needs, and links this to the necessity to prepare children adequately for the future during their early education.

Exploring sound: knowledge and understanding of the world

2   CHILDREN ARE WHOLE PEOPLE WHO HAVE FEELINGS, IDEAS AND RELATIONSHIPS WITH OTHERS, AND WHO NEED TO BE PHYSICALLY, MENTALLY, MORALLY AND SPIRITUALLY HEALTHY

Kellmer Pringle's (1974/1980) thinking, which she built on Maslow (1962) and Susan Isaacs' work (1968), asserts that children have primary and secondary needs, both of which must be the concern of early childhood education and care. The fulfilment of primary needs – nourishment, shelter and clothing – is necessary for survival. Secondary needs relate to love and security, new experiences, praise and recognition and responsibility.

Kellmer Pringle stresses the importance of the child's health and living conditions as part of development and that the child's education needs to address itself to these primary needs. School meals, outdoor play and appropriate clothing are all aspects of this.

- The early childhood tradition has always placed great importance on meals in early childhood group settings. These need to be of good nutritional value and presented attractively, served in a setting conducive to enjoying food and good conversation in small groups.
- Children in early childhood settings should have access to indoor and outdoor activities, with suitable clothing being an important element in these (for example, for jumping in puddles a child needs wellington boots).
- Attention to primary needs has implications for early diagnosis of children with disabilities and special educational needs of various kinds, and for issues such as identifying and alleviating poverty. The distinction needs to be made between special needs and special educational needs (Bruce and Meggitt, 1996 p.470–472).

Kellmer Pringle's statement of secondary needs calls for a focus on relationships which are important for the child. She quotes Elizabeth Newson (1972, p.37) who considers that every child needs someone in his or her life who is prepared to go to 'unreasonable lengths' for that child's sake. This has implications for those working with children in the context of their families.

It also has implications for multi professional work because early childhood workers are not equipped to take on responsibility for specialist help offered by other professionals, or by specialist voluntary agencies. In taking a view of the whole child, the orchestration of different kinds of specialist help may be appropriate (Whalley, 1994).

3   SUBJECTS SUCH AS MATHEMATICS AND ART CANNOT BE SEPARATED; YOUNG CHILDREN LEARN IN AN INTEGRATED WAY AND NOT IN NEAT, TIDY COMPARTMENTS

Kellmer Pringle emphasises that the child who is loved may or may not enjoy a deep sense of security. A child may be praised, but may not be given real recognition (Kohn, 1993). Every aspect of a child's need, primary and secondary, should be met in a co-ordinated, non-compartmentalised way.

> Six year-old Nikolai was working with a student teacher who praised every step in his model-making. After a while, Nikolai looked up and said, 'why do you keep saying "good"?' In this example praise was given in isolation from real achievement or effort – that is, there was no real recognition of what was involved.

Three year-old Christopher manages to make an open semi-circle which he says is his name. This has been difficult for him, and his father appreciates and recognises the effort and the achievement. The father intuitively recognises that this is a moment to celebrate and that this will encourage Christopher to keep experimenting and problem-solving as he learns to write.

Appreciation and recognition of effort should link with every other aspect of the child's needs.

Piaget's view of human development as a matrix or network emphasises the inter-connectedness of the growth and knowledge of understanding of feelings and relationships. He was a genetic epistemologist. This means that he was fascinated to study the way that knowledge and thinking develop in human beings.

He identified connected networks of knowledge and understanding – logico-mathematical, socio-temporal, physical and symbolic representational systems. He regarded the emotional aspects as implicit and everywhere, and that it is not possible to separate emotion (affect) from thinking (cognition). Each are aspects of the other (Piaget, 1968). Every aspect of knowledge and thinking connects with every other aspect of development, ideas, feelings and relationships as well as physical, moral and spiritual development. It is the same for Kellmer Pringle, although she articulates this using very different language.

4   CHILDREN LEARN BEST WHEN THEY ARE GIVEN APPROPRIATE RESPONSIBILITY, ALLOWED TO MAKE ERRORS, DECISIONS AND CHOICES, AND RESPECTED AS AUTONOMOUS LEARNERS

Kellmer Pringle says:

> *Given the inborn potential for development; given the impetus of maturation; given environmental opportunities of an appropriate kind and at an appropriate time – what can still be missing is the willingness or motivation to learn and make progress. The essential driving force of the will to learn has its roots in the quality of relationships available to the child right from the beginning of life (1980, p.33).*

Thus, while she recognises intrinsic motivation, she stresses early social relationships as the mechanism which harnesses the will to learn.

Lilian Katz (1993) more recently writes about self-motivation in terms of dispositions as educational goals. Katz states that the development of dispositions and attitudes to learning are crucial. These include mastery orientation, the overcoming of stereotypes, curiosity and the desire to explore, being autonomous and taking responsibility, concentration and involvement, persistence and problem solving. Issues surrounding gender, social class, ethnicity and special educational needs are important considerations in the development of dispositions conducive to quality learning (BBC, *Teaching Today*, 1996).

Piaget's work has a different orientation. He also stresses self-motivation, but he emphasises self-regulation, which he calls the 'process of equilibration'. This process of equilibration has two aspects: 'assimilation' and 'accommodation' (Piaget, 1968, pp. 7–8). Piaget suggests that children absorb experiences into structures which they already possess through the process of 'assimilation'. This contrasts with the process of 'accommodation' during which structures within the child have to be modified and adjusted in order to take in experiences which do not fit into the structure already in existence.

> Two year-old Robert had established that wheels are round. This view had been well assimilated through a variety of experiences, but he was then confronted with a long toy caterpillar with square wheels, which moved along when pulled by a string. This was surprising and novel, and he had to adjust his thinking to take this in (accommodation). He was active in his own learning.

Piaget's concept of equilibration (his process of self-regulation), involving both assimilation and accommodation, occurs throughout life. It supports the notion that children are intrinsically motivated through a lifelong ability to self-regulate. A range of emotions is part of the self-motivating, self-regulatory process. Assimilation brings with it the satisfaction of recognising the familiar, of repeating and practising. It brings the joy and pleasure of playing. It brings the delight of humour, or the boredom that comes when familiarity brings contempt.

Accommodation brings with it surprise, fascination with the new, even anger that something does not fit in with that has previously been experienced. It can bring struggle and frustration. Intrinsic motivation is deeply valued by the Piagetian approach, as well as in the different perspective of Kellmer Pringle.

Keeping a balance between children's and adults' initiatives is difficult. There is a difference between adults intervening to help children, and adults interfering. There is also a difference between leaving children to do as they like and helping children to have initiative, develop their own ideas, and make choices and decisions. Vygotsky's notions of actual, potential and future development are useful analytical tools which help the early childhood educator to encourage child directed activity.

The zone of actual development: 'defines functions that have already matured, that is, the end product of development' (Vygotsky, 1978, p.86). Vygotsky sees these functions as the fruits of development. They show what a child can do alone and independently.

In contrast, **the zone of proximal or potential development**: 'defines those functions that have not yet matured but are in the process of maturation, functions that will mature tomorrow but are currently in an embryonic state'. He sees these functions as the buds of development. They show what a child can only manage in the present, with help. This help may come from an adult, or from a more advanced peer. The zone of proximal development, in other words, shows the point where the child is on the edge of his or her capabilities. This is why the child needs support at this time.

The zone of future development. This is what the child will be able to do on their own at a later point of development.

> Four year-old Hannah wanted to choreograph a dance and share it with her teacher, for whom it was intended as a present. (Her teacher, Charlotte, had been away for a few days.) Hannah has an idea that the dance will be called 'Looking for Charlotte', but she needs to talk to an adult (her mother) about it. She needs someone to listen to her, but not to interfere with her idea. She needs an adult to find appropriate music, take it to school, help prepare furniture in the classroom, ask the teacher to come and watch, and explain the content of the dance to the teacher.
>
> Without adult help, her idea would not have developed so that it was translated into a dance and shared with Charlotte. Four year-olds often manage to draw pictures and give them to people as gifts. It is more difficult to give a dance as a gift without help.

Vygotsky says: 'What a child can do with assistance today she will be able to do by herself tomorrow' (1978, p.87). Play is one of the most important settings for the development of child-initiated self-directed activity. Play is also a very important setting for encouraging the zone of potential development.

> *In play a child always behaves beyond his average age, above his daily behaviour; in play it is as though he were a head taller than himself. As in the focus of a magnifying glass, play contains all developmental tendencies in a condensed form and is itself a major source of development.*

The child acts in the imaginative sphere, creates situations, voluntary intentions, forms real-life plans. In play children must subordinate their actions to the meaning of things, and behave accordingly.

> Adults need to develop skills in recognising when children need to be independent and when they need help. Three year-old Anthony, playing with the dolls house and talking to himself, needs to be alone. He is, with physical props, telling himself a story. At a later stage he will try to write stories and will then need plenty of adult help.

In this next example intervention was crucial. A group of three and four year-olds playing shoe shops needed an adult constantly in attendance in order to sustain the theme of the game, and the roles they adopted. Neelam (aged four) was a customer and the adult was the shopkeeper. The children began to come towards the activity, watching what the adult did. The latter invited children to try on shoes, addressing them, as if they were customers. Neelam decided to be the shopkeeper and took the money, gave change and bills and so on. The adult became a customer in order to make way for her. At one point, the adult was called away – the game collapsed.

Four year-old Nishaan would not let anyone have the football boots and a quarrel broke out. When the adult returned, he agreed to be the shopkeeper again and let children put the shoes on briefly. In this way, he kept control of the football boots, but let other children try them on too! This game was clearly in the children's zone of potential development and needed a co-ordinator – the adult.

Ferre Laevers (in Pascal and Bertram, 1997), working in Belgium at the University of Leuven, has over many years developed the 'Involvement Scale' which helps adults to see when children are deeply involved in their learning. This also helps adults working with young children to take a deep look at what they are offering children, since unless children are in a context which is conducive to concentration with energy being devoted by the child to the learning they are doing, unless this is in place, the ability of learning is not likely to be high.

This section has drawn out some of the practical implications of the principle that intrinsic motivation leading to child-initiated and child-directed play is important. Play inevitably involves children in self-directed, child-initiated situations. The adult's role and that of peers is as helpful partners in both actual and potential development. The degree of intervention will vary in relation to the context.

5   SELF-DISCIPLINE IS EMPHASISED. INDEED, THIS IS THE ONLY KIND OF DISCIPLINE WORTH HAVING. REWARD SYSTEMS ARE VERY SHORT-TERM AND DO NOT WORK IN THE LONG-TERM. CHILDREN NEED THEIR EFFORTS TO BE VALUED.

Vygotsky believes that when children are involved in imaginative play they will renounce what they want, and willingly subordinate themselves to rules, in order to gain the pleasure of the play. He argues that in play they exercise their greatest self-control.

> Three year-old James wanted to hold the Teddy in the home corner and 'feed' him. But he allowed three year-old Matthew to feed Teddy, because Matthew was pretending to be the zoo keeper. In order that the play could progress he gave up what he wanted.

This principle links with Principle 4. James initiated the constraints on himself in the play. He voluntarily and willingly gave up what he wanted because he could see a need – the roles he and Matthew had taken on were protected and so was the theme. Seeing the sense in a course of action through being in a meaningful situation (which play is) helps children increasingly to decentre. Seeing things from other people's points of view by taking another role encourages self-discipline.

Melian Mansfield (Pen Green Conference, February 1997) suggests that since the introduction of the National Curriculum, in conjunction with Standard Assessment Tasks and League Tables of Results in schools, there has been inevitably an increased need to deal with disruption and the management of behaviour of children in school. She links this with the greater emphasis on requiring children to conform to adult requests and tasks at the expense of encouraging self-discipline. This is not to say that children do not need clear boundaries.

Children do need clear boundaries. If they do not find them they begin to test out situations which are inconsistent or unclear, as they quickly grow to feel insecure and unanchored. Predictable environments make children feel safe. They know where they are with adults and other children, with care of equipment, or procedures for using tools and materials. This is closely linked with the development of dispositions (Katz, 1993) and attitudes towards learning, which were mentioned in a previous section of this chapter.

Mastery orientation, exploring, being curious – all become possible in a predictable environment with clear boundaries. This is very different from controlling children in ways which require children to do as adults want, without encouraging them to reflect, analyse and tease out why things should be done in certain ways.

Marion Dowling (1995) gives this example:

> In one study in a nursery school, a group of children were provided with drawing materials and told that they would receive a prize for drawing which, in due course, they did. Another group were given the same materials but with no mention of prizes.
>
> Some time after, drawing was provided as one of a range of optional activities. Significantly the children who chose to spend least time on drawing were those who had been previously rewarded.

This example shows that adults can encourage children to do what adults want through giving children rewards, positively reinforcing their behaviour in particular ways, or giving punishments. The problem is that this does not help children to reflect, analyse or think about why they want to do things or behave in particular ways which move them forward in their moral development. It might have a short-term favourable result, but in the long-term the emphasis on encouraging the process of self-discipline rather than the product of adult-led discipline is more effective.

6   THERE ARE TIMES WHEN CHILDREN ARE ESPECIALLY ABLE TO LEARN PARTICULAR THINGS

Anyone who has been with children a lot will know that at different stages they seem to be much more interested in some activities than others.

> Seven year-old William was intensely keen on skate boarding for several months, as well as being fascinated by bows and arrows, aeroplane flight paths, sledging, roller skating, BMX bike riding, tiddly winks and ice-skating.

> Three year-old Kate made a model of her classroom out of bricks and junk material. She put the 'furniture' in a cardboard box on its side. She kept infilling more furniture and people until there was no more floor space left. During the same week she went to the newspaper box and spread sheets of it all over the floor. She said she was making a road. She had a pancake for tea and spread sugar, jam and lemon juice all over it with meticulous care and then did not want to eat it, even though she loved pancakes!

These are manifestations of what Piaget has called **schemes** or **'schemas'** (in William's case, a trajectory schema and in Kate's an infilling one). Piaget says (Piaget and Inhelder, 1969, p.4) that a schema is '. . . . the structure of organisation of actions as they are transferred or generalised by repetition in similar or analogous circumstances'. The importance of the schema to the early childhood educator is that it provides a mechanism for analysing 'where the learner is' and helps predict other situations which will be of interest to the child.

Schemas change in complexity as the child grows up. For the first eighteen months to two years they are sensori-motor (based on the senses and movement); from two years or earlier the schemas also begin to be represented symbolically, and a cause and effect relationship (known as functional dependency) begins to develop.

> One year-old Amanda paints a line. This is a sensori-motor action. At eighteen months, she is calling a line she draws 'Doggy' immediately after seeing a dog. This is using the line or trajectory schema at a symbolic level of functioning. Children begin to establish the function of dependency aspects of situations.

> Four year-old David, having just painted a thick line on the paper, changes paint
> brushes. He now draws a thin line. 'See this brush?' he asks. 'It's fat. This one's thin,
> Look!' He uses each in turn and laughs. 'Fat', he says, pointing to the line the thick
> brush made. He has established the cause and effect relationship between thickness
> of brush and thickness of line.

Observing the network of schemas of a particular child at a particular time, and the level
at which the child is predominantly functioning, helps the early childhood educator to
respond effectively during the early years of education. This aspect of Piagetian theory
has been developed through the work of Chris Athey at the Froebel Institute, London,
while directing the Leverhulme and Gulbenkian Research Project 1972–76, and has been
widely disseminated through in-service work and publications such as Athey (1990),
Nicholls (ed. 1986, Cleveland), Sheffield (1980), Matthews (1993), Whalley, E. (1993),
Nutbrown (1994), Bedford County Council (1994), Meade with Cubey (1995), the 0–8
Series edited by Bruce (from 1993) and the Pen Green Conference Papers (Summer 1996,
Spring 1997).

Athey (1990, p.107) in her pioneer work describes the importance and usefulness of schemas
for identifying the consistent thread of interest that a child may have. This can be hidden
from the educator if he or she concentrates simply on the content of the child's interest.

> . . . . naming (if viewed from a content point of view) could be taken as instances of
> 'flitting'. Randolph (3½ years) for instance, cut out a zig zag pattern to which he
> attached three different names: 'a bird's wing', 'a fish tail' and 'a fan'. He was
> 'fitting' different but appropriate content into his latest 'form'.

He could be accused of flitting, but as Chris Athey emphasises, he is fitting the content of
his experiences of nature in his latest form, or schema, which is the zig zag.

One of the most frequent schemas for children aged two to five is interest in what Piaget
calls 'enclosure'. Athey gives an example of the children in the project using large wood
blocks (bricks) to build an enclosure and then using it representationally over a short period
of time as a car, boat, taxi and ambulance. In other words, the content may be flitting, but
the dominant schema is not. Athey quotes (1980, p.8) the example of Louise and her
envelopment schema:

> Over several months, Louise systematically explored enveloping space and certain
> associated schemas. She always carefully wrapped things up. For instance, she wrapped
> her clay pancake up (it was too hot to hold). She went round covering things up. When
> she has covered up the windows of her model house she said: 'now its dark inside'. She
> covered a worm with sand saying: 'you know they live under the sand . . . at night
> he'll be asleep'. She made a small hole right through her home book. Her mother was
> embarrassed and carefully mended the book. Louise made: 'a sofa with a hole in it'.

She wrapped 'sausages' in tin foil to 'cook' them. She wrapped up her mother's shoes at home and 'posted the parcel' in the rubbish bin, 'the postbox'. When she arrived at school she painted 'a parcel with Mummy's shoes in it'.

Using different materials, Louise told a long story (on audio tape) about her cat. The persistent theme was the cat going inside and outside the dustbin and bringing what was inside the dustbin into the house and so on. Her persistent concerns had become sufficiently internalised for her to have an interesting conversation about them.

Some of the most frequently-used schemas are enclosure, rotation, trajectory and grid. Teachers and advisers in Cleveland, following Athey's in-service work, have developed a 'schema spotter's guide' listing seventeen schemas they were able to work with in the classroom (Nicholls, ed., 1986). Athey argues for the greater use of schemas in the construction of the early childhood curriculum:

It is possible that the nursery school curriculum could be planned along more rational lines if teachers could make the shift from arbitrary 'content centred' provision (tomorrow we will 'do' frogs) to provision based on a recognition of children's persistent concerns (1980, p.9).

Chris Athey (1990, p.83) goes on to say

Focusing on 'content' at the expense of 'form' can lead to the conclusion that young children 'flit' from one theme to another and that they are unsystematic or even idiosyncratic.

More is written about schemas in Chapter 5.

7 WHAT CHILDREN CAN DO (RATHER THAN WHAT THEY CANNOT DO) IS THE STARTING POINT OF A CHILD'S EDUCATION

Vygotsky extends the meaning of this principle when he stresses the need to aim for the ripening structure of potential development, which require the help of adults and other children. He sees a good education as one which stresses what children can do as their capability begins to emerge. Concentrating on what children can do does not mean emphasising what they can do unaided. It means emphasising what they can do with sensitive, appropriate help. Concentrating on what children can do unaided undervalues the emerging competencies.

Vygotsky points out also that, given the right help, children are capable of higher levels of functioning than if they are left without assistance. Children should not be underestimated. In play with other children, the problem of underestimation diminishes, since they can set the level of complexity, control their own rules, and make their own actions subservient to the meanings in the game. They can self-pace their developing abstract thinking. Vygotsky says that learning 'awakens a variety of internal development processes that are only able to operate when the child is interacting with people in his environment, and in co-operation with his peers' (1978, p.90).

In play children can operate at a higher level. The same applies when children are introduced to new activities, such as cutting with scissors, using glue and so on, with the help of an adult who extends their learning and enables them to do something which they would not be able to do on their own. During play, or in a problem solving situation that is supported by an adult, the child is using what he or she can do. Vygotsky (1978) believes that instruction helps to bring consciousness and deliberate mastery to the child's abilities, but only providing the child is 'within the limit set by the state of his development'.

The BBC booklet for the *Teaching Today* series on Child Development (1996) quotes both Froebel and Katz with regard to supporting children in what they are able to do. Froebel says in Liebschner (1992, p.25):

> *to awaken the pupil's urge for learning by concentrating on what he can do well. For every being ultimately wants to be completely what his inclination and ability allows him to be.*

Katz and Chard (1989, p.30) emphasise that

> *Of particular concern is the risk that introducing formal academic and direct instruction in the early years may jeopardise the development of desirable dispositions.*

It continues:

> *Early achievements may threaten development of the dispositions to be readers and appliers of mathematical skills given the amount of drill and practice usually required for success in applying these skills at an early age. This issue can be referred to as the damaged disposition hypothesis.*

The same applies when children are introduced to new activities, such as cutting with scissors, using glue and so on. Vygotsky states: 'The child acquires certain habits and skills in a given area before he learns to apply them consciously and deliberately' (Donaldson *et al*, 1983, p.266). During play, or in problem-solving supported by an adult, the child is using what he/she can do, but at the same time the game or the adult's contribution will '. . . awaken and direct the system of processes in a child's mind which is hidden from direct observation and subject to its own developmental laws' (Donaldson *et al*, 1983, p.267).

Instruction helps to bring consciousness and deliberate mastery to the child's abilities but only providing he or she is 'within the limit set by the state of his development'. The aim is therefore to establish 'the lowest threshold at which instruction in, say, arithmetic may begin, since a certain minimal ripeness of functions is required'. The child who can use scissors competently and use glue with skill, who can wipe his nose, do up shoes and so on, is in a position to make models or go outside when he wants. This involves maturation of structures biologically. It also involves partnership with adults, and actually being taught.

8 IMAGINATION, CREATIVITY AND ALL KINDS OF SYMBOLIC BEHAVIOUR (READING, WRITING, DRAWING, DANCING, MUSIC, MATHEMATICAL NUMBERS, ALGEBRA, ROLE PLAY AND LANGUAGE) DEVELOP AND EMERGE WHEN CONDITIONS ARE FAVOURABLE

There are two aspects to Piaget's theory:

- stage-dependent;
- stage-independent.

The emergence and development during babyhood of the 'inner life' of the child, from toddler to adult, can be plotted through the stage-dependent approach. As part of this process, the stages of symbolic functioning and intuitive thought are of particular interest to early childhood educators. However, the stage-independent aspects also demonstrates Piaget's concern with the 'inner life'.

The role of processes in maturation experience, social transmission and self-regulation occur throughout life. In this section an aspect of the role of experience is taken to illustrate the 'inner life'.

Firstly, and largely separate from the 'inner life' there is physical experience which involves direct, first-hand experiences (for example, playing with water through a sieve). Children find out about the properties of objects in this way, but always relating them to what they already know through a process called 'simple abstraction'. These experiences can be directly taught.

Secondly, there is the sort of experience which leads to what Piaget calls 'reflective abstraction'. This involves reflecting on the actions performed during direct physical experiences. This kind of experience can be facilitated but not directly taught. It involves an internal co-ordination and transformation of the actions which are not included in the presence of the first-hand experience. This demonstrates the need for adults to respect the process Bruner *et al* (1976) called 'incipient intentions', or Vygotsky refers to as the 'ripening buds'.

These processes can be facilitated by the provision of appropriate concrete activities: adults can 'scaffold' the activity as Bruner suggests, or teach at the point of emergence of structures as Vygotsky requests. But it is within the child that thinking is co-ordinated and transformed. Adults cannot think for children and transfer these thoughts to them by direct transmission. They can only help children to think for themselves. Thus, to some extent, teaching has to be an act of intuition embedded in educational principles. The teacher has to have confidence in offering and organising the prepared lesson. It is an act of intuition because there is not much tangible feedback from these internal processes, especially with children of three to five. This is also often true of children with special needs. The teacher has to rely on clues from the child that the lesson is feeding the inner processes (Nielsen, 1992).

The inner life is crucial to early childhood education, including as it does the construction of images, the reconstruction of experiences, symbolic mechanisms, and imagination – the ability to go beyond the here and now.

9   RELATIONSHIPS WITH OTHER PEOPLE (BOTH ADULTS AND CHILDREN) ARE OF CENTRAL IMPORTANCE IN A CHILD'S LIFE

Kellmer Pringle stresses relationships, emphasising feelings (love, security, praise and recognition). Vygotsky, Bruner and Piaget also stress relationships but emphasise cognition (thinking).

- In Vygotsky's view, it is from social interaction that higher functioning develops.
- Bruner has increasingly come to value the adult/child partnership, particularly in relation to problem solving and developing attitudes which facilitate the process.
- Piaget emphasises the part played by culture in the process of social transmission. In this way, the child does not have to reinvent that which is already known. This links with Dawkins' recent work on the importance of social as well as biological evolution (Bruce and Meggitt, 1996, p.236).

The early childhood tradition until recently has often been perceived as emphasising the affective (feelings) aspects of development and Kellmer Pringle is in that tradition. It is important to put forward theories offering a different emphasis in order to balance this view.

Although Vygotsky puts the main emphasis on cognition, affect is important in his theory. The satisfaction and enjoyment of playing with others, the closeness of an adult/child partnership, are not in fact purely cognitive. The sensitivity of Bruner's adult/child partnership echoes this implicit affectivity. Piaget (1968) is quite open in asserting that the life of the mind cannot be dichotomised into affect and cognition. Everything interweaves. People and relationships are, albeit implicitly, central in his theory.

Thus relationships are the key to development in each of the four theories and this paves the way for the support and extension of the tenth Principle, which states the importance of the interaction of the child's internal structures with the environment represented by both people and things.

Small world play in a group and solitary play: children need both

10   QUALITY EDUCATION IS ABOUT THREE THINGS: THE CHILD, THE CONTEXT IN WHICH LEARNING TAKES PLACE, AND THE KNOWLEDGE AND UNDERSTANDING WHICH THE CHILD DEVELOPS AND LEARNS

Bruner states that a good educator is one who can diagnose the incipient intention of the child and act accordingly. He points out (1977, p.20) that:

> *Mastery of the fundamental ideas of a field involves not only the grasping of general principles, but also the development of an attitude toward learning and enquiry, toward guessing and hunches, toward the possibility of solving problems on one's own ... To instil such attitudes by teaching requires something more than the mere presentation of fundamental ideas.*

Bruner's thinking has developed over the years since he wrote this; he now gives greater stress to the context in which learning takes place and puts more emphasis on the partnership between the child and the adult (Bruner, 1990).

It is not simply assessing where the child is – for example Piaget's notion of schemas as an aspect of this, or Vygotsky's emphasis on the ripening structures – and matching this to the appropriate curriculum content. It is also a question of seeking out the way the child sees the situation (the incipient intention of the learner).

As Bruner (1977, p.xiv) says:

> *... scaffolding the task in a way that assures that only those parts of the task within the child's reach are left unresolved and knowing what elements of the solution the child will recognise though he cannot perform them. So too with language acquisition, as in all forms of assisted learning, it depends massively upon participation in a dialogue carefully stabilised by the adult partner.*

> *So much of learning depends upon the need to achieve joint attention, to conduct enterprises jointly, to honour the social relationship that exist between learner and teacher, to generate possible worlds in which propositions may be true or appropriate, or even felicitous; to overlook this functional setting of learning whatever its content is to dry it to a mummy.*

This means knowing what the child can manage unaided during the task and knowing what the child can understand but cannot yet achieve without help. Understanding precedes the ability to perform, first falteringly, then with competence. Because a child cannot 'perform' or can perform only falteringly, does not mean he or she is not ready for the task. A tottering baby is allowed to walk, and may hold someone's hand, or hang on to furniture. A three year-old may spill cookery ingredients which can be scooped up from the table. Children need to be introduced to areas of knowledge from the start, but through an appropriate environment (people, objects, places and events).

Bruner's notion of 'scaffolding' the activity helps the context and the style of teaching to be effective. His notion of scaffolding the meaningful context helps to organise how to teach. It emphasises the need to link the child's developing structures with appropriate knowledge in a meaningful context with the adult educator as an enabler.

CONCLUSION

In this chapter, the philosophies of four recent theorists who have had a major impact on early childhood education have been examined. Their writings support the early childhood tradition as described in the ten principles; they extend the application of the principles and offer a number of theoretical tools which will be given more practical use in the chapters that follow, and they provide a framework against which to set recent empirical research.

The next chapter uses this framework as a backcloth against which to set the construction of an early childhood curriculum.

Name of theorist	Key aspects of the theory	Socio-cultural context of the theory
	Although the work of each theorist could be used to illustrate each and every principle, this would become a very cumbersome exercise. Instead, in the chapter selected examples have been used to make links with some of the core principles.	
Jerome Bruner (1915–)	Spiral curriculum Scaffolding Principles illustrated in Bruner's theory in the chapter: 1, 5, 9, 10	Capitalist USA
Lev Vygotsky (1896–1934)	Actual and proximal (potential) development Higher order thinking develops out of social relationships	Marxist setting One of several children in a large family

Jean Piaget (1896–1980)	The principles illustrated using Vygotsky's theory: **4, 5, 7, 8, 9**	Capitalist European Switzerland Only child
	Networks and matrices which connect with each other to form a holistic system	
	Horizontal and vertical development	
	Child as an active learner	
	The importance of ● first hand experience ● the senses ● movement as 'windows' or access mechanisms for development and learning	
	Increasing co-ordination of networks becoming more and more complex and sophisticated	
	Principles illustrated using Piaget's theory: **4, 6, 7, 8, 9**	
Mia Kellmer Pringle (1920–1983)	Primary needs (nourishment, clothing, shelter)	
	Secondary needs (love and security, new experiences, praise and recognition, responsibility)	
	Principles illustrated using Kellmer Pringle's extrapolation of Maslow's hierarchy of needs: **2, 3, 4, 9**	

PART 2

APPLYING

THE

PRINCIPLES

4
■

TOWARDS AN EARLY

CHILDHOOD CURRICULUM

I n the last chapter links were made from the past to the present. The strengths of the early childhood tradition remain, although the language through which these are expressed has changed because of a different socio-cultural and historic era. In this chapter, the implications of the ten Principles are used to develop a modern approach towards an early childhood curriculum. This chapter forms a link between the first three chapters of the book and those which follow.

The early childhood curriculum has three aspects, each of which interact with the other.

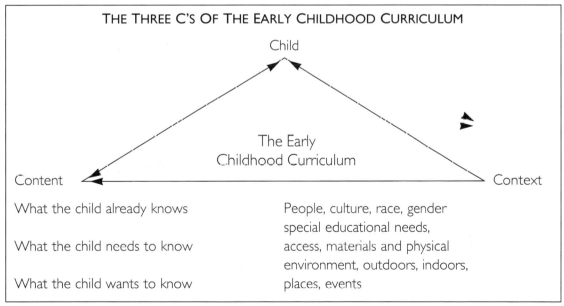

The three C's of the early childhood curriculum (from Bartholomew and Bruce, 1993, *Getting to know you*, published by Hodder and Stoughton)

Imagine you are standing on a hill. You are more aware of the top than the rest of it. Now imagine you are standing at the foot of the hill. You become more aware of a different part of the hill. The early childhood curriculum is a bit like this. At times the emphasis will be on the processes of the child. At other times the socio-cultural context will be prominent, whilst at a different time the content (what a child is learning and understanding) will be central. Only when all three aspects are integrated and in synchrony can the early childhood curriculum be of quality. If any are over-emphasised, the whole curriculum becomes out of balance and quality is lost.

It can be argued that in the mid 1960s there was over-emphasis on the processes in the child. In the mid 1970s there was over-emphasis on the context and from the mid 1980s there has been over-emphasis on the content. Achieving balance is crucial, but unless adequate care is given to the child-in-context there is little hope that children will acquire understanding and knowledge of any real or lasting depth in the content that they attempt to learn.

Understanding of the early childhood curriculum requires consideration of the processes of the child's development, the context (both the socio-cultural and physical) and the content (what is offered to children).

THE CHILD: WHO ARE YOU HELPING TO LEARN?

It is important to remember that children are part of the culture in which they grow up. They are also deeply connected with the people they live with and meet. It is probably best not to use the phrase 'child-centred' because of this. It is more helpful to refer to the child-in-context. Even two children in the same family have different experiences depending on whether they are first born, boys, girls, or have a disability, are of a second marriage, are living in a reconstituted family, as well as the influences of ethnicity and cultural background.

There are important processes which are part of a child's development, which need to be studied meticulously and in detail by adults while working with young children in every kind of early childhood setting. These include knowledge and understanding about the development of children's language(s), their play, and symbolic life, their spiritual and moral development, their physical development, their feelings, ideas and relationships.

THE CHILD IN THE SOCIO-CULTURAL CONTEXT

Material provision

Material provision makes the bones of environment. It gives children first-hand experiences. It needs to be wide ranging, both indoor and outdoor with natural and manufactured objects. Frequent lack of attention to the external environment must come from some bizarre assumption that knowledge acquired indoors is superior to that gained outside. Pat Gura (1996) provides many examples of broad material provision, both outdoor and indoor. It is important not to let emphasis on material provision lead to under-emphasis on the child.

The important thing for early childhood educators to remember is, how will the provision be used to serve the child, and how will it help the adult to help children develop further their ideas, feelings, or relationships. It depends where and when children grow up, and whether or not they attend group settings before the age of six or seven years. Many children are at home during these years in many parts of the world. Where children do join early years groups, it is important to bear in mind that material provision makes the bones of the early years environment.

The environment in which children develop and learn involve the people with whom the child interacts, the objects or material provision they encounter, and the places and events experienced. The way that children are helped to develop skills in using the provision, the way they are helped to develop competence and mastery and dispositions and attitudes that aid learning, are of crucial importance. The environment is the mechanism by which the early childhood educator brings the child and different aspects of knowledge together. 'Observing, supporting and then extending' (Bruce, 1987, p.65) is the key to good learning.

Interest tables and displays are an aspect of material provision which require care. The central aim is to give children direct experiences, to allow their initiatives and extend them, to support intrinsic motivation broadly and in depth, and to facilitate the development of dispositions and attitudes which are helpful to learning (Katz, 1989). Therefore children must be allowed to interact with the interest table and help to make the displays. They cannot be static.

Some early years educators have a wall near the drawing/writing area where children can put up their work if they wish. Sometimes an activity becomes an interest table after it has finished (for example cooking apple pie). A recipe book, utensils and ingredients are put on an interest table near the home corner, and children are likely to try to cook or to touch. In this way the children can reflect on, and use, what they have learnt, and practise and consolidate their learning free from adult domination. In this way, interest tables and activities blend towards future worthwhile knowledge.

Themes, topics and projects are another way of approaching material provision. However, most early childhood educators who use a topic, theme or project approach do not take up the children's initiatives. They simply decide on a topic, perhaps linked with the National Curriculum or with the Desirable Learning Outcomes documents (1996). This is more in keeping with the transmission model of education. It does not support the principles of the early childhood tradition.

When adults use observation as the base of their record-keeping system (Bartholomew and Bruce, 1997; Drummond, 1993), a topic or theme can be an added source of interest and learning for children. However, it is by no means necessary and many early childhood educators prefer to work entirely from observation without introducing a theme which seems to them contrived.

Dispositions towards learning

Developing mastery and skills is considered at some length here because it is not considered as an entity elsewhere in the book. They key message is that the early childhood educator should introduce skills which the child needs in order to become increasingly competent and be in a position to use.

This approach is very different from one in which the adult sits each child down in turn and 'teaches' him or her to cut, and then ticks the skill off on a check-list. Such an activity lacks function, purpose or meaning for the child. It does not build on what the child initiates, or is implicitly trying to do. It makes an error into something to be avoided, and there is a complete absence of any negotiations of shared contexts and meanings with the adult. In fact, this approach is totally at odds with the early childhood tradition.

Skills need to be taught and mastery encouraged, but in an embedded context which relates to what children strive to do. The same principles apply when children are learning to tie their shoelaces, cut their food at meals, swim, draw or write their name. Having a sense of control and mastery is deeply linked with self-confidence and feelings of self-esteem (Roberts, 1995).

For instance, the moment to introduce correct letter formation is at the level Ferreiro (1983; 1987) describes when children try to write their names, or their first 'fixed string'. In Chapter 6 on language, it is suggested that the first fixed string is the moment when children resolve the conflict between their own personal symbols and those which can be shared with others. At this point, the child can see the purpose of legibility, speed, formation and aesthetic quality. He or she begins to use clear semi-circles in drawing and to use emergent writing. This behaviour is an indication of readiness to tackle lower case letter formations, provided the understanding that written forms are made out of fixed strings is also emerging. At this point, tuition will give the child the skill needed to undertake legible, speedy and well-formed handwriting, which will usefully serve the writing process. It will also help children to present work well.

Tracing, using templates or stencils, completely cuts across this process and is contrary to the principles of early childhood education. It is more in keeping with the transmission model of education. Being able to represent someone else's idea of a cat by means of a stencil is low level work. It keeps children busy, but it has little to do with education. Helping children to use what they can do – draw circles and lines – tells them that they can draw their own cat, which is unique and imaginative. This is a higher level skill in the child and needs careful encouragement from adults.

A class of six year-olds had fully established the repertoire of marks on paper which are needed to form letters in the English language. (Some languages use lines predominantly, some curves, in the written form. Written English uses mainly lines for capitals and a mixture of lines and curves in lower case). This class was involved in a project on the Middle Ages, stemming from an interest in castles by a group of children in the class. Each child wrote his or her name and decorated the first letter. Some moved on from this to write poems which they later presented beautifully. The aesthetic possibilities of handwriting were highlighted in this way. Mastery and skill in presenting work and sharing it with others became appreciated.

Three year-old Paul sat in the book corner. He picked up a book and ruffled it, dropped it and opened it in the middle. The early childhood worker sat with him and opened it, explaining about beginning where the story starts. She helped him to look at it so that he could benefit from the experience. At storytime she used a book with an enlarged text with a group of children. She asked Paul to show her how to begin and he was pleased with his success. He liked becoming skilled in the use of books. Lack of skills brings lack of confidence.

Eight year-old Hannah and six year-old William went with their parents to a Barn Dance in the local park. Hannah joined in with gusto after initial hesitation. She had in fact learnt to do-si-do at school during country dancing. The following week the family went again, and this time William joined in. He was meticulous in getting the do-si-do exactly right and would only take part in partner dances with the family, so that he could get it correct.

A few days later Hannah made up a dance at home using a pop song. In it she used some of the steps she had learned when Barn Dancing. The newly acquired skills were being used in a new dance context, choreography.

It is important that equipment is readily available for children to practise their newly acquired skills. If the woodwork bench is only put out once a week, this is not possible. Children need opportunities in becoming proficient when they are ready, not when educators are ready. If children only use climbing frames once a week, the 'ripening structures' Vygotsky talks about are not adequately catered for in the environment. In this situation, where skills and the dispositions towards learning are not encouraged, accidents are more likely (Pascal, BBC *Teaching Today*, March 1996).

This is another reason why it is important that children have access to outdoor play every day. The clumsy child needs to become more proficient in using the shoulder, because the shoulder affects movement of the arms and hands (Sheridan, 1973). The woodwork bench, climbing frames and dancing are excellent provision for this need.

Places, events and culture

Places and events which are part of the cultural background are also important aspects of the context of the curriculum. For example, visiting the police stable, the mosque, museums, the train guard's van, or the park and shops, being visited by a puppet group or celebrating Diwali, are all important. The context is both indoors and outdoors beyond the school. Places, events and culture cannot be separated from people.

Outdoor provision complements indoor provision

People

People are the most important part of a child's education. The contribution made by both adults and other children is stressed throughout this book. The child's family and socio-cultural background are deeply influential. Children do not leave the socio-cultural aspects of their lives behind when attending a group or school. Their culture and the people they live with are a part of them (Whalley, 1994, Rogoff, 1933, Bruce, 1997a).

THE CONTENT OF THE CURRICULUM

The content of the curriculum, what it is considered worthwhile for children to know about and understand, is culturally defined. There are stark contrasts between the content of the National Curriculum in, for example, Norway, New Zealand, or in the Pacific Rim. Early childhood workers need to be informed about the culture in which they work and its curriculum emphasis, but thinking about the knowledge children acquire is also enhanced by knowing how other cultures approach the growth of knowledge and understanding, and how narrowly or holistically the concept of curriculum is viewed. Some cultures emphasise performance according to teacher-led tasks, whilst others place more emphasis on reflective, critical, imaginative and creative aspects.

THE EARLY CHILDHOOD CURRICULUM IN ACTION

This chapter so far has given a broad framework for approaching the three 'C's' of the curriculum

- the child;
- the context;
- the content.

In addition, certain basic elements in the learning process need to be built in, namely breadth and depth of knowledge and the pursuit of excellence, with high expectation for each child. The curriculum needs to be relevant and to have meaning for the child as it is experienced.

The remainder of this chapter gives a series of examples of the early childhood curriculum in action which brings out the points made so far. The chart on page 64 illustrates the active role of both the early childhood worker and the child if education is to be open and interactive and in the early childhood tradition. Early childhood settings, where both adults and children are active learners together, are likely to create a curriculum of quality. Where the early childhood worker dominates, or has stopped learning, or the child is given the lead most of the time, then quality is likely to be diminished. When children are taught, mainly by worksheet, the learning of which children are capable is seriously constrained.

A quality curriculum:

- sees adults and children as active learners;
- engages children both broadly and deeply with the content of the curriculum;
- has high expectations of what children do and high expectations of the learning opportunities adults provide for children;
- is based on narrative observation of children;
- emphasises adults knowing and understanding how children develop and learn, as well as being informed about the subject to be studied (the content);
- emphasises the need for adults to be informed also about the context in which learning takes place so that children are given access in which their learning is both supported and extended: this is particularly important in relation to equality of opportunity;
- uses observation (assessment and evaluation) to inform the planning of the curriculum so that adults begin with observation and move to support and consolidate what they learn, and also extend the learning into less familiar aspects of knowledge and understanding;

- depth of knowledge is important to the teacher if he/she is to respond flexibly to the child's interest: every area of the curriculum has a particular pattern, order, set of relationships within it.

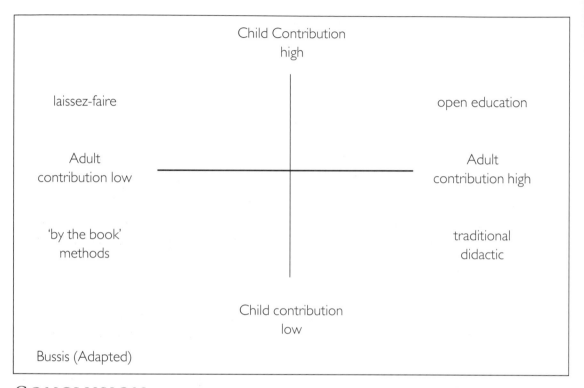

Bussis (Adapted)

CONCLUSION

The early childhood curriculum is constructed from three different elements. First it concerns the child and the processes and structures operating within the child. Secondly the curriculum deals with the context in which the child learns, whether or not the situation is conducive to learning, and whether it provides access to learning. Thirdly, the curriculum involves knowledge and understanding. A quality curriculum brings the child, knowledge and understanding together in an integrated form, appropriately and relatively using the environment which is made up of people, objects and material provision, places and events.

The key to the early childhood curriculum is that adults should

- observe the child;
- support the child in developing and learning;
- extend the child's development and learning.

(Bruce, 1987, p.65)

5

■

SCHEMAS

INTRODUCTION TO SCHEMAS

The study of schemas, which is the study of biologically determined patterns in the way children behave, helps adults to understand children better. But perhaps most importantly understanding schemas also helps adults to relate to children more easily and to enjoy their company more, as well as helping the children to learn in deep and thorough ways.

A schema is

> *a pattern or repeatable behaviour into which experiences are assimilated and that are gradually co-ordinated. Co-ordinations lead to higher level and more powerful schemas (Athey, 1990, p.37).*

Children do not act randomly, but in ways which are patterned, through the influence of their genetically, predetermined biological development and also through the way socio-cultural influences interact with their biological make-up. Beneath the apparent randomness and chaos in a child's behaviour there is order (Gleick, 1998).

The pioneering work of Chris Athey

The study of schemas began in the UK in the 1970s. The work was first pioneered by Chris Athey, who was Leverhulme/Gulbenkian Research Fellow for the Froebel Nursery Research Project, 1972-77, based at the Froebel Institute. The author was the teacher at the school set up in the grounds of the Froebel Institute College to focus on working with parents in a close partnership, and together learning about children's schemas within the context of traditional good nursery practice.

It is very important to stress that schemas should not be studied in isolation from other aspects of the child's development and learning, but within the context of traditional good nursery practice and a high quality curriculum. The findings of the Froebel Nursery Research

Project were published in book form in 1990 in a seminal work by Chris Athey: *Extending Thought in Young Children: A Parent Teacher Partnership.*

As Ann Hedley pointed out at a conference (in November 1996) at Pen Green Research and Development Base, in her presentation 'Beyond Desirable Learning Outcomes – A Schema Story', Chris Athey had shown, by introducing colleagues to schemas, that:

> *we know a lot about 0 to2 year-olds;*
> *we know a lot about 5 year-olds and upwards;*
> *We don't know very much about 2 to 5 year-olds – only what they can't do, not what*
> *they can do – we have a deficit model of them and we have to change this.*

Schemas give practitioners and parents words for what is intuitively known

Often when people begin to study schemas they exclaim: 'But I know all of this. I just never used this terminology to describe it'. One of the problems early years educators have had during the last 100 years is difficulty in expressing and articulating in words what good practice is, and what 2 to 5 year–olds in particular can do. Those who can speak and write effectively and clearly about their work, as well as put it into practice, are more likely to be listened to. The study of schemas helps early childhood practitioners to develop a vocabulary of observation which in turn informs curriculum planning.

SCHEMAS ARE NOT ISOLATED: THEY DEVELOP IN CLUSTERS AND ARE PART OF WHOLE NETWORKS

Schema clusters seem at times to rise and dominate what the child does, and at other times it is as if they have gone into hibernation. At first it was thought that one schema was dominant for a period of time in a child's development. As the Froebel Nursery Project developed, and in subsequent years as more practitioners began to study schemas in their own early years settings (Cleveland, Sheffield, London) and the New Zealand Council for Educational Research (Meade with Cubey, 1995) undertook research into schemas, it became clear that schema clusters dominate for a time, with contextual influences, socio-cultural aspects, raising others from periods of quiet. This fits with recent brain studies which suggests that the brain is stimulated by use (Athey, 1990, Greenfield, 1995).

SCHEMAS ARE AN OBSERVATION TOOL – BUT NOT THE ONLY ONE

Schemas help us to add to our knowledge of child observation. Understanding schemas and learning how to observe them has emerged out of a time-honoured tradition which uses narrative observation to describe:

- what children are doing and saying
- interpreting and analysing what is happening using currently available theory
- planning the next steps in a child's learning.

Susan Isaacs used observation in this way in her famous Malting House School in the 1930s, analysing her observations using the then current psychoanalytic theory of Melanie Klein. Klein's work, developed in the 1930s, emerged out of Freud's theories and were influential for the work of Susan Isaacs.

The current framework for Inspection, OFSTED (1997), emphasises observation-based record keeping, and plans which allow for differentiation in the curriculum according to the individual needs of children as well as those of the group as a whole. The tradition of observation and analysis continues.

The basis of good teaching is informed observation. Once observed and identified, knowing about the schema clusters that children have can help adults working closely with them to plan interesting and appropriate learning experiences.

Schemas should not be viewed in isolation from other aspects of observation or good practice. Schemas enhance existing and well tried observation strategies and will only be useful to practitioners if used in an integrated way alongside what is already known about both observation, good early years practice, and a high quality curriculum.

Those involved in studying and using schemas need to incorporate observations into their philosophy and curriculum practice in a holistic way. Otherwise, schemas will be seen as just another educational fashion or become a very narrow method which leaves out whole aspects of the curriculum.

SCHEMAS ARE NOT A CURRICULUM METHOD OR A CURRICULUM MODEL

When used as an integrated part of traditional early childhood practice, schemas enhance our ability to observe, reflect, analyse what children are learning and act on our observations in the light of what we find. They are not a curriculum method like the American High/Scope structured programme or its British adaptation (See Bruce and Meggitt, 1996) emphasising Plan, Do, Review, or the Montessori Method.

Schemas are part of being human: the biological and socio-cultural paths of development and learning

There are two paths of a child's development: the **biological path** and the **socio-cultural path**.

BIOLOGICAL ASPECTS Schemas have both aspects. A baby is born with a repertoire of schemas which are biologically pre-determined and which, as they mature, co-ordinate, integrate and transform into ever more complex and sophisticated forms. Trevarthen (1996) believes that many aspects of the baby's behaviour are genetically pre-determined.

SOCIO-CULTURAL ASPECTS The socio-cultural aspects of schemas are to do with the way that experience, as opposed to biological maturation, influences the development of schemas through childhood and also through our adult lives. Because the two are in a perpetual state of interaction, each influences the other causing changes, modifications and transformations.

SCHEMAS ARE PART OF HUMAN DEVELOPMENT

Schemas are part of human development, from birth to death, but they are not in a constant state. They are always adjusting and changing in the light of experience. This is why they are such a powerful learning mechanism. Children with disabilities have schemas, but are often challenged in their use and development. For example, the typical rocking of a child with autism is an example of a narrow range in the use of trajectory schemas.

Helen, seven years old and growing up in a musical family in England, experiences and is taught by her parents several different ways a violin bow can produce sounds. The development of some aspects of the trajectory schema will be particularly enriched and strengthened through her developing violin playing. The pleasure and deep satisfaction of music making with people she deeply loves, and is loved by, is part of Helen's schematic experience.

In the same way Depee, two years old, growing up in Sarawak, North Borneo, would experience everyone taking off their shoes on entering people's homes. From the time he can walk, inside/outside schema (with feet in and out of shoes) would be influenced by intermingling this action with the feelings of being welcomed and warmly greeted by friends and relatives and the relaxed conversation following. Feelings of love, pleasure and this relaxed state are linked with feet in this setting.

In many cultures adults lose this sense of ease in their bodies, but the vogue for aromatherapy and massage and movement sessions, using Tai Chi for instance, indicate that many in the UK are trying to address the feeling aspects of their schemas intuitively.

Biological form and socio-cultural content

As Chris Athey (1990) emphasises, form and content both play an important part in the development of schemas. The biological (form) and the socio-cultural (content) paths have central places in development.

SCHEMAS FUNCTION AT DIFFERENT LEVELS IN EARLY CHILDHOOD (0-8 YEARS)

- **Sensori motor level** – through the senses, actions and movements. The sensori motor level emerges first, but is used throughout life when occasion demands.
- **Symbolic level** – making something stand for something else.
- **Cause and effect** – sometimes called functional dependency (if I do this, then that will happen).

The symbolic and cause and effect levels of schemas develop alongside each other in an integrated way, once the sensori motor level is established, and these three levels of schematic behaviour continue to be present and to surface, influenced by the context and situations which arise throughout life.

- The **abstract** or **operational thought level** manifests itself – when there is increasing understanding of reversibility and transformations and a co-ordinated understanding of these. This emerges over time.

Neither children nor adults stay at one level all the time

Children, like adults, do not function at one level all the time. It depends what they are doing, who they are with or where they are, how tired they are, if they are hungry or need the lavatory.

Children and adults move in and out of the different schematic levels but cannot go beyond their biological capabilities at any time. As always, the biological and socio-cultural aspects of development interact, co-ordinate and are integrated with each other.

The dynamic aspects of schemas

*   **Dynamic** – movement and actions

The dynamic aspect of a schema is like a video film, linking thoughts together.

When six year old Koor spins around and says 'I'm mixing a cake', this is the dynamic side of the schema.

The configurative aspects of schemas

*   **Configurative** – based on perceptions and the senses

The configurative aspect is like a still photograph which stands alone. When Daniella (four years) draws with circular scribble and points out a tangled ball of string on the floor and says 'it's the string', this is the configurative aspect of the schema.

Chris Athey (1990, p.37) suggests that of the early schemas, when babies are gazing at people or objects, or following them with their eyes (tracking), 'gazing leads to knowledge of configuration. Tracking leads to knowledge of the movement aspects of objects, including self and other persons.' She suggests that babies quickly begin to co-ordinate these two behaviours – gazing and tracking – integrating the two into an early network, and realise that the same person or object can be still or can move about. From the beginning, the dynamic and configurative aspects of schemas seem to co-ordinate with each other.

ADULTS TEND TO ENCOURAGE CONFIGURATIVE ASPECTS OF SCHEMAS   Early childhood settings, schools and parents, tend to encourage the configurative aspects of schemas more than the dynamic aspects. Drawings, paintings and models are usually more celebrated than children creating dances or songs. It is more difficult to 'keep' a dance or a song than a model. After all, the configurative often leads to a product, such as a painting of the string. This can be kept as an example of the child's work in the child's folder, or put on the wall or the display, or taken home. It might be carefully labelled with what the child said – 'it's the string'.

Whereas the configurative aspect of the schema can be 'kept', the dynamic aspect of the schema cannot. It is here and gone. Nevertheless, it contains deep thinking and has much greater possibility for transformations. Transformations are changes into new forms, adjustments and adaptations which children need to make because they are crucial for the development of abstract thinking, which develops during what Piaget calls 'operational thinking' in the later part of early childhood (usually 4 to 7 years).

Chris Athey (1990) and John Matthews (1994), using the theoretical insights that schemas give, demonstrate how children's early mark-making develops in their writing, drawings and paintings. These echo, using different theory, the earlier findings of Rhoda Kellogg in the 1950s or Michaela Strauss in the 1970s.

Enclosure, trajectory and core and radial schemas

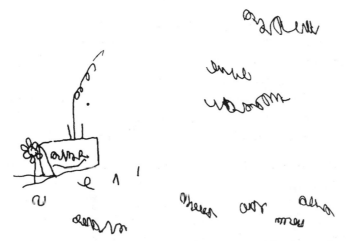

Drawings and writing together - zigzag schema

Morag (five years-old) lives in Scotland. She arrives in school (Primary 1) proudly wearing a kilt of a Gordan Tartan. 'This is my new kilt', she says. In her school she is helped to value her Scottish heritage. She knows it is a Gordan Tartan. It is interesting that this aspect of heritage fascinates her at this time. She has a strong concern with grids. She spends time at the water tray, sieving and using the water and fish nets. She also likes the home area windows and peeps through the net curtains frequently. 'I can see you, its net, so I can see you'. She is enthusiastic about sewing and enjoys simple tapestry work and willingly learns how to use the thread when directly taught by her teacher.

Grid is not her only schema, but it seems to be in particularly active use for a few weeks. There is already good classroom provision in Morag's case. The teacher enhances her interest in the Tartan aspect of grid by introducing a display of tartans and helping interested children to see how tartans are constructed.

Morag began to paint tartans and people wearing them. She often mixed the colours of paints that she needed in order to make a Gordan Tartan. During this time she showed little evidence of schemas such as core and radial. However, she learned to make charts showing data about the weather. In these, although grid was the framework for the chart and gave her enormous pleasure to draw the frame, she used other schemas in the symbols that she chose to represent the sun (core and radial) rain (dab) and clouds (continuous co-ordinated semi-circle).

Core and radial schema

'Not flitting but fitting' (Athey, 1990)

As we saw in Chapter 3, Chris Athey (1990, p.107) gives the example of Randolph who cut out a zig zag pattern. He first said it was 'a bird's wing', then 'a fish tail' and then 'a fan'. As she points out, he was 'fitting' different but appropriate content into his latest 'form' (Schema).

Ann Hedley (1996, p.3) gives the example of Nicholas,

> We were worried about Nicholas because he was due to go to school after Christmas and he didn't seem to settle to anything – how wrong we were! He wrapped himself around in the curtains hiding. He wanted to dress me up and cover me over, he dressed the teddies, he tried to block himself in on the bottom shelf of the hollow blocks, using them as a barricade. When listening to a story, he sat on the chair, always trying to wrap himself around the legs of the chair.

> When at the end of the session his mum Sandra arrived, we told her what we had learned on the course and that we had observed Nicholas covering, enveloping and enclosing. She said 'Oh yes, he is always doing that. When I go shopping in the clothes department, I can never find him, because he is always hiding in the racks of dresses and at home he is behind the settee!' (envelopment schema)

This is also an example of fitting, not flitting. Unless adults observe children carefully, in an informed way, they may mistakenly think a child lacks purpose, or is 'off task' when in fact the child is systematically learning. It is important to recognise the difference when working with young children.

CONTEXTUALISING THE STUDY OF SCHEMAS

Schemas are both biologically pre-determined and socio-culturally influenced, and so they change and modify according to who children meet and grow up with, where and when.

The historic roots of the study of schemas are also important to consider, so that the social context is understood across time, space and cultures.

The historic background to how schemas came to be studied

When Froebel, Montessori and Steiner were developing their curricula, nothing or little was known about schemas. Because they were good observers of children, each tuned in to what children naturally do, and so they intuitively facilitated the children's schema clusters in the curricula they developed. A high quality curriculum is based on the observation of what naturally interests children. It is likely to be an effective curriculum too, since children do not have to be goaded into participation most of the time.

FROEBEL   Froebel, in developing the Gifts, Occupations and Movement, Mother Songs and Garden in his curriculum, together with his study and increased knowledge of play, sub-consciously supported and extended the schemas in the curriculum that he developed. He was working before schemas were a known concept.

His first Gift was the soft ball (Bruce and Meggitt, 1996, p.353; Bruce, Findlay, Read and Scarborough, 1995; Liebschner, 1990).

The subsequent Gifts were early sets of wooden blocks, ancestors of the modern unit and hollow blocks which are now regarded as essential in a high quality early childhood curriculum. Children would build towers and knock them down.

The more obvious schemas used in block play are vertical and horizontal, lateral trajectories, enclosure, connection, on top, inside/outside, transporting, up/down, dynamic trajectories, dab, clashing trajectories. Both the dynamic (transformations) and the configurative (static) aspects of schemas were encouraged in Froebel's curriculum.

Children are naturally drawn to aspects of the environment which allow for opportunities for the consolidation of schemas. As Chris Athey says (1990, p.46), 'functioning improves with use'. It is almost as if children actively seek people and things in the environment which echo their schemas and encourage them in their use. Chris Athey calls this 'recognition' (1990, p.69).

Froebel's curriculum encouraged children in the possibilities for both consolidation and extension of schemas. For example, a set of blocks has endless opportunities for rearrangement, new ways of setting out instructions and using schemas in ever new combinations.

MONTESSORI   Montessori's notion of sensitive periods, drawn from the Dutch Biologist De Vries, also unwittingly facilitated the development of schemas in a child's development and learning. Unbeknown to her, for she, like Froebel, was working before schemas were known, her Exercises of Practical Life, the pink tower and the didactic materials gave highly specific and pre-structured opportunities for children to practise and repeat as they exercised their schemas. Transformations were not aspects of schemas which were encouraged in her curriculum, but configurative aspects of schemas were (Bruce, 1976).

Schemas included were trajectories, vertical, horizontal, connection, on top, inside/outside, envelopment, transporting.

STEINER   Steiner's facilitation of schemas is more akin to that of Froebel. Whereas Montessori's curriculum implicitly supports schemas, Froebel and Steiner's curriculum both support and also extend the child's schemas. Steiner's use of silk materials and drapes to wrap around dolls, wooden blocks of irregular shapes, beeswax to mould into different shapes, the use of candles in aesthetic patterns, the circle, songs and movement, games, the sticks for eurhythmics, do not pre-structure or stipulate the way in which a schema is practised or exercised on the environment, but instead invite experimentation, variation and transformations of many kinds. Steiner's curriculum, like Froebel's, encourages transformation as much as configurative aspects of schemas.

Examples of facilitation of support and extension of schemas in Steiner's curriculum might be envelopment, enclosure, trajectories of all kinds, push and pull, inside/outside.

DARWIN   The study of schemas has emerged from Darwin's biological theories of evolution. Gradually, the disciplines of biology and psychology have moved closer to each other (Trevarthen, 1997). In recent years, biologists and mathematicians have also influenced each other more closely, for example the biologist Richard Dawkins (1993), or mathematical chaos theorist James Gleick (1988).

Schemas help us to see the order behind apparent chaos and disorder in a child's behaviour (Bruce, 1991, Chapter 7). It is very helpful to parents in particular, but also to professionals working with young children, to understand that children do not act in random ways, but that there are underlying patterns in what they do. This can ease difficult moments and phases as a child grows up.

PIAGET   Piaget developed his work on schemas from the 1920s over a period of 50 years, adjusting his terminology as he did so. In this book, the later terminology is used, as it is in most books referring to schemas (Athey, 1990; Matthews, 1994; Nutbrown, 1994). According to Piaget, babies are born with a repertoire of patterns in their behaviour which are generalised as they are put to use. These patterns of behaviour, such as sucking, gazing or tracking are called schemas. As they are generalised across different situations which the baby experiences, they become more and more sophisticated as the patterns increasingly co-ordinate into networks. Co-ordinated networks of schemas bring about the integration of one schema with another, so that schemas change, modify and transform into new schemas.

For example, the early gazing and tracking, reaching and grasping and sucking, all form a network of schemas which become co-ordinated and transformed. By four and a half months the baby can look at an object, reach out for it, grasp and suck the object. This is a new schema or network, often referred to as hand-eye co-ordination, or cluster schemas. Later, the ability to use and understand the purpose of a pulley, rotation or trajectory becomes linked with these early behaviours in more co-ordinated and sophisticated form.

The range of Piaget's theory

One of the reasons why it would be unhelpful only to use schemas in looking at the development and learning of young children is that every theory, including Piaget's, has its range (Bruce, Findlay, Read and Scarborough, 1995 p.28). It is important to look at the fitness of purpose of any theory, and to draw on theories which complement each other and so have some philosophical cohesion. This is very different from taking an eclectic approach where bits and bobs of different theories are taken in isolation, unconnected ways. This leads to inconsistency, confusion and classroom practice which constantly contradicts itself.

There is work to be done in linking Piaget's schemas with other theories, but the work of interactionist theorists such as Vygotsky, Bruner, Piaget and Dunn, and the psychodynamic theorists Winnicott and Erikson, have areas which blend comfortably with each other in important respects. (See Chapters 3 and 8.)

Of these theories, those of Dunn and Winnicott in different ways address socio-emotional issues most explicitly. Vygotsky emphasises language and socio-cultural aspects of thought, whilst Bruner emphasises representation, cognition and the role of the adult in scaffolding a child's learning. Piaget's theory, John Oates (1995) suggests, is the most over-arching and comprehensive theory to date. Even so in spite of some extensions, adjustments and modifications, Piaget's theory still has a narrow range and looks at socio-emotional and socio-cultural issues only implicitly. A theory that is all-encompassing has yet to be developed, and it may well be that this is not possible.

Piaget's theory: stages and networks

The most widely known aspect of Piaget's theory is his stages of development (Bruce, Findlay, Read and Scarborough, 1995). This was seized upon because it expanded the work that had been done on normative development by pioneers such as Gesell and others during the 1930s. This concentrated on milestones in a child's development (Bruce and Meggitt, 1996, p.31).

An example of the normative development approach would be:

- a two year-old jumps;
- a three year-old hops;
- a four year-old skips.

In Piaget's more sophisticated stage theory, children move from sensori motor (at 0 to 2 years approximately) to pre-operations (2 to 7 years) and then to complete operations (7 to 11 years) and formal operations (from 11 years onwards). The ages at which children develop have been found to be highly inaccurate, with huge cultural variations. For example, children growing up in the Swiss mountains understand and see things from different view points much earlier than children growing up in a flat town.

In moving into a new stage of development children transform quite literally. In fact, Piaget's stage theory (this aspect of his theory is called **hierarchisation**) is only one small part of his whole theory. Piaget also emphasises that a child's development progresses as a more and more complex network just as developing through a hierarchy of stages.

Piaget also gives a central place to biological maturation, experience and the socio-cultural context. These are called the 'stage independent' aspects of Piaget's theory. Another aspect of his independent theory is his concept of **equilibration**, which shows that children try things out according to what they expect and know (**assimilation**) and then adjust, transform and change when things are other than expected (**accommodation**).

Schemas are best seen as being linked with both the stage dependent (hierarchical) side of his theory and also with the stage independent aspects. Those using Piaget's theory have tended only to draw on selected aspects, rather than to use it holistically. It is best if it is used holistically, so that both the stage dependent and stage independent aspects are seen as co-ordinated and integrated.

Schemas do not disappear in later life, but they certainly change and transform as they co-ordinate and integrate as ever more complex and sophisticated networks of behaviour, and according to the socio-cultural context.

The way children are supported in the early use of their schemas has a deep emotional impact which remains. It is perhaps significant that Seymour Papert, inventor of the Turtle Computer, writes in his book *Mind Storms* (1980) of the way his early love of cogs at about the age of five years was encouraged by his parents. He left a transparent cover on his computer so that children could enjoy seeing the movement of the cogs. Unbeknown to his parents, they were supporting and extending his core radial cluster of schemas. The outcome of their support during his early childhood for the things which seemed to be fascinating to him was that in adult life he developed pioneer work on computers.

SCHEMAS AND THE TEN CORE PRINCIPLES OF EARLY CHILDHOOD EDUCATION AND CARE (0-8 YEARS)

Effective practice has always drawn on the theory available to inform it. Not all theory is useful to practitioners, but the core principles help those working in early childhood education and care to select and use theory in ways which illuminate and enhance consistent approaches which have a logic and sense of direction from the past leading to the future.

1   THE BEST WAY TO PREPARE CHILDREN FOR THEIR
     ADULT LIFE IS TO GIVE THEM WHAT THEY NEED AS
     CHILDREN

Where do schemas go after childhood and later in life?

Helping a toddler who is transporting, scattering and heaping objects everywhere by
providing objects which will not break or be dangerous when thrown, such as baskets
and other containers as well as space to move about unhampered, is contributing to a
child's preparation for adult life. It is doing so in ways appropriate to childhood for a
toddler.

Objects look different when scattered about, or when heaped together. But they are of
the same quantity even though their appearance changes. The transporting schema leads
towards a concept of quantity. A toddler who has rich transporting experiences is likely
to benefit as an adult and develop a sound concept of quantity. There are cross-cultural
variations. Some cultures stress transporting food and transferring it from large sacks to
small containers rather than buying food in pre-packaged form. Children in these cultures
will differ in their early experiences of quantity and transporting in relation to this.

Some examples of where schemas lead in developing into later concepts

These are only selected examples which can only give a glimpse of the importance of early
schemas for later development of concepts. Each of these concepts has feelings, ideas,
social relationships and object relationships as part of it which contribute to why we like,
dislike and are interested or not in particular things. The feelings about angles, clashes,
being covered up and so on are an important aspect of schemas. We are only at the beginning
of understanding this. Because Piaget's theory is so cognitive in its orientation, it is not
easy to explore feelings and relationships in looking at schema clusters. It may be necessary
to enhance and extend Piagetian theory because of this.

Early Schema	Later Concept
Vertical trajectory	Height
Horizontal trajectory	Length, time lines in history
Lateral trajectory	Angles
Intersections	Graphs in mathematics and co-ordinates, joinery in woodcraft (for example dovetail joins)
Grid	History charts, structures in buildings such as scaffolding
Trajectory scribble	Shading in art
Dab	Targeting a point (aiming at a point, using a compass, for example radius of a circle, point on a circumference) geometry
Enclosure	Maps, geometry, regular shapes, art, figure drawing and so on
Envelopment	Surrounding and covering, area in mathematics, greenhouses in biology and horticulture, hot air balloons and the physics of gases, concept of run off in geography as in rain running down a slope, camouflage colour and shading in art
Core and radial	Mini beasts in nature (biology), flowers and plants (botany), molecular structures, DNA (chemistry), snowflakes
Containers	Capacity and volume
On top	End points and what is between, that is exact length and exact height
Transporting	Quantity and understanding of number
Infilling	Volume, capacity, marquetry, roofing, fish scales, mosaics

Developing language and schemes

Cathy Nutbrown (1994, p.57), building on the work of Chris Athey (1990), stresses the importance of using appropriate descriptive language which links with a child's schemas during conversations. She gives the example of Stuart, looking at a hand-operated sewing machine. He tells the teacher 'it goes round and round'. The teacher replies 'Yes, it turns, it rotates', giving him the language to support his schemas.

Often children do not immediately incorporate new vocabulary into their vocabularies, but recognition gives meaning, which leads to deepening understanding and widening vocabulary. As Marian Whitehead (1996) points out, children begin to be able to use language to comment on their world.

2   CHILDREN ARE WHOLE PEOPLE WHO HAVE FEELINGS, IDEAS AND RELATIONSHIPS WITH OTHERS, AND WHO NEED TO BE PHYSICALLY, MENTALLY, MORALLY AND SPIRITUALLY HEALTHY

Ideas, feelings, relationships and physical development

Piaget (1968) stresses that movement, thinking, feelings and relationships cannot be separated. He wishes there were not two separate words for thinking and emotion. Schemas are about the whole child. They involve the physical and spiritual development of the child as well as ideas, feelings and relationships. They adjust and develop differently according to the cultural context, but schemas are a mechanism for co-ordinating and integrating development and learning.

Having things that can be predicted helps young children to settle into a group setting.

Amandip (three years) is new and every day the first thing he does is to go and find two planks in the wooden block area. He holds them upright and seems reassured by this start to his day. It is like his teddy bear. This anchors him and makes him feel secure. Further observations will give clues that he has a strong vertical (up/down) trajectory schema. It turns out to be significant that he holds the planks upright every day. The vertical trajectory schema co-ordinates and help him to make sense of what he finds in the nursery. It helps his feelings to be anchored and find calm as he settles into a new environment.

SCHEMAS AND FRIENDSHIPS Cath Arnold (1990) studied children in her family group and identified their schemas. She found that children who played together, either in parallel or co-operatively, shared similar schemas, or schemas that complemented each other. When quarrels occurred it often seemed that children had conflicting schemas.

> Josh wanted to make a row out of the wooden blocks (horizontal trajectory). Wanda came and took the end block and put it on to the tower he was building. She wanted to build upwards (vertical trajectory). Josh strongly objected and snatched back his block, accidentally knocking down Wanda's tower. A quarrel broke out with adults needing to intervene swiftly.

It would not be helpful to emphasise the importance of sharing and working together at this moment. These children are trying to do different things. Gradually it might be possible to suggest Josh makes a row of blocks which end at the base of Wanda's tower. This might encourage the children to co-ordinate vertical and horizontal trajectory schemas, but not today. Instead, each child's schema needs protection from an adult in order that each has freedom to learn.

Schemas and everyday life: living as a whole person

Every day we wake up, get up, do things, go to bed and sleep.

For a toddler and young children, teenagers and even for adults, getting dressed is a whole schematic experience. Putting on a T-shirt or pants involves going through, inside/outside, over and under, enveloping, enclosing, to name only some of the schemas.

The first dressing up clothes that children enjoy putting on and wearing in an early years setting tend to be hats, shoes and belts. These involve very basic schemas (in, out, containment and enclosure) in great evidence when observing toddlers. Soon they enjoy wearing capes or surrounding themselves with drapes. This is envelopment.

> George, (four years) was Zorro for several weeks, wearing an eye mask, hat, cape, gloves and long baggy trousers. He was almost completely covered by these clothes.

Schemas are not just to do with ideas that children are developing (pretending to be Zorro) they are also to do with feelings, relationships and physical development. It is easier to put on a hat than a cape. It is an emotional experience to pretend to be someone else.

Meal times are very emotional for children. It is a serious sadness for a child when an adult pours custard on the treacle sponge when they had wanted it beside their sponge cake. The schema is on top or enclosure. Putting curry on the rice, rather than beside it is a similarly emotional experience for adults. If a toddler, who has just begun to take note of enclosures is given a broken round shaped biscuit, there is likely to be a strong reaction.

There is often a fashion for wearing pony tails and plaits and an interest in Afro-Caribbean hairstyles when children are developing a core and radial schema cluster. Nancy would not go to her nursery until her hair was done as she wanted it. Her mother had to allow extra time to plait her hair each morning for several months.

Bedtime rituals involve schemas. It matters whether teddy is under the bed covers or on top of the pillow when the 'on top' and 'underneath' cluster of schemas is strong.

Helping with everyday chores (envelopment schema)

Children helping with everyday chores

The following few examples show how important this can be, providing children are not cajoled and nagged into helping. A positive approach is more likely to encourage children to positively want to help. Children 'recognise' what is involved in helping before they can 'perform' competently.

- **Infilling** – put the blocks in the box in patterned order.
- **Trajectory and containment** – children can sweep up sand with the dustpan and brush.
- **Trajectory** – sweep the floor or the playground. Remember the child may not be aware of beginning and ending of the handle (trajectory) and might concentrate only on the end with the brush on it. This is an important safety factor.
- **Envelopment** – wipe over the table tops to clean them.
- **Vertical trajectory** – (inside and outside) - stack the saucers and the plates in the home area and put them away in the cupboards.
- **Inside/outside containment (divided space grid)** – sort and put the cutlery away in a divided cutlery box in the home area.
- **Envelopment, inside/outside, containment, transporting** – put away the dolls in their beds in the home area.

SNACKS AND WASHING UP **Rotation of the taps in order to fill the jug and pour water into the washing up bowl.** This involves containment and rotation and transporting. The soap bubbles are spheres. The dish mop might be a core and radial type. Wiping up with a tea-towel involves a child in envelopment of crockery and cutlery.

Schemas and the child's sense of identity

Children use and explore schemas first of all in relation to themselves. Babies spend time putting their hand into the mouth of those they are close to. Where do I end and where do I begin? Toddlers put the whole of their body into a cardboard box and love to climb in and out over and over again.

> Three year-old Jean Paul (who is bilingual in French/English) arrives in the room and announces, putting his hand inside it, 'J'ai une poche'. He puts a walnut into his pocket from a bowl of nuts on the coffee table. He also enjoys putting pebbles in and out of different boxes.

Dens are popular and dressing up clothes too, when children use their whole bodies to exercise the inside schema cluster, but gradually they use objects as well as self. Going inside a den is about feelings and physical behaviour as much as it is about relationships, ideas and thoughts. Cosiness, completeness, safeness, feeling anchored, these are feelings, but also intellectual ideas are integrated within the schema clusters of envelopment, inside and outside. Recent studies of the brain emphasise that the chemistry of the brain brings feelings as well as thoughts (Greenfield, 1996; Nash, 1997, p.36-7). For example, anger, frustration and joy are all associated with chemical changes in the brain.

Schemas and feelings

Ferre Laevers, working in Belgium, has developed an Involvement Scale which is now in widespread use in the UK as a result of the Effective Early Learning Project directed during the 1990s by Professor Christine Pascal at Worcester College of Higher Education (Pascal and Bertram, 1997). Observations taken at Pen Green during the data gathering stage of the EEL Project suggest that the child who is an involved learner is a child whose schema clusters are being enhanced by a quality curriculum.

Recent work on brain studies suggests that the electrical activity of brain cells actually brings changes in the brain's physical structure. The schema clusters are modified and changed by experiences the child has. Experience has a huge impact on the 'blueprint' the child's brain is at birth (Nash, 1997, p.36). Experience, good or damaging, brings refinement or atrophying of thinking, feelings, relationships and physical developments. Children who do not play are not exercising their schema clusters. They are therefore not firing and wiring their brains optimally. This means that they learn less (Nash, 1997, p.37).

In his foreword 'The Gears of my Childhood', Papert (1980, p.vi) traces back to the way he developed a positive affective tone towards Mathematics to the early enjoyable experiences he had playing with cogs, cars and gears. Cogs are resonant of the core and radial schema, usually very strong in four year-olds, which he was. Emotionally and intellectually rich childhoods which allow involvement and play in natural biological schemas, quite literally lead to richer brains.

Relationships, feelings and interactions between adults and children, as well as the material provisions offered, both contribute effectively to the child's learning.

Listening, talking, negotiating, sharing ... and involved in a transporting, in/out schema cluster

3   SUBJECTS SUCH AS MATHEMATICS AND ART CANNOT
    BE SEPARATED; YOUNG CHILDREN LEARN IN AN
    INTEGRATED WAY AND NOT IN NEAT, TIDY
    COMPARTMENTS

Schemas are integrated, co-ordinated networks of behaviour through which children can gain access to knowledge and understanding, and sort out their ideas, feelings and relationships. They are part of the way the child's brain is wired. Depending on where the child lives and the socio-cultural context, children will be encouraged to develop schemas in relation to, for example in the UK, the Desirable Outcomes Documents for four year-olds, which are different in England, Wales, Scotland and Northern Ireland, before moving on to the legal requirements of the National Curriculum (See Somerset County Council, 1997 and Birmingham, 1997).

Curriculum for 0 to 3 years in relation to schemas

Although not explicitly designed to empower children's schema clusters, the treasure baskets developed by Eleanor Goldschmied (1994) for sitting babies and her bags full of objects for heuristic (exploratory) play for toddlers, do in fact lend themselves to the rich development of children's schemas.

Curriculum for 3 to 8 years in relation to schemas

> In an early years setting, a teacher helped the children to extend their mathematical learning. She rigged up a pulley with a bucket and hung it above the paddling pool. Four year-old Nayam and three year-old Shazia worked with this most of the morning. Nayam was concerned with filling the bucket before it was released. He focused on fullness, sometimes with water, sometimes with toys he had collected. Shazia, on the other hand, was concerned with holding the rope right until the bucket reached the top and then releasing it. Her interest lay in the splash, which she enjoyed enormously. She and Nayam tended to argue, as their concerns were different.

ADULTS CAN SUPPORT SCHEMAS WITH APPROPRIATE LANGUAGE   With the help of the teacher, they reached a compromise by which he filled the bucket, and she hoisted and released it. The role of the adult here was, as Bruner would assert, to diagnose the incipient intention of each child in order that the mathematics in the situation could be developed. The teacher used the mathematical language of 'full' and 'empty', 'half full', 'nearly full', and so on for Nayam.

One of the important functions of language in mathematics is that it should help children to comment on the world (Whitehead, 1996). There is a need for adults to extend learning through appropriate language in genuine conversation. Genuine conversation seems to arise more often when adults have an understanding of schemas and so tune into what the child says (Meade with Cubey, 1995, p.70).

> Shazia had also shown great interest in the paper aeroplanes introduced by the teacher, and the balloons which were blown up, but not tied, so that when released they darted across the room making a squeaky noise. These were other experiences of hold and release which added to Shazia's knowledge of trajectories. She would repeat the trajectory action with her finger where it met, using words like 'up' and making squeaky noises in imitation of the balloon. This was a mathematical experience.

> In a different nursery school, three year-old Perry's teacher introduced paper aeroplanes and noted that Perry was fascinated by the vapour trails left in the sky by the aeroplanes which passed over the school She brought in some streamers and he ran, with streamers unravelling behind him. She was helping him to make tangible a trajectory path rather like the aeroplane's vapour trail.

TOPOLOGICAL SCHEMAS   Shazia and Perry were both using a repertoire of topological concepts to explore trajectories (Athey, 1990, p.83-85) as well as their 'hold and release' structure which they have had from the age of three months (Davies, 1994).

Williams and Shuard (1976) point out that:

> *Children notice what are called topological properties first, i.e. not those involving measurement but those concerned with such things as the general outline of a shape, whether it is open or closed or has one or more holes in it, the nearness of one thing to another, the position of a thing between two others. Thus, though distance has little meaning for them, they understand what is meant by such concepts as 'next to' and 'between'.*

ON TOP, UNDER, OVER, NEAR AND FAR   The relationship between the bucket and the top of the pulley, the throwing of the paper aeroplane, the starting-point of running with the streamer, the bucket in the water in the paddling pool, the aeroplanes landing on the floor, are all an exploration of beginning and end points, and the relationship between them, or order (Athey, 1990, p.85). The topological notions involved are proximity, separation, connection and relationships between them, or order. These link with Piaget's notion of schemas.

In this case, Perry and Shazia are presenting a trajectory schema – a generalisable and repeatable pattern of behaviour. Identifying this can be valuable in formulating teaching strategies, and presenting young children with a balanced curriculum. This needs to be based on awareness on the part of the adult of the area of knowledge to be developed.

LINKING SCHEMAS WITH MATHEMATICS, DANCE   However, although it is certainly true that here mathematical knowledge is being introduced which matches the child's developing schemas, these schemas could also be developed in ways which are not purely mathematical. Schemas also contain the 'stuff of dance' (Davies, 1969). The child's schemas are a resource, an access mechanism, which can be used to tackle any area of knowledge. Observing and identifying schemas informs curriculum planning. The adult needs to be aware of the child's schemas, and then to consider different curriculum possibilities and next steps in learning for the child at that stage. The adult needs to bring the two together, as Perry's teacher did in introducing the streamers, or Shazia's in introducing the pulley.

SCHEMAS INFORM CURRICULUM PLANNING   Knowing that a child is exploring trajectories is not enough. The adult can extend this exploration using different areas of knowledge, and introducing material and engaging in appropriate language or conversations. Knowing the schema informs the adult's curriculum plans, and helps the adult to plan with appropriate selection and flexibility (Pollard, 1997, p.181).

MOVEMENT   Mollie Davies (1977, p.3) writes: 'Types of movement activities in which children spontaneously engage should lead to structured opportunities in the school situation'. The structuring of the curriculum can be direct or indirect, but it is an essential contribution to the child's broad and rich development. For children of 0 to 8 years, the emphasis is on indirect structuring of the curriculum.

Davies (1995) also says: 'If exploration goes on for too long without giving dance opportunities for consolidation and extension, it holds children back'. She suggests that children need free exploration in their movement education but also adult led experiences and opportunities for consolidation and extension the child's natural schema clusters. Lydia Gerhardt (1994) shares this view, and extends it to working to include children with special educational needs.

> Four year-old Kuang was using a remote controlled computer toy. He wanted to push it. The adult showed him that he needed to instruct it to move forward, backwards and sideways by pressing the appropriate key (marked with a direction arrow) and another key (marked with a number) telling it how many paces to move. He quickly understood this, and made it go forward to the end of the room.

Then he wanted it to go to the other end. He picked it up and turned it round, ready to go back. The adult showed him how to use the backwards arrow to reverse the direction, but he found this intervention annoying. This demonstrates his stage of development. Kuang could deal with trajectories going in one direction, but not with reversing the direction.

He was taken to see trains at Waterloo Station. Since this is a terminal, when trains reached the end of the line, they had to retrace their direction out of the station. After seeing the trains he enjoyed action songs about trains reversing their paths – for example, 'Puffer Train' and stories by Rev. W. Awdry such as *Thomas the Tank Engine* with shunting and so on.

He was also encouraged to play games like 'What's the time, Mr. Wolf!' in which children reverse in their tracks when the 'wolf' comes. It was six months before he began to retrace his steps in games. Once he did this, he used the reverse button on the computer toy. He was using a horizontal trajectory schema in developing these understandings.

COMPUTER WORK   Computer work does not teach children concepts which they do not yet possess. It is simply another experience through which to broaden what they can already do. It was a useful tool for the adult in diagnosing Kuang's schema level, and a worthwhile additional experience once the structures of reversing a trajectory were emerging.

MUSIC

In a reception class, children four years of age had a huge magnetic board with magnetised musical notes in a box which could be put on the board. They would sing a tune and put it on the board without inhibition.

Sonya, four years, made a flat line of notes, and sang it 'da, da, da, da' pointing as she went. Her sounds were the dynamic aspect of the horizontal schema and the notation on the board was the configurative aspect of the schema.

The teacher played an arpeggio on the piano, pointing out that it went up and then down. Sonya asked her to put it on the board. Sonya saw an open semi-circle. She was just beginning to use these in her drawings and paintings. This was why her teacher thought she might enjoy arpeggio. The teacher's observations and identification of the open semi-circle scheme informed her curriculum planning so that she directly taught Sonya about arpeggios.

She learnt to start practising singing arpeggios going up and down the scale again and again. Her teacher began to wonder whether it had been such a good idea to introduce arpeggios since she sang them non-stop for several days!

> She also learnt to play her flat da, da, da, da tune on the drums, the piano, the xylophone, the shakers and the African talking box, as well as the descant recorder. This was a trajectory schema – horizontal in this instance.

DRAWING AND PAINTING John Matthews (1994, p.41 and p.43) in his study of his three children as they grew up, followed their development in painting and drawing as well as their model making. He writes about his son Joel, who at thirteen months has learned to toddle:

> *Joel also likes to carry his cup of milk around with him. However, co-ordinating these two new skills is not easy and he frequently spills milk. On one occasion, the milk falls on to a smooth, shiny, concrete floor. Joel, his jaw dropping, watches with great interest the spreading white shape. Then, he puts his right hand into the milk and starts to smear it, using the horizontal arching motion. He quickly brings his other hands into play, so that both hands are fanning to and fro in synchrony, meeting in the midline, until they become out of phase. In this way, he makes the two sectors of a circle in the spilt milk.*

Over the next few weeks Joel is introduced by his father to paint.

> *Between 13 and 14 months Joel keeps repeating vertical and horizontal arcing movements. Because we know that Joel at this time has a range of options open to him, we can be fairly certain that when he reaches out into the milk, or applies the brush to the floor, he does so with the intention of making a movement.*

SUMMARY OF SCHEMAS

Name of child	Schema clusters – mainly trajectories in the examples used.
Nayam	space as a container inside/outside/fullness (topological schemas)
Shazia	crashing and moving trajectories, vertical and horizontal action schemas, release
Perry	horizontal trajectory recognition of the beginning and end of trajectories
Kuang	horizontal trajectory moving in one direction and then reversing trajectories
Sonya	horizontal trajectory – her sounds are dynamic aspects, her notation is the configurative aspect
Joel	arcing trajectories (Matthews, 1994)

Each child is unique

Joel, like children trans-globally and cross-culturally, is, in his own unique way, using basic schemas in his early mark-making. The way he uses his schema network links with this statement by Judith Jamison, an American contemporary dancer (in Davies, 1995, p.160): 'There is only one of me. There is only one of anybody. That is why steps look different on different people'.

Pat Gura (1996, p.55) also emphasises the universal aspects of the schema clusters.

> Schemas have remained the same since the dawn of human kind and this is why we can detect similarities between things like megalithic structures and children's block play. Points, lines, boundaries, connection, enclosure, envelopment are all examples of schemas. All occur in block play and all occur in the early dry stone building of our ancestors.
>
> …If we are looking for connections between our human past and the world we live in today, schemas may be a promising way to go.

Schemas connect us with our past, with humans on a trans-global scale, and help us to metacognate (reflect) on who we are as unique individuals. To use Donald Hebb's phrase they show us 'the difference in the sameness' of being a human.

Children with disabilities

The work of Lillie Nielsen in Denmark is interesting. She designs a Little House for a child with disabilities based on her observations of the child's needs and the observations of the parents, and yet, schema clusters are both supported and extended through the Little House.

First, the child is observed over a period of time, and when the team of parents and staff feel that they have some idea of what captures the child's awareness or interest, a 'Little House' is built around the child. This links with the time honoured tradition of den building, participated in by children all over the world.

> Barry, a child with cerebral palsy, liked to feel enclosed and to reach out and touch the walls, and to reach up and touch the ceiling in his little house. He did this lying on his back. He tried to catch hold of circular objects which were hanging, especially those which were of the bracelet or ring type. Envelopment, enclosure and rotation were strong interests. He selected objects with these properties as they hung from his ceiling. He cooed to himself contentedly as he reached out for them.

From Roman roads to blockplay road building

The dominant schema cluster (envelopment, enclosure and rotation) helped the less dominant action schemas of reach, grasp, hold and release, and also encouraged their co-ordination. By working with Barry's strengths and interests, the aspects of his development which need attention are also developed. In order to reach the weaker aspects of a child's development, it is best to access these through the child's strengths.

The work of Lillie Nielsen has been developed in the UK, particularly through the influence of Robert Orr (1993) working with children with profound disabilities. Whereas Lillie Nielsen's work can be linked implicitly with schema clusters, he has made direct links with schema clusters.

Adam Ockleford (RNIB Education Service) has developed work with music for children with profound disabilities with an emphasis on visual impairment, but these would also be suitable for all children in the spirit of inclusivity. The music implicitly uses schema clusters such as rotation, enclosure and trajectory.

4   CHILDREN LEARN BEST WHEN THEY ARE GIVEN APPROPRIATE RESPONSIBILITY, ALLOWED TO MAKE ERRORS, DECISIONS AND CHOICES, AND RESPECTED AS AUTONOMOUS LEARNERS

Schemas enable children, in a natural way, to make decisions and choices. Schemas help children to learn from errors. Schemas encourage autonomy. Without autonomy children would not become successful learners. They will always be reliant on others controlling and leading their learning throughout their lives.

Mark, three years, began spitting at people. He could target someone's eye with unerring accuracy. The schema was a targetting 'trajectory' with 'dab' (the spit was the dab schema).

His mother bought a pea shooter and suggested he could target cereal boxes on the kitchen table. He played happily for hours. He had a straw and newspaper pellets as objects. He willingly picked them up when he had finished and helped throw them in a rubbish bin (targetting the rubbish bin by throwing things into it).

In the bath he blew water at floating objects. The pleasure of these pursuits and his enjoyment of the company of his mother and other friends far outweighed the frustration of people's reaction when he spat in their eye. This was a better use of his targetting trajectories. He stopped spitting in people's eyes.

> The learning possibilities of targetting trajectories have given him autonomy of
> learning about forces in physics, but he needed an adult's help to do so in an
> acceptable and worthwhile way.

5   SELF-DISCIPLINE IS EMPHASISED

Children who develop self-discipline have high self-esteem and behave 'better'. (See
Chapter 8, the Ability to Decentre.) The four year-old (often in reception class with a
teacher untrained to work with the age phase) who is required to sit most of the day at a
table, involved in fine motor activity and adult set tasks, is either likely to become 'naughty'
and to fidget and stray from the table, pull the hair of neighbours, roll pencils on the
ground, lose concentration, or to behave in school but become bad tempered and tearful
at home, perhaps returning to bed wetting.

This is because asking children to sit for long periods involved in fine motor activities is
flying in the face of the natural behaviour of a child of this age, and denying children the
opportunity to learn in the ways their biological make up is programmed to do (Davies,
1995). Young children should be active and interactive learners (as the theories of Piaget,
Vygotsky and Bruner emphasise). Being told to sit down, sit still, stand in a nice line, stop
talking, listen and colour in worksheets is never going to develop a child's self-discipline.
It will at best produce conformity to the voice of authority.

Children will persevere when they initiate and choose

Kevin at three years old loved to climb. He climbed furniture and was reprimanded constantly for doing so, but he had no access to climbing frames or gymnastic equipment, except 20 minutes a week in school from the age of five years. By the age of nine years he was scaling walls and stealing from houses and flats. He loved the danger and the thrill of heights.

By the age of 13 he was sent to an experimental unit where he was closely observed, assessed and given appropriate therapy and education. It was decided, amongst a variety of measures, that he should be taught to rock climb. He loved it, quickly learning the techniques.

During the years 13 to 16 he slowly began to change from delinquent to ordinary citizen, and remained so in adult life. He spoke of the importance of being set clear boundaries in the unit, not stealing other people's property. He was taught to think about the cause and effect of this and the implications of his actions. To steal was not acceptable.

Later, as an adult he spoke of his experiences in the unit, of being able to find an acceptable way to fulfil his joy of climbing heights, of being valued in his own right and having his needs specially thought about, being nurtured and feeling that he mattered. His vertical trajectory schema and the thrill of the danger of climbing remained important from childhood, through adolescence and into adulthood. It became an important access tool or mechanism which took him from childhood 'naughtiness' (climbing furniture) to adolescence (delinquency) into ordinary adult life (with a passionate hobby of rock climbing).

Recognising a child's schema does not make it acceptable behaviour

Chris Athey (1990) points out that it is not necessary to love a schema when it is identified. The schema itself is morally neutral, it is simply a biological pattern of behaviour. However, the way that it is used socio-culturally is not morally neutral. Its use can annoy others or be morally unacceptable. It is very important that adults do not feel they must support unacceptable behaviour just because it is a schema cluster. Allowing a child to be unacceptable does not help the child. It makes children dislikeable and often they are emotionally rejected or shunned by children and adults alike. However, finding acceptable ways in which a child can use a schema cluster enhances a child's self-esteem as it did for Mark and Kevin. When children feel disliked or disapproved of, their behaviour usually seems to deteriorate and their self-esteem plummets (Roberts 1995). When they feel liked, valued and approved of, their behaviour improves.

Children need to be unconditionally accepted by adults who work with them professionally. Some adults have problems in managing to achieve this with some children, but children are deeply aware when this happens and sensitive to it.

> Jenny, 7 years, has a visual impairment. Like many children disabled in this way she often rocks to and fro. Her family do not want her to do this. At school she is taught a tune on the piano and thoroughly enjoys it. The rocking as she plays is acceptable, in fact it brings pride and pleasure to those close to her. As she learns more tunes she begins to rock only when playing at the piano. She begins to inhibit rocking in other contexts. Her trajectory schema is appropriately used in the piano playing situation.

> Rebecca's mother became ill, and Rebecca carried paper tissues to her whenever requested, and sometimes spontaneously. Her behaviour was, fortuitously, appropriate for the occasion. She felt that it had been a success, and when some flowers were delivered for her mother, she regularly took these to different points in the room. Her mother and her friend praised her for looking after her mother so well.
>
> She used her ability to transport objects to care for her mother (for example transporting tissues, flowers, drinks and slippers). In this way she experienced being kind, caring and responsible. Not only were her efforts praised, but they were recognised and genuinely appreciated. Since her mother had not been ill in this way before, Rebecca was also gaining a new experience caring for the sick.

Judy Dunn (1988) suggests that children learn self-discipline if they are helped to see the results of hurting and helping people and showing them that you care. The concern children have for themselves develops and becomes concern for others too. Helping children into the appropriate use of schemas helps in this.

6   THERE ARE TIMES WHEN CHILDREN ARE ESPECIALLY ABLE TO LEARN PARTICULAR THINGS

Paul, three years, is observed to be often involved in a schema cluster of rotation, enclosure and connection with trajectories. He does not yet draw using the core and radial schema. He loves to unlock doors with keys and turn door knobs, which annoys adults. He spends ages at the sink turning taps off and on. He is removed from the bathroom when the floor constantly becomes flooded. He does spiral shaped scribble when he draws and paints.

He is interested when an older child brings a conker into the nursery on a string. He swings it dangerously and has to be stopped.

He likes the windscreen wipers on the car, and wants to put the umbrella up and down and up and down, but he is very rough with it so it is taken from him to save it from being broken. He is frustrated. It seems that each time he is stopped when he tries to exercise his partial rotation schema.

In the light of these observations, the staff decide to introduce a pulley into the outside area.

Indoors a tea urn is introduced and he spends long periods turning the tap off and on and making the water spray out as he puts his hand over the tap (a dynamic core and radial effect). The classroom provision and experience offered helps cause his schema cluster to be exercised in ways which are more acceptable to adults than before. When using the pulley he is concerned with the cause and effect aspect. When he rotates the handle, the bucket goes up. When he rotates the handle the other way, it comes down.

He does not yet understand how the pulley or the tea urn works at an abstract or operational level of the schema. However, he can see the cause and effect relationship of turning and twisting the handle one way or the other on either the pulley or the tea urn.

The cluster of schemas in evidence is:

- rotation;
- connection of trajectory to enclosure;
- emergent core and radial.

The level of schema in this example is cause and effect.

- Both his emotional well being and his involvement (Laevers, 1996) in experiences are good.

- The learning in relation to the English Desirable Learning Outcomes documents is mostly in relation to 'knowledge and understanding of the world'.

It is important to note that Paul does not yet draw or paint using the core and radial schema, but he does seem to have some embryonic understanding of it. Children use schemas embryonically and are attracted to the way their schemas are echoed in the socio–cultural and material world long before they can 'perform' them at will. In other words, recognition of a schema and some early awareness of it comes before the ability to perform.

> Tom, three years, spent an afternoon throwing a stick into a bush in the garden. His mother could not understand what he was about, but left him to it, staying near because of the potential dangers of stick throwing. It was months later when he began to draw core and radials, and yet sticks in a bush made the same prickly effect. Prior to this he had picked out pictures of beetles and ladybirds in books. Recognition of the core and radial schema comes before performance of it (Athey, 1990 p.69).

Children are born to learn

Children are born to learn. We only need to help them. We don't always know exactly what is needed. If we observe and support a child's schema clusters and see what the child is serious about, we find this informs us over time, but we can begin to extend the learning because we know the general direction that the child is taking.

By supporting what he knows of partial rotation, in educationally worthwhile ways, Paul is less frustrated (and so are the adults!) and he learns more effectively.

Tom is safe playing alone, throwing sticks in the garden with his mother nearby, but this would not be acceptable in a group situation. He could be offered other choices over and above the basic provision of large numbers of clay and wooden twigs at the clay table, or a dartboard with suckers on the darts, splash painting, dish mops, buckets of water and a wall to bash, or a hose on a hot summer day, and fountain making in the water tray.

7 WHAT CHILDREN CAN DO (RATHER THAN WHAT THEY CANNOT DO) IS THE STARTING POINT OF A CHILD'S EDUCATION

Schemas help adults to enhance what children can do naturally but in socially worthwhile directions. In a traditional early years setting, children make relationships with adults and other children and are given materials, equipment and experiences which emphasise 'can do' rather than 'cannot do'.

Chris Athey (1990, p.41) writes: 'an important role of the teacher is to feed spontaneous structures with content, not necessarily found at home, or in the street or playground'. She goes on to say: 'Within the highest concept of education, teaching facilitates and "fleshes out" spontaneous and natural concepts with worthwhile curriculum content'.

The traditional toddler group or nursery/infant classroom has always implicitly made good provision for the 'can do' aspects of schemas and given children access to learning. The traditional equipment and provision, and the garden which is an important part of the curriculum, offers children opportunities to 'recognise' and reflect their emergent schemas, to practise and consolidate their repertoire of schemas, and so gain access to higher order ideas and deepened feelings and relationships which they can actively use in their lives.

In offering a 'can do' quality curriculum which integrates within in an active understanding of schemas, early childhood workers need to be aware of three things. These involve being able to:

- observe and identify the child's schemas;
- support the child's schemas through effective use of the material provision and interactions with people in the environment;
- extend the child's learning from the starting point of what the child can do by enhancing and adding to material provision, environment and interaction with people.

An example of how observational schemas can lead to informed planning in the curriculum is shown in the following chart. It is taken from case studies by Sue Rice (1996, p.72-6).

Observing the Schema cluster	Supporting the Schema cluster	Extending the Schema cluster
Joanne (3 yrs, 11 mths) at home, mother reports she likes to overfill containers and cover surfaces, and to be wrapped in a large towel, and to wrap toys in towels or blankets. She likes to dress up in flowing clothes and veils and collect toys in her arms until they overflow. Swimming, she loves to feel waves of water breaking over her head. Mother was concerned that she did not seem to make friends easily. Schemas – envelopment cluster.	Filling containers and covering objects, and fitting them inside boxes at the workshop area. Using a selection of boxes on a display of boxes with cones, acorns, conkers, leaves etc. to put in the boxes. A particular interest (with Edward a fellow enveloper) in a ring box, and a box with a sliding lid, and a pencil box. She was drawn to a bowl of cornflour and water and smothered her arms and hands in the green slime with great energy and enthusiasm. She spent increasing amounts of time in the home area when she wore layers of dressing up clothes. At home she used more veils for dressing up and covered her hands in chocolate when making crispy cakes. She was interested in the number of mattresses on which the Princess slept in the story of the Princess and the pea. Joanne's mother expressed her pleasure in what she had observed and said how Joanne's activities seemed to have taken a new meaning during conversations with staff about envelopment and how she and Joanne were enjoying their time together.	Kim's game, involving covering a selection of objects when guessing which one had been removed (with an adult and two other children). Wrapping baked potatoes in foil to bake at a Barbecue to celebrate Divali. (Small group and adult) She enjoyed a bowl of paper mache (small group and an adult) Water play – involving polythene bags filled with different coloured water. She pummelled them until they burst. Parcels buried in the sand tray, when she approached, the sand looked smooth and she looked disappointed. As she pressed her hands in, she discovered a parcel, and her face gleamed with a smile. She opened the parcel carefully to avoid tearing the paper, and then gathered all the objects revealed, scooping and pushing the sand with her other hand to make sure nothing was missed. She found a box with a lid in which to collect the treasures until they could be shared.

8   IMAGINATION, CREATIVITY AND ALL KINDS OF SYM-
    BOLIC BEHAVIOUR (READING, WRITING, DRAWING,
    DANCING, MUSIC, MATHEMATICAL NUMBERS,
    ALGEBRA, ROLE PLAY AND TALKING) DEVELOP AND
    EMERGE WHEN CONDITIONS ARE FAVOURABLE

The traditional early years curriculum appeals to children because it creates conditions favourable for the development of symbolic behaviour. It is tuned into every level of complexity at which a schema can operate.

As we saw at the beginning of the chapter, schemas have different levels of complexity within them, and a child may be functioning at an earlier or later level of the schema, by moving in and out of levels according to the newness of the materials and experience, or the intimacy and relaxed nature of the relationships with other children and the family worker enjoying being spoken to in a small group.

Schemas may function at:

- **Sensori–motor level** (senses and actions/movements);
- **Symbolic level** (making one thing stand for another);
- **Cause and effect level** (sometimes called functional dependency);
- **Abstract thought level** (when reversibility and transformation are co-ordinated in thinking so that ideas can be held in mind in the absence of any concrete reminders)

(See Athey 1990, p.171-2; Meade with Cubey, 1995, p.3-4)

Chris Athey divides the symbolic level (1990, p.69) into sub sections:

- graphic representations of people and objects which are still;
- action representations of the movement (dynamic) aspects of people, objects and events;
- speech representations of either static or dynamic aspects.

SYMBOLIC BEHAVIOUR HAS LAYERS   Symbolic behaviour has layers which become more and more co-ordinated as the network strengthens. This also links with brain studies (Greenfield, 1996), and Gardner's (1980) notion of multiple intelligences. Schemas continue to be important throughout life from birth to death, as adults continue to use both the senses and the movement aspects of schemas. Actively seeking out things in the environment which echo, match and resonate with schemas biologically within the person, or raising schemas to the surface through recognition that what is 'out there' matches with internalised schema clusters, are both important socio-cultural influences on schemas.

- Dandelion clocks resonate with the core and radial schema, both configurative when still and dynamic when blown.
- A fencing tournament resonates with dynamic trajectories of all kinds.
- Written English lower casement letter formations resonate with configurative grids, semi-circles and core radial schemas.

9 RELATIONSHIPS WITH OTHER PEOPLE (BOTH ADULTS AND CHILDREN) ARE OF CENTRAL IMPORTANCE IN A CHILD'S LIFE

Schemas have a huge impact on the way we relate to each other. We saw in an earlier section that Cath Arnold (1990) found that children often become friends when they have similar or complementary schemas.

Chris Athey (1990, p.63) states:

> ...*most adults know when they have struck a chord in a child. The child's closely focused attention usually signifies that a good match has been made between an adult stimulus and some particular or general concern in the child.*

The TTA-funded parent-staff partnership practitioner research project at Pen Green Research and Development Base (1996/97) found that intimacy was important if young children were to learn effectively in education and care settings when their parents were not present. Tuning into children's schemas was helpful in developing this project (Whalley & Arnold, 1997).

Natasha, two years, made constructions with the wooden blocks. Each time she did this she seemed concerned that her construction should look symmetrical at each end.

She was videoed in the nursery making these constructions while her family worker sat alongside her gently protecting her block play by his presence. Other children came and looked interested in her construction.

As soon as the video was shown to Natasha's mother, she recognised her concern for symmetry, and linked it with the mathematical concept of quotity (this kind of twoness which has symmetry). She loved to hold two identical objects, one in each hand, and to set them down opposite each other. Wooden block play lends itself to experimentation with quotity. Adults were able to be more sensitive to her.

She regularly attends a group that the staff run called 'Understanding Your Child's Learning'. Because the family worker and parents shared what they knew of Natasha's interest in symmetry, they were able to be more sensitive to her both at home and the early years setting.

Natasha's mother felt justly proud of her daughter's mathematical achievements, and this warmth was felt by Natasha. The family worker felt that his work with Natasha was being valued by her family.

Children thrive when the adults around them work well together and respect and value the contributions that each makes to the child's schema clusters as they develop and learn.

'Nothing gets under a parent's skin more quickly or permanently than the illumination of his or her own child's behaviour' (Athey, 1990, p.66).

In 1993, Elizabeth Whalley, inspired by her visits to Pen Green where schemas were studied, undertook a project for Buckinghamshire LEA introducing schemas to parents and staff. Parents willingly kept observations of their children at home, and shared them with staff. One very positive parent said: 'It's so personal'. A teacher said: 'I feel more confident about what I'm saying'.

Ashley (four years) made lines of cars on top of the sofa, used hoopla to drop rings on hooks on a board, connected pegs together in a line, helped wash-up, and enjoyed seeing water run down the plate as he squeezed the sponge. He tied things up with string and rope, and found his toy hand-cuffs, hand-cuffed anyone willing (such as the milk lady!), made traps out of rope for Daddy, and enjoyed the film 'Home Alone' at a friend's house. He painted hand-cuffs at nursery. His schema cluster is trajectory, connection and enclosure.

When adults spending time with children enjoy their company, and can understand more about what they do and why, both children and adults relax, and the result is more quality in every respect.

10 QUALITY EDUCATION IS ABOUT THE CHILD, THE CONTEXT IN WHICH LEARNING TAKES PLACE AND THE KNOWLEDGE AND UNDERSTANDING WHICH THE CHILD DEVELOPS AND LEARNS

Schemas make an important contribution to a child's learning and development:

- through the socio-cultural context in which they develop;
- schemas support children in what they know;
- schemas extend children into what they do not yet know about, ideas, feelings, relationships and physical development;
- schemas are genetically endowed mechanisms, biological 'rough blueprints' (Nash, 1997), through which children are helped to think, feel, move and relate to other people and environments.
- Schemas influence and enhance a child's uniqueness.
- Schemas modify, change, transform and sophisticate as they develop.
- Schemas challenge those who argue that there is only fragmentation of humanity across cultures and no common ground across child development transglobally.
- Schemas help us to tune into children and families and so help development and learning.
- Schemas help us to make progress as we develop in an evolutionary (not revolutionary) way towards best practice building on the early childhood traditions.
- Schemas help us to link and find shared ground but not to become standardised and uniform in our practice.
- Schemas help us to celebrate human and cultural diversity.

Although schemas are very complex to study and need plenty of time to observe and come to understand, over time they help adults working with children and their children and their families to enjoy their time together more easily. It is worthwhile making the effort to study them.

6
■

REPRESENTATION

When we represent, we find a way of bringing back something or someone from a previous situation. The process that is called 'representation' is the way that we manage to keep hold of our past experiences in an orderly way. The more we learn about how humans develop, the more it seems that everything links and interacts in a web or a network. When we represent something, we might:

- remember back and have an image in our mind of something or someone from a prior experience, and replay it in our mind;
- we might actually make something stand for something that is not present.

Bruner (1981) says that this process of representation, works in three inter-related ways:

- through the enactive mode;
- through the iconic mode;
- through the symbolic mode.

The **enactive mode** is the way that we represent experiences through the doing. For example, after a while we only have to get on a bike and we can ride it. Early childhood educators have long believed in the importance of 'learning by doing' for young children as this quotation from a nursery school prospectus shows:

> *The children are learning through the doing, at this stage of development. This means that they will experiment with materials and get messy, very messy. Please do not send your children in good clothes that cannot take glue, paint, cooking mixture, pet food and many activities that we provide.*

The **iconic mode** is the way we represent with an image which stands for the person, event or object. Take, for example, a photograph. The traditional early years curriculum (0–8 years) has always encouraged children to make images in their minds, as well as using books, pictures, photographs and interest tables to keep fresh in the mind experiences that the children have had. For example, after a visit to a pond to collect frog spawn, the interest table might be set up complete with photographs of events in sequence and displaying the equipment used (for example nets and jars). As children interact with the interest table, they keep their experiences alive and learn from them. The emphasis that Bruner places on doing ('active learning') – imaging and making things stand for things symbolically –

demonstrates the importance of real and powerful experiences, which children can reflect on and use to learn through.

Learning outdoors is equally as important as learning indoors. Young children do their best learning outdoors because the enactive mode can be used to the full. Every aspect of learning interacts with every other aspect in a network or interwoven web. It is important to remember that children will find drawing and early attempts to write easier if they also use the 'doing' and 'imaging' modes to the full.

The **symbolic mode** means that we can represent something in a code. Language is a code. We can say the word 'cat' to stand for a cat. The word is not the real thing. It is a symbol of a cat. It stands for a cat.

Children are encouraged to develop symbolic codes through, for example, drawing and painting (Matthews, 1993), dancing (Davies, 1995), imaginative play (Gura, 1996), making models and language and literacy, writing and reading (Whitehead, 1996), arithmetic, algebra, geometry and so on.

Children need experiences which give opportunities for all three of Bruner's modes of representation – doing, imaging and making things stand for something in a symbolic way. Traditionally, the early childhood curriculum has done this. It is important that the traditional early years curriculum (0-8 years) is not neglected so that the process of representation in children is safeguarded. It is, after all, one of the most important of all human developmental processes.

A workshop area offers children opportunities to carry out complex ideas.

THE BEGINNINGS OF REPRESENTATION

Some children need a teddy or some other favourite object to sleep with. It helps them to feel safe and secure as they sleep. It links the child with other people, especially parents and close family, when they are separated from them, perhaps by going to sleep, or when going to the early childhood setting, or when spending the afternoon with friends or neighbours. Winnicott (1971) said objects such as these are 'transitional objects'. Some children use their transitional objects (for example the teddy bear) as a substitute for important people in their lives whilst they are away from them. Other children need important people to be present if they are to fully enjoy their teddy bear, or transitional object.

I spent a weekend with a two year-old girl called Ellen and her transitional object 'Baby Lion'. I had not met Baby Lion before. He became a new friend.

Baby Lion was taken up by Ellen when her mother started leaving her with a friend one afternoon a week. Baby Lion is truly transitional, standing for the mother who returns at the end of the afternoon, the link across the separation between them. Also, Baby Lion can stand for Ellen, who goes to a friend's house and has adventures without her mother, yet with her once removed. Baby Lion is also Ellen's companion while she is there. He is both Ellen's possession and her creation. The transitional object belongs only to the child. No one else can presume to alter it in any way. This situation has strong links with children's early attempts at writing, which we shall explore later (in Chapter 7 on communication, language and literacy).

At the weekend, Baby Lion had a pony ride. Ellen did not. Baby Lion ate lunch and slept. Baby Lion is quite a character, having moods and ideas which have to be accommodated.

Something significant is happening here. Imaginative, representational play is developing around Baby Lion. Other children and adults are willing to have him watch while they play with Ellen. He is sometimes on the edge of games with the children. Sometimes he is part of them. He was taken up a mountain (the stairs) and had adventures. He helped Ellen to find her way into group play with other children. There was a great deal of 'drama' that weekend.

Another enjoyable time was spent during a week with six-year old Raymond, for whom the selection of a transitional object varied, its attractiveness lasting for a day or two. One day it might be a camera, then two days later a whistle. Within a few weeks of joining his foster-parents, he began to require a transitional object. It always took him into group play and helped him to find a 'role' for himself. Perhaps Bruner would say it helped him to explore different modes of representation, but in Winnicott's terms it allowed him to do so with safety.

Raymond acted as a defender from wasps on the beach – he believed that they would go if he blew his treasured whistle. He lined everyone up and 'took photos' of them, legitimately controlling a group of people. He experimented with leadership, power and kindness in different contexts and in an acceptable way. Within two days, for the first time, he was 'in the game' with four to seven year-olds helping them to make a museum with their holiday treasures. Although we are primarily concerned with the first five years, it is as well to bear in mind that for some children, like Raymond, the roots of representation come later, but nonetheless healthily.

Winnicott believes that these early imaginative representational plays develop into group relationships and that they are natural and healthy. Educators of young children need to recognise the importance of transitional objects for the child and to treat them sensitively. Not all children have transitional objects, but they will use favourite toys, or special voices, or imaginary friends, depending on the socio-cultural setting in which they grow up. By observation and empathy the adult may be allowed into the world of the child's representation play.

Transitional objects and other similar behaviours are not leftovers from babyhood, but an exciting development from it. They are the essence of play, which is heavily bound up in representation, being part of a group, as well as being important in literacy and other individual representational work.

Early childhood educators need to consider how to welcome transitional objects in their settings. Perhaps they should not be put away out of sight or access. It is worth considering a special small chair, where the objects can sit when not needed, but are safe from other children. This allows them to be cuddled or carried round, rather than put away in a cupboard until home time. Winnicott would argue that to put the object away denies the child both possession and the chance to develop play and creative ideas. Ellen would not have had her adventures without Baby Lion working alongside her. Transitional objects are a rich resource of children's representational development.

THE DEVELOPMENT OF REPRESENTATION IN CHILDREN

Being able to represent (keep hold of prior experience) by making images or making symbols which stand for people, events and objects in their absence, or in their presence, is an important part of human behaviour. But two similar people who have the same experiences will in fact experience them quite differently. This is because to some extent, without realising we are doing it, we can select what we focus on. This is not a conscious process, and when it happens, which it does all the time, we call it having interests, or hobbies or favourite places and activities.

Piaget says that we have a network, a repertoire of behaviours (which he calls schemas – see Chapter 5) which influence what we are interested in at the time and which alter and modify in the light of feedback from real socio-cultural experience. This means that the biological aspects of our development interact with the socio-cultural side of our development, and so each of us is a unique person.

Piaget (1976) thought that the process of representation developed rapidly from toddler times until after the statutory schooling, which in most countries is appropriately six or seven years of age. This is the period when the process of representation really begins to flourish. For Piaget, as for Bruner, there is an important network of processes developing in the child, each of which interacts with the other in a web-like way.

It is a network or web which involves a child in:

- active learning;
- imitation;
- making images, which might be auditory (sound), visual, touch, smell or taste;
- making symbols, when something stands for something else.

Imitation

Piaget does not mean copying when he says that imitation is important as part of representing experience. Imitation differs from copying in that the child makes use of and reconstructs an event after the event.

> Three year-old William sees a friend, two year-old Charlotte, eat cheese on toast cut into small squares in a grid pattern. He usually has toast fingers. Next day he asks for his honey toast to be made like Charlotte's. He is reconstructing in the light of a new situation and context. He is adapting an idea he wants to use.

Through imitation of this sort, children experiment with different behaviours, roles, ways of painting, swimming and much more. This is a strong argument for not separating educational provision for three and four year-olds since the younger children benefit from imitating the older, who in turn benefit from the leadership and sense of responsibility involved. The practice of mixing three and four year-olds is currently being eroded. Piaget's notion of imitation gives strong justification for the mixing of ages.

Children making images

The images that children form are difficult for adults to study, because they are inside the child's mind. Piaget calls the period from two to five years the 'dark ages' in our knowledge of children. Later on, children can often describe the images that they have and put them into words, although even as adults, some of the most important images we have remain unspoken, and so they should. Words are only one way of making symbols and should not be over-emphasised in human development.

Adults can encourage imagery. For example, a teacher when finger painting with children, might comment that their handprints resembled a peacock's tail seen by them previously on a visit to the zoo. It also looks like a horse-chestnut leaf, or a fan. In this way adults are giving the opportunity of at least three images – the tail, the leaf, the fan – without imposing any of them on the child.

Adults can help children to construct images and value those that children create which are based on experiences.

> Four year-old Dominic brought home a butterfly picture made by dropping paint on the paper and then folding it, still wet, in half. He said to his mother, 'This is like a bird with its wings out. This is like a bull's head. This is like a butterfly. This is like a cloud'. Here is a series of images of his own. This is different from the adult saying, 'Today we are going to make a butterfly painting. What colours will your butterfly be?'

In the latter approach, the adult is in control of the images, not the child. If encouraged to do so, children will use real experiences they have lived through as the basis of imagery which they are increasingly prepared to articulate and share.

> Two year-old William found some pieces of wood on a beach. One reminded him of a fish. One reminded him of an aeroplane. Similarly, in their paintings and drawings children will often label their efforts because they are reminded of something - for example, a drawing that represented a maze for William at three years of age represented a honeycomb a few hours later. He had recently visited Hampton Court and eaten honey from a comb.

It is also important that adults do not offer narrow experiences to children and so restrict the processes of imitation and forming images.

> A student on teaching practice in a nursery school one day took in a model windmill for a group of three and four year-olds to make. The children were eager, but needed almost constant help, and the student found herself, in effect, making a dozen windmills. She tried a new strategy the next day, which was still to encourage the children to make a toy as a present for a baby about to visit the nursery. This time, however, she made half a dozen or so different toys, including a windmill. Again, the children were eager, but this time her offering to them seemed to trigger a range of images. They chatted about their ideas, and made a

> wide range of windmill-type toys, although they certainly used (imitated) some of the ideas presented in her model.
>
> Mary made a tube and fringed the ends of it, cutting with scissors. Gareth tore off strips of paper from a sheet and stuck them on to a box he found in the scrap material. Shanaz stood the cylinder she made upright, stuck a stick on it and another across to intersect it.

These children were imitating, taking ideas from other people, and forming images. Both are of great importance in Piaget's theory.

Symbolic representation

Piaget values the personal, highly individual symbols that children develop to make something stand for something else. He also values the shared conventions which are developed by groups, cultures and societies in different places and parts of the world:

- personal, individual ways of making symbols (which is when something is made to stand for something else);
- the shared conventions used to symbolise (stand for) something agreed by a group, culture or society;
- making links between the personal, idiosyncratic symbols children make, and the arbitrary agreed signs that groups make, can lead to a good balance between creativity and conformity.

SYMBOLIC REPRESENTATION – MAKING SOMETHING STAND FOR SOMETHING ELSE

SYMBOLIC REPRESENTATION

Idiosyncratic, highly personal symbols that are special to the person who devises them.	→	Creativity and imaginative representations
Shared conventions, arbitrary signs agreed by a group of people and the norms of the culture.	→	Using the cultural conventions and conformity in the way experiences are represented

Amanda (four years) went on a tube train. Later that day she made her legs wide apart, and then close together. She explained it was the tube doors opening and shutting. This is an idiosyncratic, personal, symbolic representation. It is very creative.

David is two years old. He goes to his grandad and makes a thumbs up sign. His grandad replies, using the same sign. This is an agreed convention for 'okay', 'all's well' in the culture in which David is growing up. He is conforming to the socio-cultural context in this example of symbolic representation.

Learning a verbal language, sign language, learning to use agreed mathematical symbols or musical and dance notation, or learning to write, are all examples of different kinds of symbolic representation which involve shared conventions of the culture. In most countries in the world children are encouraged to use their own personal symbols until six or seven years of age, while at the same time actively exploring the shared conventions of their culture (Ferreiro, 1997).

In some countries, children are expected to learn symbolic conventions from the age of two, three or four years of age and to abandon their personal symbols and experimentation with exploration. The emphasis is on using the conventional symbols of their culture. This is likely to lead to conformity and performance rather than creativity in adults.

Recently there has been much discussion in the UK (Woodhead, 1996) of education in the area of the Pacific Rim. The system seems to be increasingly successful in encouraging technical engineers, musical or dance performers and mathematical performance to set questions. It is not clear whether an emphasis on conformity and performance in the agreed conventions of a culture, performing a dance, a piece of music, arithmetical problem, piece of geometry or algebra and so on discourages creativity, problem solving, original scientific thinking, choreography, musical composition, jazz improvisation, scientific and mathematical discovery. It is almost certainly a case of balance from the age of 7 or 8 years according to the ever increasing research evidence on children developing (Gardner 1983; Desforges, 1996; Kegl, 1997; Greenfield, 1996).

However, the younger the child, the more emphasis there needs to be on the child's own personal symbols, and the active exploring and problem solving in relation to conventional symbols.

This is discussed in more detail in Chapter 7, when 'writing' is used as an example of representation.

BALANCING IMPORTANT ASPECTS OF SYMBOLIC BEHAVIOUR

A QUESTION OF BALANCE

Creative: thinking for yourself, using personal, idiosyncratic symbols	**Convention**, conforming to the culture and its expectations

Piaget and Bruner agree that active learning (learning by doing) is important. Copying is not useful, but reconstructing an experience in your own way (by imitation) is useful. Images, although often hidden inside you, are important. Children need to master symbolic codes.

Piaget values the child's own personal, idiosyncratic symbols as much as the conventional codes of the socio-cultural context in which the child grows up.

PIAGET

REPRESENTATION IS A WHOLE NETWORK

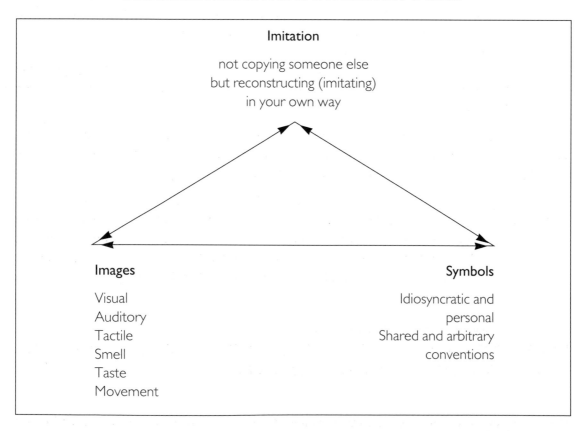

BRUNER

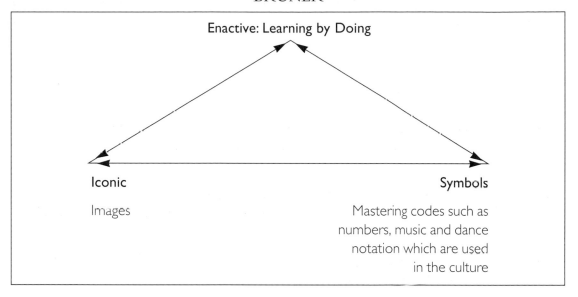

Vygotsky's work is useful in pointing out the value of play props as a way in which children represent things, events and people.

- They use play props such as cups or plates. They also represent these and make their own. Sadiq at 3 years old, uses a beech leaf as a play prop. He pretends it is a plate. He uses a daisy as a play prop so that it stands for a fried egg.
- Children move into role and dress up, pretending to be someone else. A paper plate might become a driving wheel, a long skirt might be a prop which symbolises the 'lady from old fashioned times'.

Vygotsky says that the child, such as Sadiq, sees one thing (the daisy) but acts differently towards it (treating the daisy as if it were an egg). He gives the daisy a different meaning. That is what children do when they make something into a play prop.

The theories we have looked at in this chapter, of Bruner, Winnicott, Piaget and Vygotsky, lead us to some practical strategies. We have established that children need direct, powerful, emotional experiences, and a consistent environment which offers diverse, enriching opportunities. Young children require a supportive setting in which imaginative play is encouraged, through which there is frequent opportunity to reflect.

SOME PRACTICAL STRATEGIES FOR ENCOURAGING THE DEVELOPMENT OF REPRESENTATION

Recent research emphasises the importance of context, both in social relationships and the influences of the culture.

Throughout this book, the advantages of younger and older children playing together is emphasised. Vygotsky's and Piaget's work show how important it is for younger children to see older children handling materials with confidence and pleasure, and to see moments of struggle and recognise how the adults in the environment are supportive and enabling at such times. Motivation to learn and move forward are closely linked with security, self-confidence and self-esteem. Adults can help children in these areas.

Observing children

Careful child observation comes first as illuminated by Matthews (1994) or, using a very different Steinerian perspective, Strauss (1978), so that the emphasis is on looking at and identifying what the child can do, before leaping into action. Adults working with children will also need to act on their observations of children.

Observations should inform adults so that they can plan what to do next making appropriate schemes of work for children, whether with a group of children or an individual child (Pollard, 1997, p.181).

The adult first observes the child's themes of play, drawing, models, conversations and so on, then attempts to help children individually, or as a group, to elaborate these themes. This might be through conversation, through suggestion or by providing relevant and appropriate materials and experiences in a sensitive way. There is a world of difference between intervening sensitively and appropriately and interfering when adults move into teaching without first tuning into the child (BBC/NBC, *Tuning Into Children,* 1996).

Working with young children, providing appropriate materials and experiences, might also mean that adults need to allow themselves to be used as an extension of the child – for example, holding the sticky tape while children cut it, to stop them from giving up at a difficult moment, or helping to keep a theme going in the home corner when the play is breaking down.

Two three year-olds, Barbara and Clare, wanted to play nurses, but a quarrel broke out over who should give out the medicine. The adult intervened, saying 'I am the sister. Nurse Barbara, would you take the patient's temperature? Nurse Clare, please would you wash the patient?' Both are given attractive nurse-like tasks. The adult has kept the theme and the roles going and has also extended the children's play in adding to the range of nurse-like activities.

Materials which can be used for representation

Material provision involves people, events and objects with which the children interact. It can be set out in many ways to excite curiosity and surprise, and yet there must be security for the children. There needs to be some anchor areas, always in the same places and forms, such as the book area and home area. Other areas might change regularly, and link with recent experiences of the children – for example, a Tudor Manor might be created to fit in with a visit to the Tower of London.

Different kinds of provision make different demands. Children need to experience the challenge of many different demands. Children need to experience the challenge of many different experiences, and of wide-ranging provision.

> At three years old Hannah danced a rosebud unfurling, her idea. She was very frustrated when she tried to draw this event.

It is important to bear in mind Bruner's three modes of representation, and the conflicts the child must resolve between them. This implicitly argues for a rich, wide range of media for young children to experience and work with. Children need to become proficient in the representational possibilities of different clays, doughs and woodwork as well as plasticine, mud and wet sand. They need different papers, brushes and paints, from oil to poster to powder paint, thick, thin and medium. They need to draw with pastels, charcoal, pencils, felt pens, chalks, inks and so on.

A broad material environment becomes very exciting to provide. Children need to experience and tell stories, hear and see and make music, and dance in different styles – dramatic, comforting, romantic, folk – from different cultures. Endless possibilities emerge.

The way that materials are set out, the range and variety of materials offered, the way adults help children to learn how to use materials, are all important in encouraging children to represent.

- There needs to be some anchor areas always in the same places and forms, for example the book and home areas. Other areas might change regularly to link with recent experiences that the children have had as a group, for example the visit to the park.
- Different kinds of material make different demands. Children need to experience the challenge of many experiences and a wide range of materials.

Depending on the material, the representational experience will be entirely different each time.

It will be very difficult for Georgio (4 years) to make a representation of his bathroom pipe freezing and bursting (a dramatic experience for him and his family) in clay, woodwork, sand, dance or drama, but he managed to do it at the water tray.

It is important for children to try out what it is like to represent in different ways with different materials. A broad material range becomes exciting and interesting for adults to provide and watch and help children to use when representing. Some children will show more strength in one area, less in another. Others will be all-rounders.

William at three years-old almost never paints, although the opportunity is constantly available. He rarely draws, either. He rejects dough and clay. But he models a blackbird out of Plasticine, with a black body, head, wings, a yellow beak, two yellow eyes, and yellow legs and feet. He is angry when it will not stand up, and only grudgingly accepts the suggestion that it could sit on a nest made by a helpful adult. He wants it to hop. The representation of movement is what he really wants. He knows that blackbirds have a springy hop. He represents this with his body, briefly, before a rough and tumble game develops with his sister. William prefers to represent using three dimensions, and through dance-like movements.

Kate at three and a half years rarely drew or painted, but made marvellous models. She made a model of her school classroom one day with a cardboard box and bricks to represent furniture, accurately placed spatially (Young, 1989).

Interestingly at five years old, both these children were doing meticulous and beautiful drawings and two dimensional work, but both were easily frustrated if their efforts did not work out. Kate went on to study art at 'A' Level and William studied physics.

It is easier to change clay or bricks, and reorganise them, than it is to change a drawing that has not gone according to plan. On the other hand, it is easier to fall into a stereotyped and narrow formula in drawings, and to let dance-like musical and three dimensional work atrophy as the imagination increasingly fails. Kate and William were encouraged in the early years (0-8 years) to experiment, explore and value their own personal idiosyncratic representations. They were not 'forced' to adopt cultural conventions or to draw in formulas.

Representation in all its forms is important. Dance, music, sculpture, construction toys, drawing, painting, literature and drama all offer different possibilities. Each offers something special, something worthwhile and unique. We can keep hold of past experiences of people, situations and objects by representing them.

CONCLUSION

- Representation is a process in human development.
- It gives children and adults ways of keeping hold of important experiences through images and symbols.
- Images can be to do with what we hear, see, smell, taste and touch, or do in terms of movement.
- We use symbols to make one thing stand for another usually in the absence of the person, object, place or event. Some symbols are very personal and idiosyncratic. These are understood only by the person using them and perhaps those close to them. Some symbols are shared conventions, arbitrary by nature, such as words, writing, music, dance, notation or algebra.
- The early childhood curriculum encourages children to:
    be active learners
    make images
    develop symbols, both personal and shared conventions
- Special objects or toys might become what Winnicott calls 'transitional objects', easing children in and out of situations involving separation from those they are close to and at the same time encouraging the representational process to develop.
- The process of representation leads towards children (and adults) developing interests and hobbies in life. The biological path of development (our genetic programme) is constantly in touch with, part of and influenced by the socio-cultural path of our development. Consequently, even identical twins might develop different interests.
- The process of representation develops as a web or network involving:
    the senses
    movement
    imitation
    making images
    making symbols
- The process of representation involves a sense of ownership by the child. Young children representing their own experiences, their own ideas, feelings and relationships and not those of others which are not part of their experience.

'Formula' drawings, simple and complex

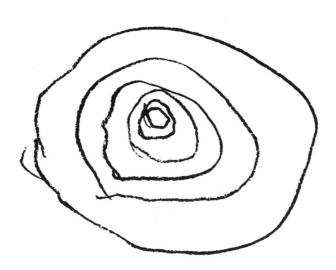

Girl, 3 years 3 months

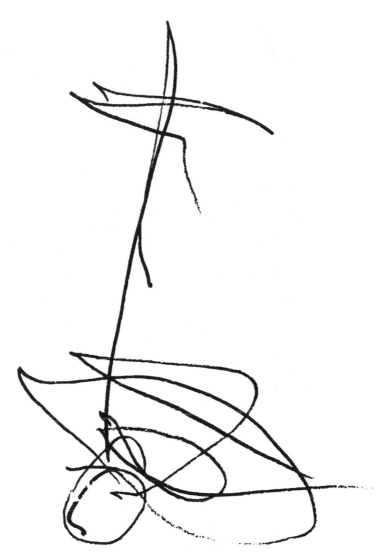

Boy, 1 year 9 months

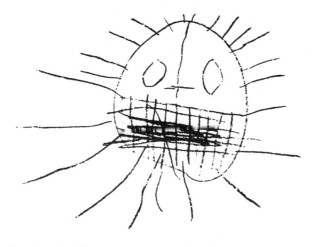

Boy, 4 years 4 months

Boy, 4 years 5 months

7

∎

COMMUNICATION, LANGUAGE

AND LITERACY

Language is about communication – communication with self and communication with others. It helps people to move from the here and now to the past, into the future and into alternative worlds. It uses agreed signs which evolve to fit the times and setting in which the language is used. It enables people to think and feel at an abstract level about ideas which are hypothetical and imaginary in effective, efficient, deep and moving ways. It normally involves talking and listening; it can involve reading and writing.

In Western culture all four elements are important areas of language in the school setting and in life generally. To be illiterate sets people at a disadvantage. To be unable to talk or listen cuts people off and brings loneliness and frustration along with the lack of opportunity to communicate with others. Language does not have to be oral. It can be 'talked' or 'listened to' in different ways. Some deaf and blind people talk and listen through touch. The language of the deaf has gained recognition as an official language: British Sign Language (BSL). This is not an oral language. It combines gesture, agreed and shared signs with finger spelling.

The work of researchers like Mary Brennan (1978) and Judy Kegl (1997) has helped those who use oral language to appreciate that sign language has a syntax and has evolved just as any living language, has regional dialects and enables abstract thinking. It contains features shared by verbal languages. It facilitates thinking, feeling and communication. It allows those who understand it to construct shared meanings together. However, like some other languages in the world, it has no written form and so cannot be read.

Communication

Work over many years by Colwyn Trevarthen (1993) shows how babies communicate and 'speak' to those close to them in non-verbal ways. They move in synchrony with the voice of the parent or sibling in a dance-like fashion. They 'reply' when spoken to, providing the person pauses long enough for them to make the reply and does not constantly 'talk at' the baby.

Trevarthen's most recent work (1997) with a group of musicians demonstrates that babies will also complete a musical phrase when sung to. The adult begins to sing and the child spontaneously completes the music in a form recognised by musicians cross-culturally. The work of Acredelo and Goodwyn (1997) shows that parents who use gesture and sign as well as talking and signing to their babies help their spoken language to develop more readily.

Listening and talking

It is not the aim of this book to raise that weary old chestnut of the nature/nurture debate as to whether language is a genetically and biologically pre-determined system, or whether it is socially learned from the culture. It is almost certainly the case that both are crucial according to evidence provided from brain studies (Greenfield, 1996) and from linguists such as Judy Kegl (1997).

Because of the Sandinista Revolution of 1979 in Nicaragua, a group of deaf children came together for the first time after the Revolution when a school for deaf children was founded in Managua. When they met in this special school, they had only a few idiosyncratic and personal signs, as they had grown up as one isolated deaf person living amongst a hearing community in their homes.

As they met, a natural development occurred. They began to develop a 'pigeon language' which was a basic language, and it gave them the means for the first time in their lives to share ideas, feelings and to communicate with each other. The older children (teenagers) continued to use this language, but the younger children developed it on until what linguists call a 'creole language' emerged out of the pigeon language. This was a fully fledged sophisticated sign language, which was quite unique in the world, using grammar and a rich vocabulary.

Judy Kegl argues, convincingly, that humans are genetically and biological predisposed to develop grammatical language systems. These children did it – out of nothing! But, and this is important in looking at the way language develops, there are two socio-cultural aspects to her findings.

- Both the basic pigeon language and the sophisticated creole language had taken in elements of gestures used in the Nicaraguan culture and transformed these in a more developed form into the vocabulary of the language.

- When Judy Kegl visited deaf children in rural areas, living at home without contact with other deaf children, they only used primitive gestures and signs without any grammatical element. When she introduced the children to each other, and taught them the full creole form of the sign language, the younger children quickly took it up and became fluent.

In other words, biology alone is not enough. A language acquisition device (as proposed by Chomsky in the 1960s) needs the company of other people to be triggered to the full. We need other people, because we are social animals. We need, literally, to participate with other people in our culture and language. It is not as simple as teaching children to talk. In this case, the younger children were teaching the teenagers and adults the creole, the more sophisticated form of the language.

Most of the time adults and children, through participating with each other in the language and the culture, will be teaching each other different things. It seems that Froebel's statement that we 'need to live with our children' still holds force today.

Bilingual children listening and talking

Judy Kegl's work demonstrates that children need to have opportunities to share language with others. There are many ways in which this can occur. Marian Whitehead (1996, p.15) writing about young bilingual children, reminds us that: 'Their language and family situations are complex and uniquely varied'. Very few children are in fact equally at ease with several languages, and so are not truly balanced bilingual speakers. Whitehead (p.19) refers to the way some children who are bilingual use 'bridge building' strategies to move from a known language to a new language. This involves using words from the new language, but with the grammatical patterns of the securely known language. This is a skilled temporary solution called 'inter language' bilingualism. Children become involved in language mixing and switching (Whitehead, 1996, p.17).

Children who are bilingual grow up more easily able to appreciate and value differences between people and cultures (Miller, 1983). This helps them to make sense of social situations. It is important that early childhood educators make every child feel that their language and culture is welcomed, valued, respected, acknowledged and visibly supported.

Encouraging language

July Fisher (1996, p.78) emphasises that, especially for children learning English as a second language, 'one of the most important elements of an environment for young learners is the provision of opportunities for children to talk together and with adults',

Children are very good at tuning in to each other, and often one child will 'translate' to an adult what another child means. Parents are also able to signal to early years workers about events and situations which will help the communication between them and the child. Similarly, early years workers can promote the parent/child relationship by telling parents what was done in school and inviting them in to show them.

Three year-old Richard was met each day from nursery class by his mother. The early years worker made a point of suggesting that, if parents were not in a rush, their child could show them round. In this way parents had an idea of the activities, models, paintings and so on in which their child was involved. Later, at home, when Richard referred to a dead worm, his mother did not have to puzzle over his meaning. She knew that he was studying newts in school and that worms were fed daily to them. When, in school, Richard talked about 'my yellow one', the teacher knew that he has a new Teddy bear because his mother had mentioned it. Shared context has been an important finding in the Pen Green Practitioner Research Project (Whalley and Arnold, 1997).

Conversation can be effectively developed to deal better with situations and ideas removed from their immediate contexts if parents and early years workers work together. As children grow up they can be helped to become aware of the need to explain and fill in necessary information in order to bring meaning to those who were not present. Listening to stories, reading and writing facilitate this process. These are strong links with the ability to decentre in the development of a sense of 'audience'.

A group of seven year-olds were going round a stately home. The guide wanted to talk about the ceramics. The teacher sensed that this held no interest for the class. She did know about some of the paintings and asked the children to look at a painting of a lady. She asked what Zoe, Mark and the picture had in common. The situation changed, from a monologue by the guide to suggestions from the children with the teacher acting as chairperson. Eventually, it was established that Zoe and Mark had both recently acquired baby sisters. The children wondered if that was the link. Had the lady just had a baby? In fact, the fine lady in the painting had founded a maternity hospital for the poor. The children asked about her, why she did this, who she was.

This teacher had taken the children into history and helped them to glimpse the social order of a different time from their own. The language introduced was rich but welcomed. The teacher had helped to establish a partnership by starting from something which the class found interesting and relevant. Her share of the partnership was achieved – it was to link up with a project on Victorian Britain, including the contrast between wealth and poverty, and the social order of the times.

July Fisher points out that this kind of whole group teaching may produce, according to Alexander *et al* (1992), 'higher order questioning, explanations and statements'. However, she stresses that the report 'Curriculum Organisation and Class Room Practice in Primary Schools' is mainly concerned with children 7 to 11 years of age (Key Stage 2). She juxtaposes this finding with the report written in reply to that of Alexander *et al* by David, Curtis and Siraj Blatchford (1992) which challenged the view that whole-group teaching is effective for children 3 to 7 years of age.

Children need to have opportunities to initiate conversations in the school setting during activities and during group times. They also need individual and small group settings – for example, when involved in music, dance, or story. In these settings they can interject and the adult can use these interjections to make the story meaningful at a deeper level.

> 'I've got one of these' may seem an egocentric response by four year-old Jason to the story of *Titch* by Pat Hutchins. However, it tells the early years worker that Jason knows about a pinwheel. He explains how it goes round if you blow on it. He wants to abandon the story at this point and talk about his pinwheel instead. The early years workers can let him talk with her because it is a small group of three children. The other children bring in information about how the pinwheel works. When the early years worker has taken each child's initiations about the subject, she takes them back to the text. Jason often returns to this story, provided it is in the book corner. Old favourites are an important part of leading towards reading.

When adults are involved in discussions with small groups (2 to 4 children) the advantages are that children are less likely to lose the focus of the conversation when it is not their turn to speak. They do not have to wait too long if they are bursting with a thought on the subject. It is also easier for the adult to draw children into the discussion, and to make use of the contextual back-cloth of what children say. Even so, there are frequent times when adults need the help of other children to 'translate' or give the contextual clues needed for the conversation to flow and make sense to everyone participating.

> Three year-old Luckdeep sat down for story time when the teacher told the story of Mrs Wishy Washy and kept saying 'in there'. The teacher wanted to respond but did not understand. Sandeep explained that Luckdeep wanted the teacher to put the scrubbing brush in the bowl to make soap bubbles. The shared socio-cultural context was not enough. It was necessary to negotiate a shared meaning, too. The teacher then built the bubbles into the story.

Children are active in their learning and need to be encouraged in this. Their active feelings affect their active thinking. One deep, powerful experience is better than many pedestrian ones.

> Six year-old Tom's mouse died. He was very upset. A story about a mouse and his experiences in a cage, and how he runs away leaving his owner sad, contains in it some of Tom's grief. He loved the story. It evoked the memory of a first feeling encounter. Tom did not choose the story, his mother did, recognising the importance of the death of his mouse.

Adults needs to choose books for children which help them to meet and extend both powerful and everyday experiences. Sometimes these will arise spontaneously, as with Jason and the pinwheel. Sometimes they need to be planned by the adult, as with Tom. Children relate their own experiences to those of others through books, shared activities and outings, provided that adults allow them to be active in the process. Sometimes the child initiates, sometimes the adult, but the child always needs to be active.

Margaret Meek (1985, p.43) stresses the need to 'foreground the emotive' in this process. She sees emotion as an integrating force in children's experiences. As well as listening to stories and being helped to interact with the text, children produce nonsense rhymes and jokes which are a very important aspect of their being active in their language development.

Chukovsky (1963) and more recently Marian Whitehead (1996) Goswami and Bryant (1990) all note the importance of rhyming sounds as an important element in learning to read. Jenny Riley (1996, p.28) emphasises the importance of adults capitalising on the way children naturally enjoy songs and rhythm.

Piaget sees playing with ideas and making jokes as the highest level of understanding. Helping children develop a sense of humour was one of the central aims of Chris Athey's project during 1972–1977. Having fun with language, or with any area of knowledge, implies good understanding and can be used as a means of assessing what children know well.

Rearranging ideas and words is the basis of the creative process. Talking and listening, partnerships and being active in language development, lead into literature. Peter McKeller (1957) defines the imagination as the rearrangement of past experience in new and fascinating ways.

The importance of making errors free from criticism

Wells and Nicholls (1985, p.18) argue for

> *the value of errors, to learners as elicitors of helpful feedback and for teachers as a source of insight into the meanings that their pupils are making.*

In talking, children are attempting actively to formulate the rules of language. They hypothesise for example, 'I hitted the ball.' If adults reply by extending, 'Oh, you hit the ball, did you?', they give the correct form without rejecting what the child said. This helps children to adjust their 'rules' for themselves. Direct correction of children's speech is ineffective and may create stress – for adults as well as children. Self-correction is an important strategy as children check for meaning. It also tells adults where children are in their development.

The pleasure of sharing books together

Writing

In order to put the development of writing into context, it is necessary to return to Chapter 6 on Representation. Writing is an aspect of language, which is an aspect of representation.

Winnicott (1971) proposed the importance of the transitional object in the early development of representation. Baby Lion stood for the link between the mother and the child as well as the space between them when they were apart. Baby Lion was Ellen's first possession and creation.

Vygotsky, in agreement with Winnicott, goes further. He is quite clear that early representation leads directly to written language. He points out that gesture is of paramount importance: playthings and drawings initially acquire meaning supported by gesture. A pencil becomes a person. A book cannot become a person, but its dark green cover could allow it to be turned into a forest. Gradually, objects acquire a meaning independent of gesture. Make-believe, says Vygotsky (1978), is a major contributor to the development of written language. So is drawing.

Representation is one of the keys to writing. Vygotsky's thinking is very much in tune with that of Marie Clay (1975) whose work has been an important influence on research and thinking about early writing. She suggests that children need to construct their own writing system, a theory of their own which they can operate. They need to be allowed to experiment and develop their own theories.

This early writing must be unhindered by external demands for neat letter forms, proper spacing, writing on the line, and conventional spelling. Recently, the influence of the work of Emilia Ferreiro and Anna Teberosky (1983) has grown (Ferreiro, 1997). Ferreiro, like Vygotsky and Marie Clay, argues that thinking about early writing has over-emphasised the graphic shapes (the figurative aspects) and under-emphasised the constructive aspects (the rules of composition). Handwriting, letter formation, legibility and speed have tended to be the main focus of adults helping young children to learn to write.

Like Vygotsky, Ferreiro and Teberosky believe that children first try to 'find the frontier that differentiates drawing from writing'. Initially, children begin to put letters into their pictures, but Ferreiro and Teberosky (1983) and Ferreiro (1997) suggest that the letters do not 'say' anything by themselves. There is only a vague relationship between letters and drawing.

> Six year-old Raymond uses the R to represent himself, the D to represent his foster mother Daphne, and the H, his foster father Hywel. Some letters are easier to write than others. Prospective parents choosing names, please note! Curves, such as those in C and in J with an open semi-circle, are more difficult (see page 72).

Ferreiro's work adds support to Marie Clay's. Children do not seem to be 'taught' capital letters by ignorant, tiresome parents, although teachers often accuse innocent parents of this! Children probably use them, if Piaget is right, because they select patterns to draw which they can draw easily. They use complete enclosures and trajectories, separate and in combination. This means that, broadly speaking, they tend to use capitals first, and the more difficult lower case letters later.

The alphabetic symbols used by children could well be the stepping-stones towards conventional writing. I remember using a nailfile to carve my name in capitals with painstaking care on the wooden mantelpiece. My mother tells me I was four years old.

Nigel Hall (in Martello and Hall, 1996, p.98) writes:

> *Just as they create non-conventional versions of spelling patterns, so they generate non-conventional rules for punctuation. Although their rules may be non-conventional. . .it is reasoning not guessing that is involved.*

Jo Weinburger (1996, p.11) points out that most young children 'are keen to "write" and if given materials and a context will readily do so'. Putting notepads into the home area next to the telephone, for example, seems to encourage writing behaviour. It is important to bear in mind, Weinburger stresses (p.13) that 'writing does not just happen', and she goes on to say: 'Because development occurs within a cultural and social context, children from different backgrounds will necessarily have different experiences of writing'.

Weinburger refers to the findings of Minns (1990) who in Coventry studied children in their home settings. These included Afro-Caribbean, Asian and Anglo families. The children had varied experiences of literacy which did not necessarily mirror the way literacy was approached in the schools.

As young children begin to experiment with writing, for example shopping lists, in their play, and see the writing other children and adults do, and to see print in school, Ferreiro (1997) suggests they experience a conflict. Ferreiro, giving resonance to the findings of Judy Kegl on language development, suggests that learning to write is not entirely dependent on the external socio-cultural environment, but that there are also internal organisational mechanisms at work. Children, as they learn to write, she argues, are learning about the nature of the link between oral and written representations. Jenny Riley (1996) reiterates the importance of this connection.

As children observe and write, there are conflicts to be resolved and experiments to be made in writing. For example, Ferreiro's research demonstrates how children find monosyllabic words a challenge, because they like to have between 3 and 5 characters in a cluster in order to feel that they have written a word (see page 71).

> AMA stands for Amanda, and matches the number of syllables in her name. BO + stands for Ben, but does not match the number of syllables in his name. The children tend to put in a 'dummy' (extra marks), because of their minimum role. They like to have three 'letters' to make a 'word'.

For this reason, according to Ferreiro, children find longer words, with more syllables, such as 'refrigerator' with 5 syllables, easier to tackle than 'boat', with only 1 syllable.

Again, the child's own name cannot be given too much emphasis. It may be the first 'fixed string', as Ferreiro and Teberosky (1983, p.207) call it, that the child meaningfully encounters. It serves a useful purpose in causing internal conflict in the child between the number of letters and the number of sounds between the alphabetic and syllibic codes. Striving to resolve this conflict between letters and sounds takes the child into a new level of understanding what is involved in writing. As children resolve the conflicts involved in this, they gradually, according to Ferreiro and Teberosky, break the writing code.

Ferreiro and Teberosky say, (1983, p.277)

> Let children write, even in a writing system different from the alphabetic one. We must let them write, not so (that) they invent their own idiosyncratic system, but so (that) they discover that their system is not the conventional one, and in this way find valid reasons to substitute their own hypotheses with our conventional ones.

It is a serious matter when children enter school at five years old, knowing that they don't know how to write their own names and believing that only by tracing and copying will they come to know.

The distance between copy writing and children's spontaneous writing is as great as the distance between copy drawing and children's spontaneous drawing (Ferreiro and Teberosky, 1983 p.278).

If children entering school are seen as deficient in knowledge of the alphabetic code, and in dire need of swift initiation into it, the teaching of writing will be tackled by asking them to trace letters, copy sentences, correctly forming their letters, and as soon as possible introduce punctuation, spelling and grammar.

Ferreiro is not arguing that children should be left to themselves in learning to write. Like Weinburger (1996), Miller (1996) and Riley (1996), she suggests that children need support and help as they move into the role of writers. Riley stresses the importance of children working out letter/sound relationships as part of this. Miller gives excellent examples in home and school settings brought alive with her family literacy experiences with her daughters, but also giving self-help strategies to practitioners which are invaluable, and go beyond the requirements prescribed in the Desirable Outcomes Documents or the Key Stage 1 documents of the National Curriculum.

Donald Graves (1983) works on the principle that the adult's role is to help children 'find their own voice'. Teachers can, of course, help children to use other people's voices very competently, but if we are talking about educating young children, we want our efforts to lead somewhere useful later on. This means that children need to be helped to find and then learn to use their own voice, not someone else's.

Ferreiro (1997), Clay (1975, 1977, 1989) and Miller (1996) suggest that at an early age, in the first five years, children can be truly educated in the writing process. There is a desire in this approach to build on what the child already knows and, with adult help and peer group help, progress from there. The two year-old who draws and make believes is perhaps already sharing creations with the significant people in his or her life, and this is the basis of writing.

Family literacy

Colin Harrison (1996, p.25) gives a three-part definition of family literacy.

1) The spontaneous family literacy activities.

2) Inter-generational projects to improve literacy levels of both parents and children.

3) Support or intervention programmes encouraging children's literacy development within the family.

He refers to the work of Denny Taylor (1983, p.87) who sees the family as the base of literacy: 'Literacy is part of the very fabric of family life' (*We ought perhaps to add 'in some cultures'*.)

Denny Taylor also believes that 'literacy can be a barrier between home and school, and a contrivance of familial dissent' (1983, p. 87).

> Andrew would not do word and picture matching with his mother. Instead, he made the cards intended for this purpose into an eagle, which he cherished. His mother sensibly gave up!

Some of the children in Taylor's study ran into problems on school entry. She states: 'A skills approach to writing runs counter to the natural development of reading and writing as complex cultural activities'. Taylor's naturalistic study reiterates the harmful effects of an over-emphasis on skills work in the early years of education.

The way that the family's approach to literacy meets the school's approach to it is a very important consideration in working with young children, but the way that the child interacts with his or her own family in relation to literacy is also important. Denny Taylor's work supports the view that the personalities involved, and the education style of the parents, are dominant factors in shaping the literate experiences of the children within the home. From the beginning the child is both active and reactive to his or her own family's literate experiences and presentations of them.

> Parents find that each of their children differs in responses to 'writing'. At three years, Hannah would 'write' in zigzagging cursive a shopping list whenever her mother did so. She loved to sign greetings cards with a capital H. She loved stories, often demanding them during the day, as well as expecting as many as possible at bedtime.

> At three years, William, from the same family, the second child, would just about concentrate for a bedtime story. Mother had to work hard to keep his concentration, whether he chose stories or whether she did. However, he loved to lie in bed and listen to his five and a half year-old sister read to him until he fell asleep. This also helped her reading to develop, of course! At four years, William began to enjoy his bedtime story with mother, often choosing the same one several nights in a row, for example *The Tale of Mr Jeremy Fisher* by Beatrix Potter. He would not tolerate any deviation from the text, which he knew inside out. He showed no interest in writing, except for the W of his name with which he would sign the occasional drawing.

At four years, Hannah was reading a few words, such as 'Hannah' and 'Mummy' and writing all the time. By five years, she had 'cracked' the alphabetic code. At four and a half years,

William began writing his name frequently, and then cutting it out and sticking it onto models he had made. By five and a half years, he had cracked the alphabetic code, and was always asking his mother for just one more episode of a story. He showed no desire to write, except for his name, but constantly wanted his mother to write notes as reminders to do things.

PRACTITIONERS NEED TO TUNE INTO THE CHILD'S FAMILY LITERACY   Shirley Brice Heath (1983), amongst others, has stressed the importance of the teacher tuning into the child's family. What is the family's understanding of and approach to literacy? To bedtime stories? Denny Taylor (1983, p.54) shows us how families 'salute and hurt' each other through print.

> Seven year-old Hannah writes her mother a note: 'I'm terribly sorry about the nail varnish remover'. Mother writes to father, 'You are late. Supper burnt. Serves you right.'

Hannon, Weinburger and Nutbrown (1991) stress that the gains children make through family literacy programmes are difficult if not impossible to measure reliably until children reach the age of nine or ten years. They emphasise the importance of home visits, and how parents appreciate help with how to support their child's reading at home. It emerges that parents do not naturally or automatically know how children are helped towards literacy just because they are parents. Children learn about the multiplicity of literate activities as they participate in different social events (for example birthday cards, shopping lists, bills). In fact, children often engage in writing activities of which the parent is unaware. Scraps of paper might exist all over the house, with phone messages, reminders, stories and so on which are purposeful and functional. The home is where children are introduced to functional literacy. Its importance cannot be over-emphasised.

There is a potential problem if those working with young children from outside the family setting attempt to tell parents what they should do, whether in the school setting, or the day nursery, or during home visits. This is a partnership on professional terms. An equal partnership demands a more reciprocal approach to the relationship (Whalley, 1994).

Children need to see adults 'writing for real'

In our earlier explorations of representation in this chapter, we looked at the need to give children experiences which build on those of their home life. A child might have been to the corner shop, or the market, or the supermarket. Any of these experiences can be added to or exploited further. Another consideration is the need for children to imitate. Seeing adults involved in functional writing, at the bank, making shopping lists with the children, writing notes for the milkman is important in this respect. Writing needs to be demonstrated in a functional and purposeful way, so that children can select what they will represent or write about.

> A student on teaching practice took in plenty of junk for the three to four year-olds in the nursery school. She set it out attractively, made herself very available by sitting at the table, and the children flocked to make models. John experimented with glue, covering the box! Segun had a plan to make a can. No two models were the same, and not all were representational. The student was not imposing her theme of 'shape' on this group of children, although there was plenty of skilful 'shape' talk popped in at appropriate moments, in sensitive ways. Donald Graves might say that the student was helping the children to find their own voice, rather than to echo the thoughts of the adult, which is narrow and passive, and soon becomes boring.

However, if children are to find their own voice they need a great deal of support and encouragement from adults, since to do this is much harder than copying. If they are to reach satisfaction and a sense of fulfilment, they need to be helped through the inevitable struggles involved in any worthwhile activity. Being there at the right moment to hold the glue pot still, to stretch out the sticky tape for it to be cut by the child, to hear the story the child has woven around the model, to suggest painting it – all these actions by adults are part of encouraging representation and have implications for early writing. In early writing work, representation is a key factor.

In attempting to do this it has been necessary to refer back to previous chapters. And it is also necessary to value the family's contribution. Children need a wealth of firsthand experiences to make learning meaningful, and to set it in a functional and purposeful context.

Representation is important in all its facets, in stories, dance, songs, home corners, dolls houses, constructional toys, paints, models and drawings. Amongst all this, children can be encouraged to 'write', in the classroom post office, restaurant, hairdresser, bank and so on. 'Real writing' is only the culmination of a long process towards it.

For example, when there is a fight in the home corner, or between two puppets, the children may in fact be looking for a 'lead sentence' as is necessary in the writing process. Early dramatic play helps children to explore roles and themes, beginnings, endings, transitions, all of which are vital to the writing process. When a child does four apparently identical drawings, they may be the equivalent of attempts to revise and redraft in the writing process.

> Two children, William and Tom, discuss a drawing. Both are four years old. 'Why is its mouth there?' 'It's hungry, silly. That's its tongue, going like that.' He sticks out his tongue. They break into laughter.

Frank Smith (1983) believes that at first representational work is the child's creation, to be admired, but not submitted like a manuscript to be scrutinised and criticised. He is in agreement with Winnicott in this. The creation belongs to the child. No one else can presume to alter it in any way. Vygotsky says that the willingness to take criticism, to submit a manuscript for the scrutiny of others, emerges from the social relationship formed with the 'interested person', who is invited by the child to share in and work on the creation.

Just as there needs to be a truly reciprocal relationship between parents and professionals, so there needs to be a reciprocal relationship between a child and adults who will manage to extend development in an educative way. Joan Tamburrini (1982) sees this informal teaching as the strength of nursery education (0–8 years). Teaching does not have to be direct and formal to be 'teaching'.

Reading

The importance of being read to cannot be over-emphasised. (Bullock Report DES, 1975, Shirley Brice Heath, 1983, Henrietta Dombey, 1983, Caroline Fox, 1982, Linda Miller, 1996). The bedtime story is one important way in which, in a one-to-one situation, an adult can give meaning to the text. Dorothy Butler (1980) stresses that even babies can appreciate books. By looking at books in this way, adults can take up children's initiatives, giving and extending the meaning in them. Children begin to meet different worlds with the adult as translator (Geekie and Raban, 1993).

> Children from four to seven years of age watched a puppet show of an African tale. This shared experience was important in enabling children to grasp what is involved in formal book and story language. Pictures, dancers, puppets, and songs help children relate to formal book language.

Don Holdaway (1979) stresses the importance of chants and song as the basis of 'storying' (this has been revisited in the work of Goswami and Bryant, 1990). Knowing a story well – the old favourites – help children to predict when they read. Reading is largely prediction. Children need to understand about syntax semantics and grapho-phonic aspects of texts in order to read. Their own knowledge of language, the way they have 'cracked the language code', will enable them to tackle syntax in a text.

Being read to is centrally important. Listening to stories with a rich variety of texts helps children to learn about words and sentence structures in book language. The interpretations children have about meanings, the way they bring their own experiences to bear, enables this process. The more help they have had in using language with others in a meaningful way, and in using understanding of book language and its ability to create imaginative ideas in what Margaret Meek calls 'possible worlds', the better.

The grapho-phonic aspect (how it looks and sounds) develops in synchrony with syntax and semantics. Just as vocabulary-building does not lead to rich language development, so rote teaching of letter shapes, or teaching phonics out of context, do not of themselves promote efficiency and understanding of word and letter blends, or word-building. Jeni Riley (1996, p.13) drawing on research by Bialystok (1991), points out that when children use objects, for example a cup and saucer, they know their meaning. Learning the alphabet does not have the same kind of meaning, and reciting it is not enough for a child to learn to read.

Jeni Riley says

> *Merely teaching the alphabet has no enduring value and fails to guarantee an early successful start to reading. The appreciation of the symbolic representation of letters for spoken sounds occurs slowly over time and with exposure to meaningful experiences of print and text.*

The meaningful context best promotes the teaching of these areas. Don Holdaway (1979) stresses individual reading to and with a child. He also advocates the use of enlarged texts in 'shared books' for group story times, when discussion of grapho-phonic aspects can be included in an unstressful setting. In this way children establish that the letter 'a' in the alphabet is consistently written in one way, in contrast to its phonic aspect (for example, the 'a' in 'hat' is pronounced differently from the 'a' in 'hate').

Putting stories onto cassettes, and encouraging children to listen to them through headsets while following in the book, is an activity often referred to as 'Listening Post'. This type of work gives further variety and helps the auditory aspect of reading. These are some ways in which children can be helped to move from picture books to reading the text, both at home and in school.

Marian Whitehead (1996, p.96) believes that effective reading teachers 'make it possible for beginners to draw on and use a wide range of strategies'. These include semantic, syntactic, grapho-phonic and bibliographic conventions such as 'Where do I start on the page'? Taking all this into account, it is no surprise to suggest that by the time children reach the stage of 'real' reading and 'real' writing, they are already a considerable way along the route to literacy.

8

■

THE ABILITY TO DECENTRE:

THINKING ABOUT OTHER PEOPLE

THINKING ABOUT OTHER PEOPLE

The following was heard on BBC Radio 4's 'Thought for the Day' at the beginning of the Gulf War: 'The descent into barbarism takes 48 hours'.

It is a breakthrough in the process of growing up when a child is able to see situations from someone else's point of view and to empathise with other people. Of course this does not happen all of a sudden, or consistently all the time. There is debate about when it first occurs. Even at a few months of age a baby will cry in sympathy with another child, as if recognising that someone is crying. By fifteen months or so, toddlers will often comfort a brother or sister, friend, or a loved adult in the way they would like to be comforted themselves, perhaps with a kiss or by bringing a special toy (Judy Dunn, 1991). This ability to decentre, to separate from self and 'become someone else' is crucial for the development of social and moral behaviour. In this chapter its importance is given high focus.

However, it is difficult to know at what point children can put themselves into someone else's shoes and really empathise and decentre, really think how it must feel to be that person. Catching a feeling from someone is not the same as feeling a feeling that someone else has. Of course this does not happen all of a sudden, it comes and goes. Morality, which is linked with having respect for and valuing other people, slips when a child is tired, with strangers, hungry or in a mood, or in the company of those who are uncaring or unkind. According to Celia Kitzinger, this is probably the case for adults as well as children. Nevertheless, being able to empathise and imagine what it is like to be in a situation, to be someone else, is probably one of the most important aspects of moral development. Morality is about respect for people, but also it is about creating living conditions which bring this about.

This is what we mean when we talk about living in a civilised society. These issues have significance everywhere in the world, although in some countries the rights of and respect for the individual assume greater importance than those of the group as a whole, or vice versa. This has led to a debate on the issues surrounding Human Rights at international gatherings, the problems of market forces and individual greed, or the neglect of the needs of individuals in the cause of the State's needs.

Until recently, it was thought that young children were unable to put themselves into the position of someone else to any great extent. The influence of Jean Piaget's work (1968) led early childhood educators to see children under five as 'intellectually egocentric'. This does not mean selfish. Nursery teachers were trained to become skilled in diverting children, rather than attempting what was considered to be impossible – that is, trying to get the child to look at a situation from another child's point of view.

However, one can think of many situations which did not quite fit in with this blanket view, that the child was 'egocentric' until five years.

> Four year-old Wally had been unhappy when settling into school himself. He took three year-old Peter by the hand and cuddled him when he saw that he was about to cry on his first day. He knew what it was like to be 'new' and could empathise. Six year-old Vicky and three year-old Mark were eating ice cream. Vicky dropped hers and cried. Mark offered her some of his. He knew the 'tragedy', as it seemed to him, of dropping an ice cream as it had happened to him previously.

> Tamsin (four years) was prone to frequent temper tantrums. She threw herself down and began punching the floor. Megan and Paul came over, sank on their knees next to her and Megan said,
>
> 'I'm here for you, Tamsin.'
>
> They had seen Tamsin's tantrums given firm but compassionate attention by staff in the day nursery, and showed her respect. Tamsin looked up, took their hands, and sank on the floor, becalmed by feeling cared for.

Margaret Donaldson (1978) makes some links between Piaget's notion of egocentricity and the development from this stage to that of decentration or empathising (seeing things from other view points). She reminds us that children are able to perform at a higher level in a meaningful context. Piaget's tests presented children with formal tasks which were not in such a context. Margaret Donaldson distinguishes between disembedded tasks (that is abstract tasks, not performed in a realistic situation) and the embedded tasks which confront children in everyday, spontaneous events and situations. The examples of Wally and Mark and Tamsin, quoted above, are embedded in meaning and so the children could relate to the situations. Early childhood educators need to concentrate on providing meaningful situations for children through which to encourage the process of decentration and empathising, so that children can experiment and make full use of these whether they occur in planned or in spontaneous ways.

Judy Dunn has worked for several decades in gathering data in home settings about the beginnings of social and moral development in young children in their family context. Her work suggests that there is a strong link between social and moral development and family relationships. Even in the first year babies are aware of and sensitive to the behaviour of the people who are close to them. She calls this 'affective tuning'.

During the first three years children show self-concern – when they get attention from other people close to them, or begin to understand what other people feel and say because they recognise feelings they have in others, and when they comfort them when distressed – they are both giving and taking, as we saw with Tamsin, Megan and Paul. Moral development emerges out of situations where children have sufficient sense of their own well-being to feel they can both give as well as take what they need in a relationship (Laevers, 1996).

Also, during this time, children, young though they are, begin sorting out what they are allowed to do. They begin to predict what people would disapprove of. Adults might well disapprove of kicking when you don't get what you want. A brother or sister might react strongly if you take a toy away. Young children need to explore and to discover what happens when they hurt other people, help other people or show care for other people. It is however important to remember that concern for this begins with concern for self through the feelings of personal well-being, as Laevers suggests. Children, or adults, who feel bad about themselves, are less likely to be highly developed morally as they will not so easily be able to move beyond their own needs to respecting those of other people.

Judy Dunn's research suggests that families where quarrels are followed by discussions of what went wrong, and how to make things go better next time, help children to tease out moral issues. Even before children can talk she found that children benefit from learning about situations which make them angry, or excited, or joyous. The cause and effect relationship seems to be crucial. Before children can speak they know what makes people angry, and how people might react. It is initially through their relationships within the family that children learn to be caring of those they love.

Knowing about anger and love and how to deal with each is an important contribution to moral development. Once there can be more discussion, this helps reflection and analysis around issues where children are not allowed to do something, share sadness and joy together, or play with other children.

Children in settings which are intimate, such as the family, learn to negotiate with other people, rather than to manipulate other people. Negotiation is part of moral development in that it respects other people. The process of manipulation of other people means grabbing for oneself, and indicates low self-esteem and lack of well-being in the child. It is of course normal to experience moments like this, but when adults help children to move on from these, moral development grows.

It is very unusual for someone to give their life's work over to fighting a cause involving a moral principle. In the main, from adolescence to adulthood, people take on the socially expected conventions of their culture. It is only outstanding people like Nelson Mandela or Eleanor Roosevelt, who go beyond convention to take a moral stand. In other words, most people are more influenced by what other people do than they are by their conscience. It is therefore no good to expect children to know right from wrong, if they consistently see adults doing wrong. There needs to be a strong link between inner moral values and outer moral conduct. The expression 'do as I say, not as I do' is important where moral development is concerned.

Piaget found that children in middle childhood (approximately eight to twelve years of age) were very concerned with what someone's intention was. Whereas if a child broke a cup by mistake when trying to clear the table, a younger child, for example a five year old, would say the helper was 'naughty' because the cup was broken. An older child would understand that the intention was really to help, and that breaking the cup was an accident.

In the early childhood years, it is therefore important that adults help children to tease out the importance of 'intention' as well as 'outcome'. This erodes the expression 'the end justifies the means'.

Hayley (6 years) went to fetch the pudding from the fridge to help her mother. She spilt custard in the fridge and left a trail of custard across the floor, and spilt it on her shoes and clothes. Stacey (3½ years) said,

'You're naughty. You made a mess.'

Stacey does not yet see that intention matters as much as outcome. Their mother said, 'Hayley was trying to help. She didn't mean to spill the custard.'

Motive is as important as results, and motives involve feelings as much as ideas. Hayley's mother tried to keep alive her feelings of helpfulness by emphasising it, rather than the mess. Undermining a desire to help damages a child's long-term moral and social development.

It is probably best for adults never to call a child 'naughty' for this reason. Almost every juvenile delinquent has very low self-esteem. Feeling bad about yourself holds back moral development.

Laevers' (1997) research on a child's sense of well-being is of great importance here. Erikson (1963) through his eight stages of development emphasised that through a basic sense of trust in the first year, self-esteem emerges in the second. If toddlers are constantly told that they are naughty, this soon withers. The quality of early relationships is important.

- Intention needs plenty of discussion. Words like 'meant to' and 'accidentally', 'on purpose' and 'mistake', would be part of the discussion.
- Being sorry about what has happened involves looking at a situation from another point of view, someone else's point of view. A child who can do this can be helped to try and make the situation better.

By helping to clear up the spilt custard some four year-olds can think in the empathetic and decentred way which leads to this kind of respect and sensitivity towards others. Hayley is not being blamed or ashamed or made to feel guilt-ridden. She feels sorry this happened, can see why it is upsetting to others, but knows that her mother realises that it was unintentional and is doing what she can to make it better. Hayley's sense of well-being is not undermined.

When a child intends 'wrong', for example by spilling custard on purpose, there can be discussion about it. 'I am sorry you did that. I don't like it when you make a mess on purpose.' In other words the adult is not rejecting the child, but what he or she did.

The message is not:

- you are bad;
- I don't like you any more;
- you are naughty.

The message is:

- I don't like what you did;
- but you did try to clear it up;
- I still love you, unconditionally, whatever you do.

There are strong links between the early childhood years and the teenage years. Parents and adults with teenagers often reap the results of how they tackled moral development in the early years. Children brought up in the early years to explore the following areas are not so likely to become delinquent teenagers:

- intention when things go wrong;
- empathising with how it feels to someone else when you do something that makes things go wrong;
- seeing the consequences of your actions;
- understanding cause and effect relationships of events and actions;
- how systems develop which are just and fair and which can be enforced – this means discussing rules, flexibility or not;
- how to make sure those in authority are just and fair in the spirit in which they operate the system of justice.

Young children are dependent on parents, carers, teachers, friends of the family, and older children to be fair in the way they are dealt with.

Adolescents and adults participate in the whole social justice system in their society and how it relates to their culture. Issues such as the difference between policing by consent or traffic police catching people out on technicalities will become important. If the latter becomes the norm, the general public will lose respect and trust in the police, who are in the front line of any system of social justice.

Judge Tumin (Sunday Times Lecture Series, 1995) said that one of the features of young offenders in his then role as Chief Inspector of Prisons, was that they had little understanding of the difference between formal and informal situations and formal and informal behaviour. They tended to tell him personal details when he was a complete stranger to them in his role as Chief Inspector of Prisons, when in fact he was not a friend to be confided in. Roberts (1995) reports the importance of children learning to recognise the difference between informal behaviour at home and going out, and more formal behaviour in their family lives.

> At three years-old, Hannah's mother explained the family was going to meet someone from daddy's work, and it would be important to be on best behaviour. Hannah's response was 'no-one say bloody'.

From an early age, children begin to tease out that what is appropriate behaviour in one cultural setting is not in another. For some children, the difference between school culture and home culture is slight, for others it is huge. This is important because the 'fitting in' is part of moral development. It partly involves being able to be sensitive to those you are with, but it also involves remaining who you are.

Some adults demand too much from young children in this respect, for example sitting for long periods in school assembly at three and four years of age. It is inappropriate, and likely in the long run to put children off of trying to fit in with the system, and so ironically to damage their moral development. Young children are often accused of naughtiness during assemblies. In this case naughtiness is simply not doing what an adult wants. Young children are unlikely to be clear about the difference between naughtiness that inconveniences the system and the naughtiness of hitting someone else or stealing. For the young child in assembly, naughtiness becomes what adults do not like. The crucial dialogue, central to moral development and good behaviour long-term, is missing. Without adult help, children cannot sort out the interplay between intention, motive, outcome and consequence.

If the system is utterly insensitive to the child, we cannot expect the child to be sensitive to the system. The system is not, in this case, making appropriate demands on the child.

It is also important to bear in mind that a child who can ask questions about 'why must we sit so long, it is boring' is actually thinking about the social conventions of life (in this case the inappropriateness of putting nursery reception children into assembly).

In the days of Nazi Germany, or during Apartheid in South Africa, it took great courage to question the social conventions of these regimes. The 'fitting in' aspect of moral development must be seen side by side with the development of the child's conscience. It was the voices of individual conscience which led to the abolition of slavery and Apartheid, not the voices of those who 'fitted in'. The four year-old who questions being made to sit through assembly does not yet realise the enormity of the challenge he/she is making, but that does not mean the child is wrong to challenge what many early childhood educators regard as a form of child abuse.

There needs to be a balance between encouraging children to question, explore and develop a conscience over and above conforming to the socio-cultural conventions in which they live. It is important that adults do not let young children down by ignoring the questions they ask about these things, which help them to think about what is morally right.

Research (Kitzinger, 1997, p.16) indicates that in a group, most people become passive, and the 'bystander effect' operates, so that if, for example, someone is attacked in front of the group, often no-one does anything. It takes leadership to step out of being in a group and to call the police. This has serious implications for young children.

If children are herded about in large groups for large parts of their day (as they often are in large reception classes), the 'bystander effect' is encouraged and moral behaviour is discouraged. Children in smaller, intimate, quality early years settings are more likely to respond to situations as individuals and to learn to empathise and show care.

Moral development is helped when children are:

- treated sensitively by adults;
- when there is plenty of discussion and negotiation in the family and early years settings;
- children need to feel closeness, trust and understanding with adults who explain things to them and help them to express their thoughts and feelings about issues and events;
- children help each other through the quarrels they have and the negotiating and discussing they do;
- free flow play (Bruce, 1991) encourages children to see things from other people's point of view as they move into and out of different roles and imaginary situations;
- giving rewards for good behaviour undermines long-term moral and social development (Kohn, 1993).

How adults can help moral development in the young child

The first guideline is that children need to experience sensitivity on the part of significant others towards their own intentions, ideas and feelings, if they are increasingly to respond to others in this way. People who are significant to children are those who they feel close to and admire.

> Three year-old Amandip is beginning to use English in school. He is enjoying the fact that he can express himself in Punjabi and English. He chatters throughout group time and requests songs and sings them solo, because he cannot wait for the group. He wants to answer all the questions the teacher puts to the group of children. He is irrepressible. His teacher does not stop him, she encourages him, bringing in other children's contributions around his. She recognises his 'explosion' in English, but she does gently insist that the group finishes one song before he suggests another.

In the following example, the child's ability to think about everyone present at the tea table is not encouraged.

> Four year-old Peter had a friend to tea and his mother joined in. There were soon only two scones left and Peter assumed that he and his friend would have them. His mother made no comment. Peter was not being helped to think about the problem of three people and only two scones. In a sense, his mother was holding back his moral development by not raising this.

> Six year-old Nikolai's mother thanked him for thinking of her by offering her one of his sweets. She praised his kindness (that is, decentration) but did not take one, thereby encouraging him to take such a risk again!

> Three and a half year-old Matthew and his baby sister went with his parents to supper at the house of some friends. He was used to sleeping at other houses and happily went to bed upstairs. His father asked him to call out if the newly born baby started to cry. He agreed. A few minutes later he appeared downstairs crying and saying 'I don't want to'. His parents did not know what he meant, but it emerged that he did not want to tell the adults if the baby cried. He was happy to sleep upstairs, but did not want to think about the baby.
>
> The parents reassured him and he was asleep in five minutes. His mother said that at home he took pride in telling her when the baby had woken up in order to help her. He was tired and in a different setting, but the adults were sensitive to him.

The example of Matthew contrasts with that of Peter in that the family discussions are reciprocal and at times abrasive, but adults are also sensitive to his ideas, feelings and intentions and act accordingly. Peter was not encouraged to discuss who should have the last scones with adults who are important role models for him.

The second guideline for the encouragement of decentration is that children need adults to help them discuss moral issues of good and bad, right and wrong (Dunn, 1988) so that they begin to see the consequences of their actions.

> Six year-old Jenny asked for another pancake but there was none left. She was angry. Her mother reminded her that she had had two and that there were no more eggs. She pointed out that in Ethiopia it would be difficult to get any eggs, flour or milk, and this led to an interesting discussion on why and how food ought to be taken to people. Jenny had watched a programme on TV. Every day for a time she began to invite discussion about her meals in relation to low technology cooking, food availability, climatic conditions, and so on.

Jenny's mother had helped her to link some difficult concepts for a six year-old to grasp from a television programme to a spontaneous situation which had great meaning for her. Marian Whitehead (1996) points out that it is in intimate conversational settings at which talk occurs between young children and adults.

In the following examples an early years worker and parent are working together in this way.

> At school, the early years worker was doing a project on 'flowers'. She had an interest table full of them, with some that children could take apart and look at under magnifying glasses. Three year-old Melissa enjoyed putting things inside others (a topological, spatial schema in Piaget's theory). She homed in on this interest table, and began putting flowers into vases with gusto. At home time the early years worker explained this interest to her mother and asked her if she would like to take the pot of flowers home to follow up the school work.
>
> The mother had had problems in getting Melissa to come to the table at meal times because she always wanted to bring her toys with her. She found that by asking Melissa to put some flowers (even weeds from the garden) in a vase on the table she could overcome this problem. Delighted, she told the teacher about this in school next day. This marked a turning point for Melissa who began to help her mother prepare the table for meals at home and then sat down readily. She had begun to decentre a little more and to make the link from bringing a toy to the table to making the objects on the table relevant to the meal. It was not purely what she wanted but what was needed at meal times.

> Seven year-old Anthony purposefully scratched a mark on a wooden table. The teacher reprimanded him and told him that he must not spoil the table in that way. He was crestfallen. So that he didn't feel that she had rejected him, but only what he had done, she praised him when he picked a toy up which might have got crushed on the floor. She was firmly operating on the principle that there should be respect for property in the classroom in a meaningful context for Anthony.

Hilda Garrard, formerly of the Froebel Institute, London, calls this 'law with love' (1986). The teacher pointed out that she had cared about the table being spoilt and she was glad that he cared about the toy being crushed. In this way she linked the two events.

> The teacher in a class of six year-olds planned a cookery lesson. The children were to make baked apples in a group of six. They made one for themselves and one extra each to give as a present. Joanna said that she wanted one for her brother and one for her mother. She, the teacher and the other children discussed the fairness of this – and eventually it was decided that she would have to cut up and divide the two apples when she got home. The teacher helped her to think of others, to see the unfair implications of giving her extra apples, and to become involved in the mathematics of division. She was helping her to consider others, justice and mathematics, all in a meaningful embedded context and yet moving slightly away from the immediate towards the disembedded context.

The importance of mixing sensitively with other children

The third guideline for encouraging children to decentre is that children need to mix meaningfully with other children. The section which follows is more extensive than the previous two because it gives an opportunity to explore practical examples of the importance of play, not only in relation to decentration, but also more generally for early childhood education.

Children need variety in the ways in which they mix with other children, ranging from partnerships to groups. Children need to work with children older and younger, more and less advanced, as well as children operating at the same level. This applies to both partnership and group situations. Partnerships can involve older and younger children, more and less advanced, or children of the same age or stage. The following examples show partnerships between two children at different points in their learning.

> Five year-old Hannah reads each night to three year-old William. The books he enjoys are at the level she can read 'approximately', from her knowledge of the story and the picture clues. She is thinking of stories that he enjoys, but she is gaining satisfaction from the giving by using her latest learning in a meaningful setting.

Turiel and Weston (1983) demonstrate that by the age of five children can distinguish between different types of rules. Moral rules (it is wrong to hit) were regarded as unchangeable. Other kinds of rule (you must tidy the room before going out) could be changed (Bruce and Meggitt 1996).

A different partnership is between two children at the same stage.

> Six year-olds Tom and William were in the garden together. Both are particularly interested in natural science and this had been the basis of a friendship since the age of three. They found a crusader spider and made an assault course for it. They were delighted when it climbed up a pole and along a string they had rigged up.
>
> William tried to help it to realise there was another pole for it to climb down. He gently touched it, but the spider bit him. He was interested in this, as there had been discussion in his family for years about whether spiders did bite people. Both boys chatted constantly. 'Let's put a dead fly out for him to eat, then he'll come.' 'No it's got to be in a web.' 'Does he have a web or is he a pouncer?' 'What's a pouncer?' 'He hides and then pounces.' 'Oh!' There was a lot of negotiating.

This is give and take of a different kind from that of the first type of partnership. It involves a different kind of looking from various points of view and is very challenging.

At times, partnerships need adult intervention.

> Four year-olds Alistair and Stuart made a tune out of circles stuck on stave lines on a board. It was a monotone. The teacher sang it for them, and moved away. Stuart changed it so that it went up at the end, but Alistair did not want to change it. He tried to put the note down again, but Stuart grabbed it and ran off. Alistair gave chase; he was furious. Stuart's mother, who was helping in the classroom, said, 'Give him back his tune, Stuart.'
>
> It was suggested by the teacher that Stuart should start another row underneath Alistair's, going up at the end. She then played this on the xylophone, Alistair played his row and Stuart played his. Here the negotiation broke down and the partnership required adult help. Neither child could decentre without help. The adult could have made Stuart apologise to Alistair, but preferred to give the message that it is more satisfying and produces better results to cooperate rather than fight.

In these examples, one kind of partnership involves an older child helping a younger child, but experiencing great pleasure in doing so. Another involves children at the same stage of development sharing and negotiating their way through a first-hand experience. The third type of partnership showed an adult intervening sensitively when co-operation broke down. There are other sorts of partnership, of course.

The importance of play with other children

Group situations with peers, more and less advanced and at the same stage, are also important during early childhood. Group play involves children in giving up their immediate wishes in order that the play can continue successfully. Vygotsky (1978) sees this as an important attribute.

A shoe shop had been set up in the classroom. The family of four year-old Neelan owns a shop. She wanted the early years worker pretend to be the shopkeeper and quickly assumed that role. She took younger children, three year-olds Shazia and Toto, as customers. Certainly she dominated the play, but she was inducting them into what imaginative play is about. They willingly stayed, but could have left at any time. Toto and Shazia needed Neelan to show them how to play 'pretend games', how to take roles and become other people, how to decentre and see other viewpoints.

Anna Maria is another typical three year-old. The teacher was working with a group of children on the large wooden blocks. They (two girls and two boys) were sitting on them as a table and chairs. Four year-old Tracy brought a small wooden block and said, 'Would you like a tin of beans?' and laughed. The teacher said, 'I'd love some – but I need to open the tin.' She pretended to do this to a rapt audience. Then she asked for a saucepan in which to heat the beans. Sade found a flatter cylinder (a thoroughly appropriate representation of a saucepan). The teacher pretended to pour in the beans and stir. Then she asked for some plates. The children found more blocks and the teacher made toast using rectangular shapes. At this point Anna Maria came in and watched the activity. She came up to the teacher and said triumphantly, 'You're only pretending, you know.' She did not want to join in, she only wanted to watch the game.

Three year-olds need to see high-level imaginative play before being helped into it. This has implications for later work in school. Getting on the inside of roles and themes in imaginative play requires the child to go beyond 'self' and to 'become' other people in other situations in a meaningful context. Becoming someone else, acting out a role and a theme, requires considerable decentration. The spontaneous scripts which develop during imaginative play are the stuff of later story-writing. This form of play encourages the embryonic sense of audience which will flower later on.

Seven year-old Hannah, three year-old Kit and five year-olds Matthew and William decide to play King Arthur. Only Hannah and William know the story and the game quickly disintegrates. All the children know the story of Robin Hood. Hannah suggests that they play this instead and she co-ordinates the story. There is a lot of discussion: 'You say "I am hurt" and I say "Get up"' and so on. The script is agreed and carried out in action. All dress up in clothes from the dressing-up box, with swords. Kit (the youngest) follows. He makes mistakes, goes to the wrong place, kills the 'wrong' person and the other children (mainly Hannah) alert him to what is needed. Interestingly, in games of mixed ages or large groups of children, there often seems to be a great deal of rushing about and follow-my-leader activity. Younger children need the stimulation and leadership of more advanced children. Older children need to lead and organise complicated games, with younger children as willing participants.

According to Piaget, from the age of approximately eight, the ability to hold in mind several factors in the disembedded context simultaneously develops steadily. If Vygotsky (1978) is correct in his view on zones of potential development, then imaginative group play in meaningful (embedded) contexts serves as an opportunity for children in the three to seven age group to start to hold in mind several factors at once.

Hannah, if the game is to succeed, needs to help Kit by trying to see his difficulties. She needs to keep William and Matthew happy about Kit's 'errors', and to negotiate, smooth situations over and make acceptable suggestions. Maid Marion, she points out, when Matthew makes a bid to become leader of the game, is as good at shooting arrows as Robin Hood.

Matthew is Robin Hood. He insists that he is a better archer. William supports Hannah. 'It's in the book,' he declares. Hannah gets round this by suggesting that they all surround the Sheriff of Nottingham (a bush in the garden), but do not kill him.

Group play, like partnership play, is important in helping children to develop the ability to decentre. In the example of Neelan's leadership of the group, the importance of mathematics was the focus. Matching, sorting, putting shoes and feet into a one to one correspondence are some instances of the mathematical situations involved. In the example of Anna Maria, she needed to grasp the drama of the position – how to 'become' someone else, in a different situation.

In the example of Hannah, William, Kit and Matthew, adherence to a text was required. The correct version of Robin Hood's story was demanded by the participants, who willingly submitted to its requirements. This links with the partnerships in which Jenny became involved with her mother in environmental issues, Melissa became involved in artistic presentation of meals (functional art), Tom and William were involved in studying natural science, Alistair and Stuart were composing music. Every area of the curriculum contributes to fostering decentration in young children. The broader the curriculum the better.

In these examples, adults have only intervened when relationships, roles, themes, shared constructions of meanings and so on broke down. Adults supported or extended the children's intentions or initiatives. They did not 'take over', nor did they leave children to flounder. They were at hand to act sensitively as situations developed. If children are not given opportunities to experiment and negotiate, share, argue, or agree, they do not become skilled in these important areas.

However, situations break down rapidly with young children. When this happens, adults are vital in order to curb escalations and fights which go beyond the experimental. In these examples also, adults valued spontaneous events which clarified children's intentions and helped to extend learning.

Strategies used by adults were:

- making appropriate provision (Neelan);
- conversations (Anna Maria);
- leaving the children alone when roles and themes were developing (Hannah, William, Matthew and Kit);
- intervening during quarrels which the children were not able to resolve (Alistair and Stuart).

The long-term undermining effect of extrinsic rewards

Extrinsic rewards for good behaviour are only effective in the short-term, and according to Kohn (1993) may well inflict long-term damage to moral and social behaviour. He suggests that:

- Rewards punish because they control us. Feeling controlled by others damages autonomous learning (Principles 4 and 5).
- Rewards damage a sense of collaboration and teamwork, or community. They are divisive because they set children against each other as rivals.
- Rewards mask problems and ignore reasons why children or adults behave as they do.
- Rewards discourage risk-taking because they assume children are naturally lazy rather than naturally adventurous and creative.

- Rewards damage genuine interest by implying that it is not worth being good for its own sake. Rewards undermine intrinsic motivation.

Adults who focus on positive role modelling, setting clear boundaries, engage in positive negotiation and conflict resolution with plenty of discussion, listening, talking and warm concern are more likely to encourage moral and social behaviour in young children, but also with a forward influence into adolescence and adulthood (Coleman, 1997).

SUMMARY

Moral development is concerned with

- moral values;
- moral behaviour.

Even babies and toddlers recognise and imitate feelings from other people. Real empathy and being able to put yourself in someone else's shoes comes from toddler times onwards, so that children:

- develop a conscience (moral values which are not just about obeying what adults and authority figures says is right and good);
- learn how to make and change rules (laws) and to see why they are needed;
- behave thoughtfully, influenced by their inner values more than by external rewards.

Knowing right from wrong means:

- judging someone's intention;
- recognising how much children know and understand;
- seeing the consequences of actions and words.

Moral development is helped when children's self-esteem is not undermined by being told they are naughty or bad children. Rejecting what they have done, but valuing, respecting and loving them unconditionally helps children to discuss the results of their actions, and how this makes other people feel (Dunn, 1988).

9

■

SIGNIFICANT OTHER PEOPLE

FOR THE CHILD

There is a range of people who are significant in one way or another to the development of a young child. In particular, family, professional workers and other children whom the child meets regularly all become important for that child in a direct way. In this chapter, the impact of the family, professional workers and other children is discussed in turn, with particular reference to the role of the early childhood educator or carer.

FAMILY AND CARERS

In the Community Education Pack for the Open University (1997), 'Confident Parents, Confident Children', the introduction states

Helping people become confident parents may be the best way to ensure that the next generation grows up to be capable and confident. There is more to parenting than just looking after a growing child. As adults we too 'grow' as we become more experienced and skilful parents

Gillian Pugh and Erica De'Ath (1984, p.169) state:

The great majority of parents are concerned to do their best for their children, even if they are not always sure what this might be.

Every family is different, and has different needs. The key to partnership with parents lies in having a network of strategies which can be employed so that different approaches are used with different families, approaches which support and build on the families rather than undermining what the parents do. Some families do not wish to or cannot come into school often. Some families enjoy being in school, or an early years setting, but in the parents' room, not the classroom. Others prefer to be visited at home. Others want workshops, meetings, films, talks in the evenings or at weekends after school, often provided that there is a crèche. Others will make equipment, raise funds, come to social functions, but do not want further contact. Some parents actively seek help in child-rearing and in the education of their children, others do not.

The early years worker's role is to build a partnership with every parent. Clearly, it is easier to do this with some parents than with others. Situations involving suspected child abuse, whether physical, mental, or sexual, are the most difficult, and where this exists, the staff need to work with other professionals as much as with the parents.

However, the tendency of professionals to undermine any parent's self-confidence with their 'expertise', and the isolation felt by many bringing up young children, contribute to the difficulties experienced by many parents.

Most parents are not interested in children in general. Their main concern is with their own child and the child's friends. They are not teachers, nor do they wish to be. Teachers and parents do not bring the same qualities to the partnership. Their roles are complementary, and should not be seen as threatening to each other.

The parent is highly emotionally linked to the child, and prepared to go to 'unreasonable lengths' for the child as shown by Elizabeth Newson's study (1972; quoted in Kellmer Pringle, 1980, p.37). Alice Honig (1984) stressed the need for parents and professionals to build specific observations together.

The Teacher Training Agency Practitioner Research Project, based at Pen Green (Whalley and Arnold, 1997), has developed strategies for doing this more effectively. Professionals can help parents to look in more detail at what their child can do, and this helps both teacher and parents to work together for the child. In this way, the early childhood practitioners can help the parents to use the power and energy of their feelings for their child, and can build and extend on the parents' work through his or her knowledge of children in general.

Parents want their children to be happy in school. So do early childhood practitioners. Parents want their children to be successful at reading, writing and mathematics, and to be well-behaved and popular. So do staff. The aims of parents and teachers in fact coincide in important areas, as shown by research at the University of Exeter (Hughes, Wikeley and Nash, 1994). Teachers thought that parents were not very interested in assessment, but they were.

Educators who look below the surface of what parents are saying can find a shared basis for work on which trust can be built. But teachers need to share what they know about child development and curriculum provision, rather than to guard their knowledge.

The Froebel Nursery Research Project emphasised parent/staff partnership (Athey, 1990) and found that different parents liked to work with staff in different ways, with different parenting styles. It was important therefore that the teacher tuned in to the particular needs of individual families. There is no one way to work with parents.

The following examples show how staff can work with a wide variety of parents, as described below.

- Parents recognising or trying to extend the learning of their child.
- Parents who are eager to work with staff in early childhood settings in ways which do not fit in with the teacher's methods.
- Parents bodily in the early childhood setting, but not active in the classroom.
- Parents whose main contact with the setting is bringing and fetching children, and perhaps attending parents' evenings.
- Parents who do not bring children to the early childhood setting, or seek contact with the staff.

Parents recognising or trying to extend the learning of the child

Three year-old Shanaz's father was a bus driver. He wanted to be with his children as much as possible, and managed to arrange his shift work accordingly. He brought Shanaz to the early childhood setting whenever he could and normally stayed for half an hour. (He brought his younger child, a toddler, with him, too.) He wanted to know what was the purpose of each activity. He took great pleasure in watching Shanaz in the nursery once he realised that water play and other messy activities could be used to teach her mathematical language (for example, 'out of the water', 'in the water', 'high', 'low', 'long way' and so on). He used these terms with relish as she played. He was 'teaching' his daughter mathematics. His enthusiasm was invigorating for the staff, who found him a positive adult to welcome into the school. His basic trust of the teacher's knowledge made it easier for the school staff to work with him.

Parents who are eager to work with teachers in ways which do not fit in with the teachers' methods

It is not for teachers or other early childhood workers to tell families how to bring up their children, or to insist that education must be approached in one way – the school's way. Just as staff need to establish a child's intentions and build on them in educationally worthwhile ways, so they need to find out what parents think education is, before they can begin a successful partnership.

All too often the parents are asked to listen to the staff's view of education, but not the reverse. Parents need to know what staff are trying to do, but staff need to know what parents consider to be important. This is the basis of mutual respect – respect for each other's expertise, respect for each other's commitment to a particular child, respect for the different skills and strengths each brings to a complementary partnership. Two examples follow which show how the teacher can use his/her skills to encourage appropriate parental involvement.

Five year-old Betty's mother liked to work in the classroom. She was eager to 'teach' an activity. The teacher suggested that she helped the children to make dough and use it. She wanted Betty's mother to see her do this activity with the children before she had a group on her own. Betty's mother couldn't resist joining in while the teacher worked with the group. The teacher asked an open-ended question: 'I wonder what we do first?' Betty's mother instantly swooped in: 'We need a bowl, spoon, flour'. She began transmitting the knowledge. This was how she saw the role of the teacher, not asking obtuse questions that didn't get to the point. The teacher suggested that Betty's mother should all the time check what children learned by asking them questions about what they were doing. Betty's mother accepted this and acted on this, as it was part of her view of education – teach the knowledge, then test the knowledge.

Over a period of a year Betty's mother and the teacher began to discuss the importance of getting children to anticipate what will happen, to plan what will happen, to organise equipment they will need. Initially, the teacher built on the parent's view of a teacher's role and so did not undermine her confidence and did not reject her views.

Some parents experience difficulty in leaving their child in school. They are sometimes unfairly referred to as clinging or over-protective. They are often parents who enjoy a very close relationship with their children, and are very sensitive to their child's feelings and deeply concerned about their child's education.

When five year-old Stephanie made a preliminary visit to the reception class, prior to beginning school, her mother instantly settled down to work with her and the group of children at the construction toy table. She talked to each child about what he or she was doing, and skilfully involved Stephanie in contributing, and in talking to the child next to her. So far, so good. When Stephanie began to attend regularly at school, her mother wanted to stay until she was 'settled'. The teacher suggested, on the second day, that her mother should take a short coffee break in the staff room. Stephanie cried. Mother would not leave her.

Next day, Stephanie began to cling to her mother all the time, anticipating that she would try to have coffee. Mother reassured her, insisting that she would not leave her at all. Stephanie wanted to her mother very close to her, and stopped attempting to relate to the other children. By the end of the week, the pattern was set. Stephanie would not become involved in activities. Neither could her mother become involved, because Stephanie thwarted any attempt she made to work with groups of children. Stephanie's mother was upset. She felt that she had done all the 'right things', and yet her child would not let her go at all. Her 'good' mothering was being punished instead of rewarded. She needed the teacher as someone to help her who was not involved in this 'eyeball-to-eyeball' situation.

The teacher could not discuss anything with the mother since Stephanie clung to her, so she asked her to phone from home. The teacher then discussed strategies, telling her that this was a not uncommon experience for very good, sensitive, devoted parents. Of course, Stephanie did not want such a treasured person to leave. She suggested that Stephanie's mother and school take a united approach, and insist that she left for 15 minutes immediately on school arrival, warning Stephanie that this would happen. In this way, Stephanie did not have the worry of anticipating her mother's going until coffee time. They would gradually increase the time in discussion together. Once Stephanie was settled, her mother would be able to come into school and work with the children, say once a week, since she wanted to be involved in the classroom.

At this stage, it would be too complicated for Stephanie to grasp that pattern. They needed to wait until she was established. In this way, the teacher reassured the mother that she could be trusted with her child, and would be sensitive towards her. She made it clear that she thought highly of her parenting, understood her child's behaviour and wanted to welcome her to the classroom in principle, but the timing of this had to revolve around what would be appropriate for Stephanie. Stephanie's mother relaxed. So did Stephanie, who settled into school happily during that term. The next term, her mother came regularly to school to help with cooking, reading, model-making and so on.

Parents bodily in the early childhood setting, but not active in the classroom

Some parents, if encouraged, will often linger in or near the classroom after having brought their child. They will also come in on other occasions, but will resist greater involvement. The early childhood practitioner needs to develop strategies for encouraging the parents' interest in their children into active expression.

Three year-old Khaliq's mother regularly brought him to the early years setting, and went immediately to the book corner, where she was friendly, but did not seek contact with the teacher while her child settled into school. Here, a different strategy was needed. Khaliq's mother was in school regularly, but as yet there was no partnership with the teacher. Each week there was cookery, and the teacher asked her if she would make chapattis with the children. She said her English was not good enough, but the teacher encouraged her to speak in Urdu. She enjoyed the cookery session, and stayed on for the end-of-the-morning singing, sitting with the teacher and children. She liked the songs, which included 'Humpty Dumpty'. The teacher explained that the song was to help the children use mathematical language ('up' and 'down'), and that tomorrow she would do 'The Grand Old Duke of York'. She invited the mother to join the session.

Mother was delighted, and was heard saying 'up' and 'down' to Khaliq as they went out. The next step was to encourage the mother to watch her child with the teacher. Khaliq was observed putting a pile of bricks into the classroom 'telephone kiosk' one by one, and then, once a pile had formed, picking each one up and throwing it into a large cardboard box outside the kiosk. He did this for some time. He was transporting, and placing objects in containers. The member of staff asked if he did anything like this at home. He had put a pile of dried chick-peas into a saucepan from a colander, but his mother could not explain this in English. She demonstrated with equipment in the home corner, and the following day brought in chick-peas and demonstrated again. Meanwhile, the staff had organised a paint-mixing activity with Khaliq in mind. This involved putting powder paint into pots and adding water. Khaliq did this for half an hour.

His mother was beginning to see how reporting his home activities to the family worker was important, as the staff used this information in their lesson planning. She began to see that activities were planned, and that mess was necessary and could lead to science. The 'mixtures' were an early chemistry lesson, the teacher explained. So was the cookery lesson, making chapattis. These were both examples of changing a substance: from powder (paint) to sludgy liquid (paint and water) and from powdery flour to a solid chapatti. This activity is a precursor to understanding chemical equations. Khaliq's mother could see that the staff wanted him to learn mathematics (up and down songs). She gradually became more relaxed about messy activities because she could see that they led on to science and maths.

Staff need to share the importance of these different curriculum areas with parents. Valuing messy home activities (cookery) and giving them high status in school, is one starting point. Khaliq's mother also liked gardening, and grew vegetables in school, as she lived in a flat with no garden.

Outdoor activities were then given high value. This is another area which is often not seen to be important by parents. Studying worms, snails, slugs and the different properties of soils (clay, sand, and gravel) is messy, but leads to natural science. By beginning with what the parent valued, cooking and gardening, the teacher was able to share the importance of messy and outdoor activities with this parent, over a period of time. Khaliq's mother also began, very gradually, to see the need to observe the child before planning lessons, so that the lesson was effective and appropriate, and to see that her observations mattered as well as the teacher's. She became active in the classroom, cooking, gardening, helping with paintings and so on, using her strengths.

She was a home garment-maker, and a sewing machine was set up for her in the classroom where she made clothes for the dressing-up corner, or for her child, out of a big box of materials which was always available – and she let the children have turns, too.

She did not see herself as a teacher. Her presence enriched the classroom activities, introduced Urdu alongside English, and helped the staff through her developing skill in observing her own child. Her interest was in her child. In doing the activities she enjoyed, in which the children participated, she enhanced rather than threatened the teacher's role.

Khaliq's father visited the school to 'inspect it' when Khaliq first came. The family worker talked about the curriculum, mainly the beginning of the three Rs. Khaliq's father came when dolls' wash day was in progress. He was about to leave this 'women's activity' and take his son to something else. The early childhood worker told him that this was a mathematics lesson. She explained to him that she and his wife had noted Khaliq transporting objects and putting them into containers.

This washing activity had been designed to help Khaliq to do both. It helped his ability to make a series (largest, smallest clothes to peg out) it helped him to classify (soapy water, rinsing water and so on). She explained that Khaliq needed to both seriate and classify in order to be ready for number work later on. She demonstrated this difficult theory in a practical context. Father and son stayed at the activity. Khaliq's father did not visit again, but gave his approval for his wife to continue bringing Khaliq (for nursery education is non-statutory).

The developing partnership in Khaliq's family took a year to become established, and a further year to flourish. Most teachers only work with a group of children for one year and so the importance of working with colleagues as a team, and of a whole-school policy in relation to work with parents, requires emphasis. The importance of five terms in the nursery where the partnership pattern is established also requires consideration.

This example also demonstrates the indirect approach to structuring the curriculum in the interactionist style. One of the central aims of this approach is to respect the parent's view, and not to demand assimilation of these views into the school's model. The indirectly-structured curriculum more easily allows for integration of the parents' view with that of the early childhood setting. Parents are not required to lay aside their own ideas, but encouraged to broaden them.

The same applies to the staff, who are also required to keep up to date through in-service training as part of being articulate in the broadening process. Broadening thinking does not mean watering it down. It means parents and early childhood practitioners clarifying their own ideas through meeting other ideas. This is not an easy, or comfortable, way for staff to work, but it is a deeply satisfying and successful way to involve parents, as the work of Lin Poulton (1979) in Hampshire, Chris Athey (1972–7) in London, and Margy Whalley and staff at the Pen Green Centre, Corby, Northamptonshire, suggests.

Betty's mother and Khaliq's parents were asked to broaden their views, but not to abandon them. The teacher reached out to touch on areas of overlap in their view of school and home, and to build from there. In the next section, the same approach was applied to Kim's mother.

Parents whose main contact with the school is bringing and fetching children, and attending parents' evening

Five year-old Kim's mother brought and fetched her each day, would have a quick chat with the teacher, but had shown no sign of wishing to become involved in the classroom. She was anxious for Kim to learn to read and write. As is quite common, she saw teaching Kim to do this as the main function of school. She had taught Kim to write her name before she came to school.

There was a problem here in that the mother was also encouraging Kim to copy words. This differed from the school's approach, which advocated children constructing their own letters when writing and where children are introduced to conventional spelling as involving problem solving. Here was a clash between home and school. Kim's mother was not going to be convinced that the way she herself learned to write 'was wrong', because she successfully learned to write that way.

The teacher organised an exhibition of written work from reception to top infants, asking her colleagues to help her. As parents brought their children in or collected them, she referred to this. She showed Kim's mother what the school did. Kim's mother was reassured to see the high standard of spelling and large amounts of creative writing many children achieved later in the school. She was interested to see writing including stories and poems, describing outings or events, annotating of models they had made, or writing up experiments they had performed.

In this way, Kim's mother was introduced to different modes of writing. Her concept of 'writing' broadened, but the teacher did not undermine her. She congratulated the mother on teaching Kim the alphabet and especially on starting with the letters of her name. She was pleased that she had taught Kim to be enthusiastic about writing and feel that she could write. She asked her to write down stories Kim wanted to tell, so that she (as teacher) could make them into a book for Kim. As Kim was not used to 'inventing' spelling with her mother, the teacher worked on this aspect with her in school. In this way, she protected the child/parent relationship from possible failure during what might have been a difficult transition.

Once Kim became confident in her own ability to 'have a go' at spelling, she began spontaneously to do this with her mother. Her mother did not automatically 'correct' the spelling. She left it unless it was one of the spellings she and the teacher had decided to work on (for example 'wood' for 'would'). The teacher said, when Kim's mother met her from school, that she wanted to work on the 'ould' family of words, since Kim consistently spelt this sound 'oo'.

Home and school were working together successfully. Kim's mother had not been asked to abandon her views of how children learn to write. She had broadened it, which had been an exciting rather than an undermining experience. In this partnership, it was the ten minutes before and after school which were of critical importance. Kim's mother also attended any evening 'talks' to parents about different aspects of the curriculum.

Parents who do not bring children to school, or seek contact with school

Behaviour of this sort is unusual and ought to be an instant signal for the teacher to attempt to make contact with the parents, in a sensitive way. The problem is how. Three year-old Jerome's parents are an example of this type. They did not attempt any contact with the school until the teacher sought it. Indeed, they seemed quite antipathetic and involvement with them required intermediary help from the Health Visitor. This example is discussed in full in the next section (on professional workers) because, as in many instances of complete lack of contact with parents, the support of other professional workers was necessary.

A NETWORK OF STRATEGIES

In this section a network of strategies that early years workers can use has been discussed. Different families have different needs. Having a variety of approaches helps the parent/staff partnership to develop with success, which means that significant people in the child's life are working together for the child.

In the next section, which looks at the way professionals in statutory and voluntary agencies work with parents, the need for early childhood practitioners to work with a variety of adults as well as parents is emphasised. Being child-centred is too narrow an approach. It is more appropriate to consider the child–in–context, and that includes the different skills and strengths that different professionals and voluntary agencies have to offer in strengthening the child, as a member of a family.

Professionals in statutory and voluntary agencies

There are two facts which need to be borne in mind when thinking about this group of significant adults. First, the range and types of educational and care settings are varied, and this can have a significant impact on the types of professionals involved with children of 0–8 years of age. For the under–fives the variety is bewildering and difficult to justify. Even for the five to eight year-olds (that is, after the statutory school age), the variety is wide.

A considerable proportion of children under the age of five attend groups affiliated to the Pre-School Learning Alliance, which is a voluntary agency.

In many parts of the country children attend nursery classes in primary schools or nursery schools run by Local Education Authorities (LEAs). Some children attend private nursery schools or day nurseries. A very few children attend family centres or combined centres jointly funded by both LEAs and social services and health departments. Other children are placed with child-minders, both registered and unregistered. Moss (in Ball, 1994) point out that there is considerable variety of provision according to the geographical area.

The vast majority of four year-olds now attend reception classes, often in unsuitable accommodation, with inadequate outdoor area and a teacher untrained for the age phase and no trained nursery nurse to work with staff (Blenkin, *et al*, 1996). This increasing trend has been condemned by many reports over the decade, a recent example is the report commissioned by the Royal Society of Arts (Ball, 1994).

Even at five years of age there is no uniformity of provision. There are separate infant schools, infant classes in primary schools, and infant classes in first schools. Secondly, it is important to bear in mind that, according to the *Special Educational Needs* (SEN) Code of Practice (1994) a considerable minority of children will at any one time have a special educational need and this means that the stereotype of the teacher being the only significant professional involved with the child is misleading. In other words, a considerable proportion of children will require a fairly wide range of multi-professional help which goes beyond the teacher, play leader, nursery nurse or even the health visitor and general practitioner (GP). Other professionals may include the social worker, educational psychologist, child psychiatrist, play therapist, speech therapist and so on. Very few professionals working directly with children are men.

The Code of Practice for Special Educational Needs (1994) encourages a policy of inclusivity. Of the two per cent or so of children expected to require a Statement of Special Educational Need, some will attend mainstream schools. Every school appoints a SENCO (Special Educational Needs Co-Ordinator) whose role is to bring together information, parents and professionals so that the child's needs are met, and to work with the staff to produce an individual education plan (IEP). Children at Stage 1 in the process will be registered as a cause for concern by staff, but by Stage 3 professionals outside the setting, such as the Educational Psychologist, become involved. A minority of children will reach Stage 5 when a statement of educational need will be drawn up.

Men care about young children as much as women, when encouraged

Jane

In the early stages of the child's life, the GP and health visitor are likely to be key professionals. Health visitors can act as catalysts for family development in co-ordination with other professionals.

> One year-old Jane's family disliked professional workers as they had had a number of unfortunate experiences over the years. The health visitor found it difficult to gain entrance to their flat and yet she and the GP were concerned about Jane's physical growth and weight. She was small for her age, and not eating well. She was too young to attend a playgroup, and there was no parent/toddler group within easy walking distance.
>
> Another of the health visitor's clients had been a nursery teacher until she gave up work to have her child, now a year old, and this mother ran a very small parent/toddler group which met three mornings a week. The health visitor put the two mothers in touch. Because the ex-nursery teacher was 'just another mother' with a one year-old, she was able to work well with the family. Jane and her mother joined the group of four mothers and four children.
>
> Relationships with the health visitor improved. She was seen as someone who could help, but not interfere. Visits to a specialist doctor were positive. The father attended the group when his shift work allowed. They all went to a swimming club together, and had joint outings and celebrated birthdays together, as well as undertaking joint jam-making and bread-making as part of the parent/toddler group activities. The health visitor was asked to provide information regularly.
>
> She organised visits from experts on preventive dentistry, family planning and nutrition, and gave information about different nursery provision in the area. At three years Jane attended a larger playgroup so that her mother could work in the mornings. At four years she attended the reception class of the local school. The health visitor put the playgroup leader in touch with the parent/toddler group leader when a problem arose over Jane's eating. This was quickly resolved.

In this example, the health visitor had co-ordinated and used the different local resources and called upon specialist medical advice in her attempt to help Jane's family. She was sufficiently skilled to use a volunteer worker's skills when her 'professionalism' was acting as a block in the early stages of her relationship with the family. She valued what other workers could offer at every stage.

In Jane's case, it was the statutory services which 'led', with the health visitor as the key worker, co-ordinating GP, volunteer worker, playgroup and teacher, as well as specialist medical help. In the following example, the health visitor again 'led'.

Petra

Petra was born blind. She lived in an area where there was no special education support. Her parents were helped initially by the GP and health visitor, who put her in touch with an educational home visitor from a voluntary agency for the blind (Royal National Institute for the Blind). This professional worker helped the family through the first five years of Petra's life, and co-ordinated resources and professional help to such an extent that Petra was able to attend the local primary school. Her role was also to offer emotional support to the family, and to act as a bridge between teachers in the school and the family when problems arose, which they did frequently.

There was a gap in statutory services for this family – no advice on how to stimulate and manage Petra in the first five years, and no school for visually impaired children at statutory school age. The LEA bought special school places from the neighbouring authority. The parents wanted Petra to attend school more locally and to have friends in the community if possible.

The educational home visitor marshalled resources for the family with specialist equipment and advice on working with Petra in the earliest years. She supported them in the educational decisions they made and bridged the gap between home and school She was a highly-trained paid worker, employed by a voluntary agency, who had more impact on this family's life in the first five years of Petra's life than any statutory worker because of her skill in co-ordinating the medical and educational resources available.

In the example of Jerome which follows, the specialist nursery teacher was the key worker.

Jerome

Three year-old Jerome's parents did not come to school. On his first day at school he was sent on the school bus alone under the care of the bus supervisor and driver. He was 'deaf', but his hearing aid was in his satchel. It would be easy for the teacher to draw the conclusion that here was an uncaring family, insensitive to their child's needs. The teacher in this special school used a home/school book with each family since children were spread over a large catchment area and brought to school by bus. She immediately, on that first day, sent a book home in Jerome's satchel, asking if she could introduce herself to the parents, and wondering if they might like to visit the school.

The next day, the book had not been written in. The teacher could not phone the family as there was no phone, so she phoned the GP. He was wary of divulging any information at all, but grudgingly gave the name of the health visitor for the family. Contact with the health visitor revealed that both parents worked, and were bewildered by their son Jerome, who had seemed to hear and had begun to talk at two years. He had recently been sent to Jamaica to stay with his grandmother for six months – and had stopped talking. On returning home he had been tested and found to have a hearing loss.

The health visitor agreed to find out if the family would like the teacher to visit. Two days later there was a note in the home book suggesting the teacher might like to call one day after school. The health visitor had found that the parents never looked in the satchel, so were unaware of the existence of the home book. The teacher set off on the school bus with Jerome on the suggested day and, at the set-down point, found herself to her surprise at Jerome's child-minder's flat. He was picked up from there at 5.30 p.m. (It was now 4.30 p.m.) The childminder was obviously embarrassed about this, and so the teacher said that she had some shopping to do and would go straight to Jerome's flat later, which she did. When she met the parents at 6.00 p.m., a situation potentially damaging to the parent/teacher partnership had arisen. The parents were clearly embarrassed. To them 'after school' meant after work. They had not wanted the teacher to know that Jerome went to a child-minder. They clearly thought that a teacher would disapprove of this.

If an atmosphere of trust and mutual respect was to develop, the teacher's training needed to be used. She had received considerable help in working with parents during her specialist training in working with hearing-impaired children. Over tea, she established an atmosphere whereby she made it clear that she was actively seeking the parents' views, and needed their help in order to do her job. The focus was on everyone working for Jerome. The parents admitted their anger that he had been sent to a special school and their perplexity that he had suddenly stopped talking. They talked about their dislike of the hearing aid which labelled him. They did not want to come to school: they thought they would be upset to see other deaf children.Education to them meant learning to read, beginning with the alphabet, and they supposed that as Jerome was deaf there was no sense in trying to teach him. They just wanted him to be as happy as possible considering his disability. During the visit the teacher listened rather than talked. She also conveyed her delight in teaching Jerome – she wanted them to see that she valued their child.

When parents ask, 'Has she been good?', they are perhaps really asking, 'Do you like my child?' Jerome was pleased to see his teacher, but she made sure that she emphasised how relaxed and purposeful he was at home, what appropriate toys for his age he had, how she worried because he was always so beautifully turned out and his clothes might get spoiled for school.

By the end of the visit, the parents knew that the teacher sympathised with their work pattern and understood the need for a child-minder, and that she obviously liked their son and was committed to working with him. They could trust her to be kind to him. She believed he was learning and she thought them caring parents who fed and clothed their child well and stimulated his development with toys. They invited her to visit again.

The partnership developed positively, through home visits. The teacher contacted the Ear, Nose and Throat specialist, who was very helpful in getting a different hearing aid with automatic volume control. Jerome began to wear it in school. Then the mother took a day off work to come to a coffee morning/talk that the teacher had asked the school's educational psychologist to give. She met other parents and enjoyed it, finding they had similar experiences and difficulties. At the next home visit, the teacher suggested to Jerome's mother that she might like to visit the classroom in action with one of the mothers she had particularly liked. In school the mother was struck by Jerome's speech when he was wearing his hearing aid. She watched the teacher working with the children, and took comfort that Jerome was showing off and in fact that her new friend's child was, too. All the adults laughed about it and the atmosphere was relaxed.

Gradually the home visits became more focussed on Jerome's learning, the curriculum, and care of the hearing aid. Ideas for follow-up activities at home were given. The parents told the teacher what they observed Jerome doing and the teacher shared what happened at school. The parents began to write in the home book. At six years Jerome was beginning to read, talk and lip-read well and was a more relaxed child. He transferred to a partial hearing unit and a year later was integrated successfully into his local primary school, where his parents were able to give him the necessary support.

They trusted his teachers, respecting their knowledge, felt able to ask for help and information, felt included in his education, knew they were important, and that the professionals regarded them as good, loving parents.

The key factors in this successful parent/teacher partnership were that the teacher built up the parents' self-confidence and extended what the parents thought education was about rather than displacing their view with something totally different. The teacher marshalled resources and information through a multi-professional approach, working with the health visitor, specialist doctor and educational psychologist. Not all professionals welcomed this contact (in this instance, the GP did not), but the teacher kept going until she found those who also valued a multi-professional approach. She put the parents in touch with other parents to form a self-help group, and used an away-from-school setting prior to encouraging the parents in school.

Where there is little or no contact between professional workers, parents can be left confused and let down.

Kaplan (1978; quoted in Honig, 1984, p.65) talks about the awakening of the unloved self in the parent in the case of a child with a disability. This may well also apply to the parents' relationship with a child at the toddler stage of temper tantrums. Parents need to feel supported, not undermined, by professionals.

John

Two year-old John's mother cared deeply about his healthy development. He attended a dentist as soon as his teeth came through. The dentist assured her that his thumb-sucking was not a problem. His mouth would need orthodontic treatment at nine or ten years anyway, and he was likely to grow out of it by five or six years. Mother relaxed.

When John started at a play group, staff discouraged him from sucking his thumb during storytime. Mother began to worry again when John reported this. She did not like to mention it to the supervisor, who obviously knew more than she did (in her view). At six years of age, John was still sucking his thumb. At eight, the dentist suggested a visit to the orthodontist in preparation for later treatment. She insisted that the thumb-sucking was no problem. The orthodontist greeted John with, 'And what do you do that you shouldn't do?', and was unpleasant to him about it, saying she would do nothing for him until he gave it up. John's mother ventured to say that she had thought treatment would not begin until ten and that John now only sucked his thumb on going to sleep, or if distressed. The orthodontist gave a smile, but no information.

At the next visit to the dentist, the mother reported this back. The dentist closed professional ranks with the orthodontist, and said, 'Well, he's nearly stopped now, hasn't he?' John's mother felt confused about the conflicting professional views displayed in educational and medical contexts. She worried that as a parent she had failed to do right by John, but felt frustrated and angry because she had tried her best.

Cathy

> Four year-old Cathy's family were visited by a number of professional workers. Her fourteen year-old uncle was under the supervision of a probation officer. The whole family was visited by a social worker and the health visitor called very regularly. The nursery teacher visited Cathy and her mother once each term as part of the school's home visiting policy.
>
> The teacher and probation officer arranged for fourteen year-old Paul to come into school and work with his niece, Cathy. This bought out skills he could not use elsewhere – gentleness, patience and so on. Officially, he was mending electrical equipment, which meant that he could hold his head high among his peers. The teacher, social worker and health visitor worked together on financial benefits, nutrition, and stimulating Cathy and her younger sister Sharon.
>
> Obviously areas of confidentiality had to be respected, but within that proper constraint the professional workers found that they could ask each other for co-operation and support because of the 'willingness of spirit' and basic trust which had developed between them.

The teacher–nursery nurse professional relationship

The foregoing examples emphasise the variety of professional partnerships which can be significant in the development of a young child. However, the most common partnership, especially within the school, is likely to be that of teacher and nursery nurse.

It is one of the most important professional partnerships that can exist. It is worth noting that nursery nurses also work in day nurseries, hospitals and other services dealing with health and social services. They are highly skilled in their knowledge of the whole of the first seven years of the child's life, and in their training pay more attention to the under threes and health and care aspects than does the teacher, as well as studying the child's educational development.

The training of the teacher emphasises education, albeit of the whole child (not just the child's thinking) and concentrates on the three to eight years period. When the partnership is strong, the roles of the nursery nurse and the teacher complement each other.

In this book examples of the work of nursery nurses are given which highlight this often powerful partnership. There are times when the teacher leads, and times when the nursery nurse leads. That is the essence of a partnership. One of the difficulties of multi-professional work is that it is often unclear who the acknowledged 'leader' is at a particular time. Some professionals take on the role of leader all the time as if it is their right. GPs and educational psychologists are often accused of this by teachers, health visitors and social workers. Nursery nurses often accuse teachers of this same attitude.

The way each profession sees itself is linked with its status, which is linked with how it is regarded by the society in which it functions. A sense of being superior (or subservient) makes a bad starting point for multi-professional work. Both attitudes lose sight of the real work, which is to promote the development of the child in context. If one member of a partnership dominates, it will not be much of a partnership.

Whalley (1994,1997) stresses the need for different early childhood workers to be clear about their roles, what is expected of them, what their contributions should be. Because the early childhood educator and the nursery nurse literally work in the same room, this becomes particularly important.

A new teacher came to work in a nursery school. The nursery nurse knew all the families, the school routines and how the team operated in the school. She helped the new teacher by reminding her about storytimes, that each child must be welcomed by the teacher each morning, that reminders of medical examinations must go out. She took responsibility for new children and took the teacher on a home visit so as to introduce her to a family where the mother had just returned home with the new-born baby and so had not yet met the new teacher in school. She made sure that children with allergies had the right food, and that a child with eczema did not play with soap at the water tray, while the teacher got to know the class. She also organised the main activities until the new teacher was able to share and contribute more fully.

In this school the teachers and nursery nurses would meet at the end of the day to check that they had tidied up properly and together jot down observations they had made of children on cards they kept for that purpose. They would plan for the next day, each saying what she wanted to do and why. They would help each other with practical suggestions, especially in relation to their long-term plans.

The teachers tended to lead in drawing up these plans formally after they had been discussed and agreed. The teachers kept official records and co-ordinated the curriculum. The nursery nurses made observations both broad and deep through their knowledge of the different facets of child development, which enhanced the teachers' view of each child and family and helped them both to plan activities relating to the different curriculum areas of knowledge.

In a partnership it should not be possible to say who is the stronger. Both partners need each other – and both are useful for different purposes. If the teacher simply absorbs the nursery nurse's contribution into her own, the situation is too much dominated by the teacher. If the nursery nurse absorbs the teacher's views into her own, the situation is too much dominated by the nursery nurse.

Both approaches to the child are valid and of use in different ways. They are separate, but overlap. They need to be integrated so that each participant is aware of and proud of their distinct contribution to the development of the child. In this school the partnership between nursery nurses and teachers had developed into one of mutual respect, resulting in a strong team.

So far in this chapter, significant others in the child's life have been the immediate family and friends, and the professional workers in statutory and voluntary agencies with whom the family has contact. In the next section, relationships with peers are explored. Children relating to other children is a theme which pervades this book, and many examples relevant to the section which follows can also be found in Chapters 6 and 8, under the titles 'Representation' and 'The ability to decentre'.

Early childhood friendships can last for life

OTHER CHILDREN

Adults are not the only significant others for children. Children are also of great importance, both younger and older, both within and beyond the family setting.

Siblings

Judy Dunn (1984) writes about the chemistry of relationships in different families between brothers and sisters.

> Five year-old Ella and seven year-old Tom were spending a day with friends. They were introduced to a visitor to the house. 'This is Tom, and this is Ella.' Tom quickly said 'She's my sister.' He was protecting his sister from being made to speak to someone she did not know. He knew the things that tended to worry him, and applied them to his sister.

This brother and sister were very close. Being close does not mean no quarrels. In fact, quarrelling is an important part of developing relationships with other children. In the early stages children tend to hit each other. This is typical of two year-olds.

> Two year-old Hilary wanted a toy car from her three year-old brother Joseph. She snatched it, and hit him with the car when he tried to grab it back. The situation was not left here. The father took the car back and gave it to Joseph explaining that she must not grab and hit. Hilary had a temper tantrum. Joseph felt sorry for her – he gave her the car. Father praised Joseph's kindness, and reasserted that Hilary must not hit and grab, but 'ask nicely' for the car next time and that she was very lucky to have such a kind brother. Next time, Hilary again grabbed what she wanted from Joseph. Immediately Joseph shouted, 'No, ask nicely'. She shouted, 'Please'. He said pleadingly, 'That's not nicely', holding the car high up. She said, without shouting this time, 'Please can I have it?' 'Yes.' Hilary was learning from her brother the social rituals involved in negotiating what she wanted. Joseph was actively helping this process, but also learning to protect himself.

He had also learned to use the adult intervention from the time before. Adults are important in helping children to learn to resolve conflicts. Children use adult strategies in developing their own. Here, Joseph used his father's mode of intervention in a similar situation. If the situation had again broken down, he might well have called for adult help. This is more advanced than 'hitting', but is often seen as 'telling tales'. Initially, adults can help children by demonstrating conflict-removing strategies. The next stage is to act as chairperson while the children argue things out.

Some brothers and sisters seem to relate to one another as 'friends' most of the time. They actively seek each other's company and negotiate well most of the time, protect each other and extend each other.

> Three year-old William was afraid of the dark. Each evening his mother would tell him a story, tuck him in and leave him with books to look at. Before he settled he wanted to go to the lavatory. He was afraid to go on his own at that time of night. Five and a half year-old Hannah would wait for him to call, take him and tuck him back in. They enjoyed this nightly ritual which began when she moved to her own separate bedroom. It was during this period that the children began to play with each other when they woke (early) in the mornings, rather than waking their parents.

Brothers and sisters are usually together more than friends outside the family. Even so, some relate to each other more easily than others, and parents use different strategies in different families, often based on their own relationships with their brothers and sisters.

Groups

The ability to get on with people is one important part of mixing with other children. This means being able to hold on to your own ideas, to negotiate them, modify them when appropriate and share them. This requires skill! Zick Rubin (1983) suggests that there are four ways in which children need to develop skills in getting on with other children. These are:

1 To be able to gain entry into a group.
2 To be approving and supportive of one's peers.
3 To manage conflicts appropriately.
4 To exercise sensitivity and tact.

In the examples, so far, Tom was supportive to Ella, Hannah was supportive to William, and Joseph was supportive to Hilary. Joseph managed and resolved a conflict situation appropriately. Hilary responded sensitively and tactfully to her brother's efforts. Tom, Hannah and Joseph were all sensitive to a younger sibling's needs.

The examples which follow show Rubin's (1983) four strategies in action.

In a nursery school, a group of children were playing pirates. The pirate ship was a scrambling net on a prism-shaped climbing frame. The game involved climbing the 'rigging' and, when another ship was spotted from afar, rushing out and capturing treasure from it, and returning with the booty. The enemy ship would be an agreed place where there was a pile of leaves. The leaves were then brought back as booty.

> The children were predominately four years of age. Four year-old James was the pirate leader. Three year-old Alice wanted to join in. She watched from a distance, walking round the edge of the playground.
>
> She approached and stood hopefully at the foot of the climbing frame/pirate ship. She was ignored. She began to climb the net with the others, smiling at her success. As James shouted, 'Ahoy there – a ship. Let's go!' and scrambled down, hotly pursued by the others shouting 'Let's go!', she imitated them. She had been watching for long enough to know that she needed to pick up leaves from the pile. She had successfully joined the game.

William Corsaro's work (1979) suggests that Alice's tactics were typical of successful 'access strategies' for entering into the game. She encircled the game, made careful 'verbal overtures', joining in with the other children's 'Let's go!', did similar things to them, and so was not rejected.

> Four year-old Mathilde wanted to join a group of children in the home corner. She tried to walk in through the door, saying, 'Can I play?' 'No,' shouted the other children in chorus, and shut the door on her. She had not had the opportunity to encircle, and her opening conversation invited rejection.

Corsaro's (1979) work suggests that children need to use 'similar behaviour' in order to be accepted. Mathilde could not see what was behind the door, so she was not in a position to engage in similar behaviour in her actions, or to back this up with remarks like, 'We're moving the furniture, aren't we?' William Corsaro calls this kind of remark 'reference to affiliation'.

The way that the classroom is set out has implications for the way that children are able to relate to other children. The home corner, as Sara Smilansky's work (1968) suggested, is an area where quarrels develop, and where children are often rejected from games. It may be that the influence of the nativist model, and the psychodynamic framework with its emphasis on children developing freely in an imaginative world of their own, could in fact be holding back the development of group play in the home corner. High walls may cut children off from imaginative games, and impede the access strategies they need to develop. A feeling of being behind walls can be created where the walls are low enough for the children outside the game to watch it from a distance before joining in.

In Chapter 8 on the ability to decentre, there are many examples which are relevant to the significant other children in any child's life. Group play offers children the opportunity to see things from other people's points of view. It also offers the child possibilities to experiment with the manipulation of others.

Catherine Garvey (1977) points out that the 'feature of control' is an important one in the formation of children's peer relationships.

Three year-old Lindsey wants her three year-old friend Barbara to be a horse. She controls Barbara. Four year-old Terry wants four year-old Alex to be a dog. He controls Alex. Six year-old Hannah wants to play 'Being rich in the old-fashioned days'. She is the Nanny and controls five year-old Anna. Six year-old Dominic leads his gang. He captures six year-old Michael, makes him a prisoner and holds him at gun-point. He controls Michael. Controlling and being controlled, leading and being led, finding out what is acceptable (and negotiating what is), are important aspects of group play.

In Chapter 6 on representation, further examples of group play have been given. Adults often find large groups difficult to justify as educationally worthwhile. Some children tend to be involved in this sort of activity almost to the exclusion of any other if given the choice. In the examples in this chapter, and in the chapters on representation and decentration, it emerges that group play is an important but undervalued aspect of what early childhood education can offer. Adults need to develop skills in encouraging and promoting this.

> At a workshop in a college of education, teachers involved in an in-service course worked with children aged three to five years old from a local nursery school. Four year-old Gavin started to put large wooden bricks round the edge of the room. Other children copied. Adults intervened when quarrels broke out, or if other equipment which children were using needed to be moved. Soon there was an enclosure of bricks round the whole room. Children began to move around them as if they were stepping stones. About fifteen children had become involved in this joint activity. Adults had taken a supportive role, letting children watch until they were 'ready' to join in, altering the physical environment in discussion with the children.

These examples refer to the least adult-dominated aspects of group work with significant other children. Group times, when children come together for stories, music, singing, dancing, or physical education, are more adult-led.

These can be difficult times for a considerable proportion of children, particularly in the earliest years. So far as this chapter is concerned, it is sufficient to say that sitting with a friend often helps children to settle into a group time most easily. The comfort of sitting with a friend is a powerful support.

Partnerships

> Lindsey and Barbara, two three year-olds are playing horses together. Lindsey puts a long belt around Barbara's waist and 'leads' her. She rehearses what she is going to say so that Barbara is in on the script.
>
> 'I say, "Whoa there!" don't I, and you go, "Neigh", don't you, and then I pat you and I give you some hay, don't I, and you bend down like this, and you eat it, don't you?' Then they act out the scene. This helps the children to plan their story in advance, to be clear about the theme and their roles in it.

It is interesting to note that at this time, both Lindsey and Barbara showed interest in things that could be made to encircle. The belt surrounds Barbara's waist. Early friendships are said to be fleeting; one possibility is that they may be based on shared interests and that when these change, the friendship loses its base. After all, the basis of any friendship lies in having shared interests.

It is also interesting that this game was based on a shared experience. The class had been taken to see the police stables, and had been shown the harnesses. The game centred primarily around harnessing and unharnessing a horse. Shared interests and experiences are fundamental aspects of early partnerships.

> Six year-old Dominic and Michael had both seen a fight on the television. They were acting out a shared secondary experience with a lot of 'stop-go' in this game: careful play punching, holding at gun-point, kicking to the ground. No one gets hurt. This is the sort of game which adults find difficult to allow. There is a tendency to think such play is boyish.

This kind of play, when indulged in by girls, tends to be firmly squashed. In fact, the skill which lies in not hurting each other, the refinement and variety of movement, the planning together, rehearsing and carrying out of the plan, is not unlike the processes of draft, revise, redraft, refine which are involved in story-writing. It is important to recognise the sophistication which may have developed. The kind of play that Michael and Dominic were involved in was not simply rumbustious. It was helping the children to develop on a variety of levels.

CONCLUSION

This chapter has explored significant people in a child's life – some in the family, some outside it, some chosen by the child, some not. Both adults and children are important, and both family and those in contact with the family are critical in the child's development. The more professional workers in statutory and voluntary agencies concerned with the child's family work together, the better for the child. Meeting a variety of other children is also important, so that the child develops the ability to form relationships, which may be deep, or of the kind which are necessary simply to cope with everyday living together.

10

THE COMMONALITIES AND
DIFFERENCES BETWEEN PEOPLE

This chapter is about the empowerment of individuals and groups, so that whether or not children and adults are in a minority situation, they have access to full lives. For early childhood educators and carers, this means helping children have fulfilling lives as they are cared for and educated, both in home life and beyond. This means confronting discrimination and oppression of all kinds.

One of the problems educators have always encountered is how to work with individual children within a whole group. Even within the family, this can be difficult. Certainly, only children tend statistically to 'get on' academically, and to be successful in careers later on. They are given very individual help by their families. It is difficult to achieve such a highly individual approach within a group setting. What is clear is that treating all children in the same way is disastrous for many, and not even ideal for children from the dominant class or ethos, or who are of high ability.

Policy-makers and educational theorists have, over the years, identified particular groups of children whose needs have been significantly ignored. As long ago as the 1960s, studies such as Douglas's (1964) alerted educators to the fact that working-class children were not being successful in the education system. This led to attempts to remedy the situation through compensatory education focusing on cognition.

Three useful features emerged from the compensatory movement. Programmes with lasting impact were found to

- work in partnership with the family and parents;
- to be geared to individuals within the group;
- to be structured in a planned, well thought-through and consistent way.

Because the whole family was involved, account was taken of what the child came to school able to do. The child's background and home experiences were valued. Observing the child and using what the child was naturally doing was also valued. Examples of this approach can be seen in Constance Kamii's work in the Ypsilanti Early Education Programme in the USA (Kamii and Devries, 1977), and Lin Poulton, George and Teresa Smith's work in the Red House Project in West Yorkshire (part of the Halsey 1972 Studies on Educational Priority) and subsequent work in Hampshire (Poulton, 1979), together with the Leverhulme/Gulbenkian Research Project directed by Chris Athey at the Froebel Institute, London, 1972–7, in Britain. More recently work at Pen Green (recognised as a Centre of Excellence) funded by the Teacher Training Agency (TTA) has focused on the importance of close partnership between families and early childhood workers (Whalley and Arnold, 1997).

The most salient conclusion from all this work has been that it is not so much that working-class children need an entirely different education, it is rather that they need more individual and sensitive treatment within the mainstream of education, and a more appropriate valuation of the contributions made by their families in their education.

In the late 1970s, a different 'disadvantaged' group was identified. The Warnock Report (DES, 1978) served as a catalyst for thinking about children's special educational needs, and how best to promote their development. The 1981 Education Act, which arose out of this report, said:

> *A child has a special need if he/she has a learning difficulty significantly greater than the majority of children of the age, or a disability which prevents the use of educational facilities of a kind generally provided in schools for children of that age.*

This broad definition covered one in six children at any one time and attempted to avoid labelling children in medical terms, or grouping them on the basis of educational need. Warnock proposed a continuum model of identifying needs rather than gross categorisation (for example, not either 'hearing', 'partially-hearing', or 'deaf', but regarding all as 'hearing-impaired' with varying needs and degrees of handicap along a continuum). This gives more flexibility. As with the more successful approaches to combatting class bias, the emphasis was, and is, on integrating children with special needs into mainstream education rather than segregating them and providing special education. However, for some children special schools will be the most appropriate form of education.

The SEN Code of Practice (Special Educational Needs) introduced in 1994 encourages a policy of inclusivity of children with special educational needs within the mainstream, but sets out a five stage process which aims to secure appropriate support for a child. Funding is a serious issue in this scheme, resulting in an increase in Tribunals whereby parents can appeal when the child's needs are not met according to the Code.

The Warnock Report (1978) also gave major emphasis to the early years, recommending quality nursery education for all three and four year-olds. The Code of Practice (1994) emphasises the importance of partnership with parents, and promotes inclusivity of children wherever possible in mainstream settings. The Code of Practice emphasises individuality by a more sensitive and appropriate treatment of children.

Guiding principles in the education of individuals, minority or neglected groups

It is understandable that some of those involved in early childhood education and care at worst regard the increased emphasis on different groups as a new 'fad', and at best find it difficult and confusing to put each new focus of social policy into practice. Some principles of approach are needed, and what follows is a first attempt to define such principles by way of an expansion of guidelines already in existence for one of these special groups, namely minority ethnic groups.

At an Organisation Mondiale pour l'Education Prescolaire (OMEP) conference in London in 1983, Yvonne Conolly spoke on the subject of the multi-cultural classroom in the early years of education. She set out important guiding principles which are adapted in this chapter, in the exploration of issues surrounding the needs of any child who is not straightforwardly part of the majority group in the education system.

EARLY CHILDHOOD SETTINGS AND THE INDIVIDUAL NEEDS OF CHILDREN AND THEIR FAMILIES

- Children need a sense of belonging and inclusion.
- Promoting a child's sense of well being and self worth is essential.
- There is a need to avoid stereotyping.
- Everyone needs to inspect their own values, assumptions and actions in the way they respect other people.
- There is a need to overcome the natural stranger fear of people through positive strategies.

One of the difficulties facing the early childhood educator is the increasing number of groups identified as particularly needing individual help. It is helpful to the early childhood educator to have guiding principles which can be applied to any child in a minority group or indeed to any child.

Inclusion does not leave people out, inclusion stresses a sense of belonging

There is an enormous difference between the assimilation, integration or inclusion of children with special needs into the mainstream of education and care. The problem of assimilation is that it demands of the person the rejection of his or her present self in order to become a part of the majority – 'like everyone else'. For example, in the UK in the

1950s and 1960s, the desire of educators was to teach deaf children (as they were then called) to talk through the pure oral method. Hearing aids, lip-reading, use of residual hearing were emphasised. Deaf children, it was agreed, should not be deprived of the right to oral language. They should be helped to be as much like the mainstream majority as possible.

Michael was an adult brought up in this way. He was a good lip-reader and his speech was clear. He attended a summer theatre school for the deaf. He related best to the hearing people on the course, but found it difficult to follow their conversations except on an individual basis. He was ill at ease with most of the deaf-course members, unless they used oral language. He could not use British Sign Language. From an early age Michael's education had asked him to deny his hearing impairment, and to overcome it so that he could live a 'normal' life. In fact, because he was profoundly deaf, he was not quite part of the hearing world, but he had rejected the 'deaf' world. He was between the two, and this contributed to his deep loneliness with few close friends.

Jim, on the other hand, was able to use British Sign Language and oral language. He, like Michael, was profoundly deaf. He had attended mainstream schools and was at university – but he had always belonged to groups of deaf people at which he had learned to sign. He had friends who were deaf and friends who were not. His bilingualism helped to develop close friendships with both groups. He said that with hearing people he often became very tired with the concentration and effort required to listen hard and to lip-read, especially in group conversations. He relaxed with deaf friends where he could sign. Interestingly, Jim's first remark when he met anyone at the summer school was, 'Are you deaf or hearing?' He was at ease with his deafness. He did not try to deny it. He did not want to. His only bitterness was that hearing people were so insensitive to the needs of the minority group to which he belonged. He felt a privileged member of his group, as he was bilingual. His parents had fought hard to help him succeed in spite of all the obstacles posed by insensitive and inflexible systems.

Michael had been assimilated into the mainstream; Jim had been integrated. Fitting in with the mainstream was Michael's only option. It meant rejecting what makes him different from most people. It meant denying his 'specialness', his uniqueness. A system which is truly inclusive goes beyond integration so that each individual is seen as a person with rights and needs.

Inclusion: a sense of well-being and belonging

Everyone needs roots and to feel that they belong to a group. Fostering a sense of belonging in an individual or minority also helps the majority by encouraging the ability to decentre – something which is very important for young children.

> Six year-old Ufoma had never been to Nigeria, but with the other children she had learnt about Nigerian housing, climate and crops. On ceremonial days her family always wore traditional costumes and she brought these to school. Her mother cooked some traditional food and sent it to school. The teacher showed the children the ingredients and cooked the food in school with them. She invited an African drummer to visit and everyone danced. Ufoma's roots were being publicly valued. She only partly knew them. The other children began to understand why Ufoma liked hot, spicy food and wore the clothes she sometimes wore, and they respected the way she could dance. She was more popular than before because the children could put her more in context. She was no longer just 'different'. She was special and unique – and yet like them in important ways. Ufoma herself had more sense of the roots to which she belonged. However, the black child has no choice about belonging to a 'black group'.

It is important that any child feels pride in the group to which he/she belongs. This applies equally to Jim, Michael and Ufoma. Children need to be able to put themselves in meaningful contexts, where everything links. A focus on the commonality between people, which in turn highlights positive variations and diversity, is helpful.

The inclusive approach can be seen in the need to value and encourage the child's home language where a different language is used in the home from that used in the school. It is also present in the need to value dialects and accents which relate to class and regional differences. It is present in the need for children of minority ethnic groups to know about their own language, cultural roots and religious ideas and for the educator to value these.

> Three year-old Pratima came to school with her grandmother, who spoke Punjabi. The teacher managed to greet her in Punjabi. Shortly after, Pratima became distressed and fearful. It was clearly something to do with her shoes and shoe-bag. Grandmother could speak not speak English to explain to the teacher, and the teacher's grasp of Punjabi was too limited. Fortunately, the school was following an inclusive rather than assimilation approach, and Punjabi was sufficiently valued in the school for there to be a Punjabi-speaking member of staff. She was asked to help and the situation was instantly resolved. Pratima's tears vanished. The wrong shoe-bag was on her peg; hers was found. Pratima's English was developing very well, but in a stress situation she could not use it and it would be inappropriate to expect her to do so. No one uses their latest piece of learning when under stress.

James (two years old) was profoundly deaf; so were his parents. The family used British Sign Language at home and in their friendship circle. At the special school he began to attend for children with hearing impairments, he was also encouraged to sign. The staff also used oral language and encouraged the use of a hearing aid. His home language was encouraged in school, but he is also learning about oral language so that he can become bilingual.

Like Pratima his home language was valued and encouraged whilst he was also introduced to English as a second language. It is important that the child's family feels included and belongs.

For the individuals to be included in the whole, societies must know about and understand individual and minority group needs.

Six year-old Nahugo's mother takes her to school each day. She walks straight past the other mothers. This upsets William's mother, who feels her smile of greeting is rejected. A friend has recently returned from Japan and explains that in Japan people do not greet each other with a smile in the street. They ignore each other unless there is a verbal greeting. Next day, William's mother verbally greets Nahugo's mother. She looks a little taken back, but immediately smiles and responds. Thereafter, the two mothers greet each other each day.

Families need to feel that they can trust those in whose charge they leave their children.

Five year-old Judith was collecting her school lunch. It was pork. She returned to her place at the table with her meal. The teacher intercepted, asked the dinner helper for an alternative meal without pork and quietly gave it to Judith. 'No one would have known', was the dinner lady's response. She did not worry that Judith's family practiced Reformed Judaism, and that they trusted the school to apply the dietary stipulations of the religion. She did not understand the importance of these, and no one had yet made her begin to think that this point needed any attention. She expected Judith to be assimilated into the majority's eating habits rather than to take it on herself to contribute to her inclusion into school mealtimes.

Five year-old Anthea attended a Church of England primary school. During assembly the head told the children about Doubting Thomas, who had the opportunity to believe in Jesus, but did not take it. This placed Anthea in a dilemma. Her mother was agnostic, her father was an atheist. Both had had the opportunity to believe and had rejected it. What did this make her parents in the eyes of the school and church? Anthea dealt with the situation by keeping secret throughout her education the fact of her parents' rejection of Christianity as a means of retaining her self-worth at school. In fact, in many respects she received a sounder spiritual and moral education from her parents than other children in the school. She experienced with her family a sense of awe and wonder about the universe (her father was a scientist). She learned about celebration at family gatherings when African music was played and danced to. She learned about 'worthship' in family gatherings which involved discussion of matters of worth – starvation, poverty, peace, human rights and oppression.

This example demonstrates that organised religion, or belief in revelationary religions, is not the only means by which children are given a sound religious experience (Desirable Learning Outcomes, Personal and Social Development, p.2, DFEE, 1996).

Six year-old Ovo's family were pantheists, believing in spirits in the trees and plants. He, of all the children in his class, was best able to understand the North American Indian tribes' relationship with their natural surroundings during the class project on this.

Five year-old Margaret was brought up as a Roman Catholic. She could understand that five year-old Diana wore a Star of David just as she wore a crucifix.

Four year-old Sadiq was taken to Westminster Abbey on a school outing. He thought the statues had no clothes on as they were carved in stone, and saw them as rude. His mother was fascinated by the outing and explained to the teacher who was a Methodist, that in the Muslim mosque there are no statues.

These examples demonstrate the examples of assuming majority views. All these children bring different religious experiences, although it is to be hoped that each will sense awe and wonder, will celebrate and experience spirituality in some form.

Studying different cultures may initially look hopelessly complicated, especially for children in the first seven years, until it is remembered that everyone eats, everyone likes to present food attractively, using crockery, or equivalent tools to eat with, sitting in a variety of ways. Everyone sleeps, on beds, in hammocks, bunks and so on. Everyone needs protection from heat or cold resulting in a need for clothing, and everyone needs shelter.

The different ways that people tackle these aspects of life then become fascinating and important. They lead to respect for differences through geographical or regional variations, or for historic reasons, which help understanding of cherished traditions and rituals. They help children to see that diversity is rich, and value the things that human beings have in common with each other.

Adults play a crucial role in a child's learning

Encouraging a sense of worth

Self-worth, self-esteem and self-confidence are probably the most important aspects of human development. The way that people feel about themselves, their well-being, affects the way that they seem to others.

Three year-old Nasreen was from a Muslim family, but her father was an alcoholic and so her family was particularly disapproved of by the Muslim community. She had been brought to school as usual by her older sister. As the teacher greeted her on arrival, a neighbour brought his child in.

He said something in Punjabi to Nasreen and mimed a drinking movement. As he turned to go she stuck out her tongue at his back and went to the teacher and put her hand in hers. She knew the teacher valued her, and would not be disapproving towards her family. In this case, the school was supporting her sense of self-worth.

Four year-old Kuang's and six year-old Ming's mother was British, their father was Chinese. Their parents helped them to understand Chinese culture through the furniture and decor in the home, the food they sometimes ate, the emphasis on stories and Chinese ideas about health, acupuncture, Tai Chi and herbal medicines. They also knew about the British cultural setting from their mother and from school. Kuang took pride in showing his friends how to write 'mountain' in Chinese. His parents helped him be proud of what he was, half Chinese and half British.

Some children have to ask themselves who they are more than others and this can put them in a dilemma about their own sense of worth. Anthea could hide the minority stance her parents took. Ufoma could not. A positive sense of self-worth is the right of any child and it is the responsibility of the early childhood educator to encourage this, and to confront discrimination of any kind, especially among those children whose sense of worth might be challenged by the majority.

Avoiding stereotypes

Knowing who you are, and being at ease with yourself, is closely linked with self-worth. Part of being able to do this lies in the way children can put themselves into context. 'Who am I?' is an important question, which all people ask of themselves at some point in their life.

Children from minority groups are at a disadvantage in this respect – be it a minority ethnic group, a disability group, a social class group or a gender group – because others tend to label and stereotype them. It is easier for some children to choose their identity than for others.

There was no question for Ufoma but that she was one black child in a class of twenty children of West European background. There is often a tendency for the majority to label those from minority groups in a gross way. Peter 'the blind boy', rather than someone who has as many qualities as any sighted child. Ufoma is black or African, rather than a child who loves maths and hates gymnastics.

Helping children to identify themselves is probably one of the hardest tasks facing a teacher, and probably the most constructive thing he/she can do is to keep the choices open. Education, to a large extent, is about the choice people have. Michael did not have the choice that Jim had.

Paul Griffin (1986) gives an interesting account of a mother-in-law's priorities for a girl's education in 1925 and her attempts to provide girls with choices. Girls in her curriculum model were to be competent house-keepers, trained for motherhood, and well-read. In this model they had the choice, he argues, of being good at serving their families, their employers, or their country. Girls trained only for careers are reduced in that choice. Serving the family is out of fashion. It is seen as exploitation, or under-achievement by women. If Griffin's argument is taken seriously, in the modern context both boys and girls should be educated to have the choice of working in the family or having an outside career. Currently, as a study by the European Network suggests, (Ghedini, 1996) men rarely have the choice of working in the family, and women are in a dilemma about their self-worth if they are in a position to opt for it.

Education needs to be broad with a wide curriculum. It also needs to avoid stereotyping people into an identity.

> A teacher on an in-service course in London came from Yorkshire. She came on a term's secondment. She thought of herself as British, but suddenly everyone began to ask her about Yorkshire. 'Oh! You're from Yorkshire.' She began to feel that she was a foreigner. She felt her Yorkshire accent becoming stronger. She found herself wanting to read about the Industrial Revolution and the wool trade. She needed to assert her identity, but it was being chosen for her by others. She was swept along by the way that other people insisted on regarding her. She was being stereotyped.

The need for individuals to assert their own identity is stressed. The need for individuals to assert their own identity *needs* to be stressed so that stereotyping is avoided.

The gender of the majority of teachers in primary education has sex-stereotyping implications, not only for the children they teach but for the whole image of the early childhood educator. In the primary school most teachers are women and Carolyn Steedman asserts (1986, p.161) that we need to discover 'how, and in what manner, we've been made to fit there'. She argues that the middle-class woman is in evidence there as the 'Mother-made-conscious', who does not have to be very intelligent, but in whom 'feeling, intuition, sympathy and empathy is all'. No doubt most readers of her article would challenge this stereotype! But the article does put the case for the 'Parent-made-conscious' rather than only the mother in primary schools. It highlights the need for more balanced staffing, with both men and women (Whalley, 1994).

> In a nursery school in Southall a teacher took positive steps to try to overcome the stereotype that boys are better at science. She wanted to do some work on electricity with a group of three and four year-olds. She took in some battery-powered electric circuits, and was interested to find that only boys sat down to work with them. Two girls came, but there were no seats for them so they went away. Four year-old Reena came back later. The boys were monopolising the activity.
>
> When Reena came back, four year-old Nisham spread his elbows across the circuits. He was not going to let her in. When he was ready to leave, he called his friend, so

that he could take his place. The teacher insisted that Reena must have the place since she has been waiting longest. Other girls began to hover on the outskirts of the activity. The teacher worked consciously to include them, but the girls were having more difficulty. They were pushed away by the boys if they tried to sit down. The teacher introduced a waiting list, which children could sign if they wanted a turn.

A week later the teacher repeated the activity. This time, there was a balance of boys and girls. It was as if the teacher's insistence that the eligibility for doing the activity should be by turn-taking rather than whose friend you are, had had an influence. In the third week, the Christmas tree was decorated – the children put electric fairy lights on it and made up the circuit themselves. This time the girls came first to the activity. On this occasion the teacher worked hard to encourage the few 'hovering' boys to join in.

In a music corner, Betty (four years) pretended to be the teacher. She held up a book to show the imaginary children in her class. Her friend, Joanna, came and sat as a pupil on the floor in front of her. John came and tried to join in, but Betty chased him away, refusing him admittance to the play. She only seemed to allow girls to join this play scenario. However, John returned, but sat at the edge by the entrance to the music corner. He stayed there and gradually moved forward bit by bit until finally he joined the play and was accepted into it by Betty. She had viewed his creeping towards the front with suspicion, but its slowness seemed to help her tolerate his gaining entry to the play.

Already, these young children had picked up their sex roles, and were stereotyping themselves and each other. Pretty lights meant a girl's activity, houses and kitchens or teachers (of whom a vast majority in nursery infant settings are women) means girls. The situation required positive strategies by the teacher to neutralise the sex roles and combat the stereotypes. The teacher needed to inspect her own thinking and assumptions, but more than that she needed to take action in relation to it. Being aware of discriminatory behaviour is not enough. It requires action.

Three year-old Sadiq wanted to go in the home corner. The other children refused him entry. Three year-old Mary said, 'we don't want Pakis'. The teacher heard, and confronted the situation directly. She told Mary that she thought her remark unkind, and that she did not want anyone in the class to be unkind. She asked Mary what a Paki was. Mary said, 'Black'. The teacher asked her if Sadiq was in fact black. She asked Mary what she was. Mary said, 'White'. She asked her if in fact she was white. She then told Sadiq to join the children in the house. They accepted him, and the teacher stayed and facilitated the play.

Later, at group time, she asked the children to look at the person next to them to see what colour his or her skin was. The children found a wide range. Then they sang 'Under One Sun' and 'Ten Little Toes'. She stressed the commonalities and differences between them – all human, all with toes and skin, but with variations in the shapes of toes and colour of skin. She made it clear that she valued each child, and respected them all. She also made it clear that it was unacceptable that any member of the school community should not value or respect any other.

Mary's and Sadiq's mothers were both present at the song time. Both knew the teacher valued and respected their child, and themselves, and expected the same of them in school. Sadiq's mother had given him the language of prejudice in describing the Caucasian children as 'Pinkies' in Urdu. Mary's mother had taught the language of prejudice by using 'Pakis' in a derogatory tone. Prejudice existed on both sides. However, racism existed on Mary's side only, because she belonged to the majority group who held power.

Stereotypes and discriminatory behaviour put children's thinking and that of adults into narrow grooves which cut across the educational principles explored in this book. It is important that early childhood educators challenge discriminatory behaviours of all kinds.

Overcoming stranger fear with positive strategies

People like to be comfortable. Thinking new thoughts, meeting new ideas, changing your ways are all inevitably uncomfortable. They involve moving out of a rut, modifying attitudes and acting differently from before. Piaget's theory of self-regulation (his equilibratory process) has two aspects. The first involves being in situations, events, experiences, which fit with what is already known, which do not require the person to modify the structures within them (**assimilation**).

The second involves meeting a situation, experience, event which does not fit with what is already known, and which requires a change in the structures within the person, and modification in his/her behaviour (**accommodation**).

When ET met the little boy in the film of that name, he was terrified; so was the little boy. They both initially experienced stranger fear on a vast scale.

Seven year–old Elisabeth had grown up in Dorset. She had never met an African person. Her parents invited an African student to earn some holiday money by digging their garden for them. He agreed and began work. Elisabeth kept going into the garden, peeping at him and, when her friend arrived, giggling and looking at

> him from a distance as if he were someone from outer space. Her parents, unaware of this reaction, did not introduce her to him, which would have helped her to see him as a person. Her stranger fear persisted.

Mixing with a wide variety of people helps to break down stranger fear, provided that positive strategies are developed which support the situation. Where children do not meet in a positive atmosphere, prejudice based on ignorance and stranger fear persists and can even be exacerbated. Attitudes to disability are more likely to change if disabled people are part of the whole, rather than in institutions away from the community.

> At a market in Halifax, a family (two parents and two children aged five and eight) went to buy some lino. They were talking in a relaxed manner with the man selling it. The father noticed a slit in a part being measured, and pointed it out. 'Don't worry, I'll sell that to a Paki' said the salesman. The father and mother exchanged looks and the father said, 'We don't like that sort of talk. We hope you wouldn't sell that to anyone.' The seller replied that the father didn't know these people and that they'd trick you if they could. The father suggested that the seller was about to trick him if he hadn't pointed out the slit, and the mother told the salesman that she worked with people of Pakistani origin who were her friends and that she had never been tricked. The family did not buy the lino.

The children in that family were being given a powerful role model by their parents. Discriminatory behaviour based on ignorance and stranger fear was not to be tolerated, even if it meant unpleasantness in public (Siraj-Blatchford, 1994, p.69).

Looking at our basic assumptions, attitudes, values and actions

Chris Athey (1990) sees the role of the early childhood educator and carer as someone who was there to help each child learn, not someone to sit in judgement over children and their families about how well they progress. At Pen Green Research and Development Base (1996) parents and early childhood workers have been engaged in a research project making a CD-Rom about their findings.

Family workers have needed to examine some of their basic assumptions about the way they introduce children to activities and tune in more sensitively to family styles of learning in order to help individual children in their learning. It seems that when early childhood workers manage to do this, their own relationship with the child leaps forward in quality, and because the child becomes more relaxed and can find more familiar features in the situation in conversations they have with their family worker, to those they experience at home, the relationship develops more easily and the learning is of a deeper quality.

It is important that the staff in early childhood settings meet and discuss issues of equality of opportunity, including ensuring the access of every child to become fully part of the group. This will involve developing as a team anti-discriminatory strategies and a policy for everyone to draw up together. It is also essential that every individual feels committed to this. Not only this, but a policy needs to be put into action, and regularly reviewed to check that it is being implemented and to make changes as it is developed (Bruce and Meggitt, 1996).

Resources

Attitudes which promote the guiding principles discussed in this chapter are of no consequence without action. Action requires commitment from people and appropriate resources. Early childhood workers need varying degrees of additional information, advice, support, special materials and amended environments if they are to work with individuals with differences.

For example, the inclusion of a child with a visual handicap will mean extra specialist teaching support in the form of peripatetic advisers qualified in the education of visually-handicapped children; additional technical equipment including braillers; microcomputers with voice output; a special materials service of braille books and tape-recorded materials; special lighting; and readiness on the part of the teacher to go for in-service training.

Early childhood workers should be encouraged to go on courses giving access to information packs and teaching materials relevant to the cultures represented in the UK. They should have access to at least very basic conversational language training if English is the second language; and should have teaching and support staff colleagues coming from the minority groups represented in the school.

In too many instances these resources are either not available or only available after much pressure and representation. But it is the early childhood workers' responsibility to press for the resources necessary to work with children with quality, and it can be the responsibility of parents to use official channels and ultimately political channels (through their local elected representative) to achieve a better level of resources.

CONCLUSION

This chapter has explored commonalities between people, and the individuality and differences between them. A range of issues have been identified as of critical importance in approaching the care and education of any child. These included the consideration of class, ethnicity, gender, special needs, child protection and children's rights (Nutbrown (ed) 1996).

The key elements to be borne in mind are that societies need to create systems which give equality of opportunity and access to all who live in them. Attention must also be given to the various ways in which to empower children and adults as individuals, but also the groups who may be in a minority. This needs to be backed up with policies developed together as a team by those working with young children and their families and regularly reviewed.

It is understandable that early childhood workers often feel overwhelmed by the enormity of the task to be done in relation to creating better access and more empowerment for individuals, minority or neglected groups of people. Principles which can be generalised across a variety of situations are helpful in this.

- Children need a sense of belonging and to feel included, to choose their own identity and have a sense of self-worth.
- Everyone needs to inspect his/her own thinking and actions, confront assumptions and move towards equality of regard for all people.
- Fear of strangers impedes this process, and needs to be tackled directly.

Practical strategies involve knowledge of self and of others. There is a need for a broad curriculum pursued in depth which includes study going beyond the dominant culture.It should help children to link what they learn to what they already know, so that a meaningful context is built around their knowledge.

Early childhood educators are in positions of power for breaking down narrow roles for children, or combatting stereotyping of all kinds.

- All people have in common the fact that they are human beings.
- There is much diversity and many differences between people, but this is different from fragmentation of society or cultures.
- It is important to begin with what is common to all people.
- Differences can be celebrated, respected and valued.

Everyone, child or adult, has in common the need:

- for a sense of belonging and inclusion;
- for a sense of well-being and self-worth;
- for a full life, not one that is narrowly stereotyped by others with access denied or restricted;
- to overcome stranger fear;
- to reflect on and look at the values, assumptions and attitudes which influence the way people act towards others.

Every early childhood setting needs a policy which the whole team has worked on and is committed to. This needs to be regularly reviewed to make sure it is actively carried out in practice (Bruce and Meggitt, 1996, Chapter 1).

11

EVALUATION AND ASSESSMENT

HOW AND WHAT ARE

CHILDREN LEARNING

Teachers can best decide on what ought to be taught by finding out what children already know   (Athey, 1990, p.28).

ASSESSING THE CHILD

Assessment helps early childhood workers to find out about the child's progress based on observations made of the child either in natural situations or adult-led tasks. In order to effectively assess what a child can do, is learning, and has learnt, early childhood workers need to know about how children develop rather than applying tests which attempt to measure a child's progress. This is because the younger the child, the less reliable the test.

Millie Almy, in 1975, wrote: 'tests given in the early childhood years are not very good predictors of the child's later status'. The Bullock Report (1975), also written in the 1970s, quotes: 'you do not make children grow by measuring them'.

Richard Feynman, the Nobel Prize winning Physicist, criticises what he calls pseudo-scientific approaches which are inappropriate – for example, he points out that it is easier to measure atoms than what is happening in a child's mind. (Bruce, 1991). In the 1990s there has been much debate about the efficacy of Standard Assessment Tasks for seven year-olds and their reliability. In most parts of the world, most early childhood workers, parents and politicians doubt their usefulness since six or seven year-olds vary greatly in their developmental possibility to read, write and be numerate. Indeed, in most countries attempts to formally teach these areas of learning do not even begin until this age because it is not considered to be appropriate.

Evaluating the curriculum

Whereas assessment is about how the child makes progress, evaluation helps us to look at what we are offering a group of children or an individual child in the curriculum. This will involve practitioners looking at the experiences planned and the materials that they have used, and the way that staff and parents work with children, sometimes in groups and sometimes alone. Documents developed in Somerset (1997), Birmingham (1997) and Southwark (1997) are examples of frameworks using observations to inform planning of an appropriate curriculum, linked to the Desirable Outcomes Document, introduced in 1996.

Assessment and evaluation need to link together

Assessment (how the child is making progress) needs to be linked with evaluation (what the child is offered). When used together in a record keeping system, the integration of assessment and evaluation by early childhood workers comes about through careful observation of children which inform the curriculum planning' (Bartholomew and Bruce, 1998, second edition). Staff can begin to work out what they will next need to offer to children, either a large group, small group or individually.

In the UK children are not legally required to follow the National Curriculum until they are five years old. Four year-olds in the UK are offered a curriculum based around documents leading to Desirable Learning Outcomes for children's learning. These differ in Wales, Scotland, Northern Ireland and England. It is widely recognised that the English document is more narrowly conceived in relation to those of the other three countries in the UK. For example, the Welsh document as well as stressing areas of learning such as language and literacy, also emphasises core principles which relate to those of the early childhood traditions and which also deeply value childhood play.

Another useful enhancement to early years documents on the curriculum is the Te Whariki curriculum recently implemented in New Zealand (1996) which also has core principles. These are:

- **Empowerment** – Whakana;
- **Holistic Development** – Kotahitanga;
- **Family and community** – Whanau-Tangata;
- **Relationships** – Nga Hontanga

Formative and summative methods of assessing a child's progress

It is simply not possible to measure most of a child's development or learning. We can only catch glimpses of a child's progress. Given this situation it is damaging to a child's education if adults believe that only the learning it is thought possible to measure is given any emphasis in the curriculum. It will bring about a narrowing of the curriculum where children are mainly taught to achieve on formal tests, rather than becoming educated in the real sense. This is sometimes referred to as the 'dumbing down' of the curriculum. This is the difference between schooling and educating children. It is the difference between helping children to jump through narrow academic hoops, as opposed to developing their intellectual, reflective and scholarly side.

If we want children to be well educated rather than narrowly schooled, it is important that the processes of development and learning are valued as much as the outcomes of learning when assessing a child's progress. This can be achieved through two methods being used side by side:

- Formative assessment
- Summative assessment

Formative Assessment

Formative assessment methods emphasise the learning children are involved in over time. The emphasis is on the everyday context in which learning takes place rather than test situations. Formative assessment is about the processes in a child's progress and the way children go through their learning experiences in the curriculum, gradually and over time.

Information is gathered continuously and regularly in natural, non-test situations. For example, collecting a child's paintings, photographing models, keeping examples of children's written efforts and notes about their dances or singing.

Narrative observation notes taken on the spot whilst a child is cooking, dancing, doing woodwork, using the climbing frame, or hunting for ants in the garden are invaluable. These can be used to inform future planning.

Formative evaluation

Formative evaluation looks at what children are being offered and how this meets their needs, and at what needs changing, or adapting and developing. It involves a long-term plan and a medium-term plan (now often referred to as schemes of work) (Pollard, 1997), which are flexible, adaptable and constantly change as observation of children informs the plan and daily plans emerge out of this.

Summative assessment

Summative assessment is about taking stock, pausing and bringing together everything known about the child's progress. Summative assessment can be staff and parents putting together key aspects of a child's progress, for example physically, mathematically, aesthetically, or in terms of special educational needs or anti-discriminatory practice and policy review. It is then necessary to decide next steps in what to offer and evaluate the impact of this on the curriculum. It might involve the formal testing of children, as in Baseline Assessment, or Standard Assessment Tasks.

Summative Evaluation

Summative evaluation occurs regularly when staff pause to evaluate what children have been offered, and how effective the planning has been. The Ofsted Inspection Process is part of summative evaluation, although this has been criticised since many primary inspectors have no experience of teaching 3 or 4 year-olds.

Both summative assessment and summative evaluation are important in giving information and clues about the kind of education and care that a child is receiving and about his or her development and learning. However, summative 'snap shots' are of little meaning without the formative and continuous gathering of knowledge and understanding which supports summative assessment of children, or summative evaluation of what children are offered in the whole curriculum.

It is always important to remember that children perform at a higher level in a meaningful context than they do in formal test situations (Donaldson, 1978) when they are often not clear what it is that adults want of them (Hughes, 1983).

Assessment and evaluation require teachers to be clear about their intentions and how they will act upon them and to consider next steps in a child's learning. This means knowing about child development and the early childhood curriculum, and keeping up to date with recent research and thinking. In-service training is an essential aspect of this approach to evaluation and assessment.

Using both formative and summative methods of evaluation and assessment education in early childhood supports the interactionist approach to early childhood education. Using one or the other does not and has severe disadvantages. For example, one of the problems of the kind of summative methods involving formal testing is that what **is** measured quickly becomes what children **ought** to know. The problem of 'deriving an ought from an is' is called the Naturalistic Fallacy.

Children become moulded to fit the tests:

- Using only summative methods of record keeping ignores the interactive approach to early childhood education. Focusing too much on narrow, measurable progress contradicts the early childhood principles, and constrains a child's learning.
- On the other hand, only using formative methods of record keeping focuses too much upon processes and ignores outcomes of learning. The possibility of celebrating a child's successes in learning relies on being able to show some results.

There needs to be a sensible balance between the experiences that children have and activities they are involved in, and their outcomes – the evidence in terms of records of the work done.

Assessment and evaluation are important to children and parents as well as staff. For example, at school Open Evenings parents often seize upon written work, drawings, paintings, models, or look for sum books. They want to see what their child has done and to compare this with what other children do. Parents enjoy 'performances' of music, drama and dance, because again there is a product to see, a tangible outcome. Outcomes such as these are often the only available means they have of putting their child's achievements, or their anxieties about their child's progress, into any kind of context. The anxieties parents experience about their child's progress cannot be stressed too strongly.

The advantage of using equally explicit formative as well as summative approaches is that parents and others, such as school governors, are included in the process of education, as well as the outcomes. They are helped to examine the education offered to the child beyond the superficial level, which tends to be entrenched in the education they themselves received. They can be supported in doing so by teachers who are confident and articulate, who constantly seek to improve the service, and are flexible in their thinking which is based on sound conceptually-based knowledge.

Explicit ways of sharing formative assessment of children's progress are in place at Pen Green Centre for Families and Children Under Five, where children regularly decide with their family worker and parent(s) what to include in their record of achievement (special books) (Whalley, 1994). This helps children to reflect on their own learning – a process called metacognition.

Parents can be helped to see a broad and more wide-ranging picture of the child develop over a period of time, based on the continual observations made, often by parents and staff, and on the plans formulated in the curriculum. Their involvement in this process working with the early childhood worker or teacher illuminates the process. Parents are then in a position to take pleasure in their child's strengths, and to tackle the weaker areas supported by the school or early childhood setting.

Seeing an individual 'interest book' develop as part of class work, or seeing different paintings displayed on the classroom wall and then made into another kind of interest book are examples of this way of working to make formative assessment more tangible and easier for parents to see in action. Parents are also able to see their child's progress in relation to other children in a less unpalatable way than when suddenly plunged into an Open Evening, where the differences between their child's achievement and the achievements of others may be startling.

Early childhood workers gaining confidence through assessment and evaluation

Confident early childhood workers have two strengths. The first is the ability to reflect upon, analyse and act upon their work with children. A survey at Goldsmith's College, (1996) suggests that this is linked with the level of training, of the early childhood worker, and the EEL Project (1996) has similar findings.

The second strength of confident early childhood workers is the ability to communicate and share with colleagues, the child's family and those beyond the school setting, to explain effectively what they are doing and gain external co-operation. In particular, teachers need continually to broaden their knowledge of how children develop. They need to be able to observe children with skill and use their observations in practice. Alongside this, staff need to develop their understanding of different and wide areas of knowledge and to see logical lines of development in them (Harlen, 1982). One of the reasons why children need to engage with the broad curriculum is that each subject has its own logic and characteristics which contribute something to the child's education. In each case they need to be able to discuss observations and action plans with colleagues, the child's family, and beyond the early childhood setting.

Developing these two strengths requires time and effort in planning and reflecting on work with children, colleagues and the child's family. Early childhood workers who have a clear approach are less likely to jump on to the latest educational band-wagon. Because they are striving to put recent developments into some coherent framework within which to set their practice, they are less likely to get in a rut, and more able to establish where they need to modify or change their practice.

Half-formed ideas are easily challenged, and this quickly threatens self-confidence. Early childhood workers who are helped to think about what they do (through staff meetings, in-service training and so on) are in a position to justify their actions (Pascal and Bertram, 1997). This means that they can share their thinking. They can meet differing ideas about education from a firm base, and do so with self-confidence.

It is one thing to be able to look at another's point of view, but it is also necessary to examine these in relation to one's own. Not having a point of view, or not knowing quite what one's point of view is, does not enhance self-esteem. Those with low self-esteem are often held in low-esteem by others.

Communication begins within the profession – through initial and in-service training, and by developing whole school and institutional policies through staff discussions and working together to formulate development plans. Communication is shared with the child's family, through open style record keeping which invites partnership. It goes beyond this to others within the profession. Efforts should be made to improve communication between early childhood educators and secondary level educators, for example. There is also a need for multi-professional work, with co-operation, co-ordination and sharing as the key.

The general public and politicians need to be better informed. The confident, articulate knowledgeable early childhood educator and carer can invite discussion. If people understand the work being done they are more likely to value it.

Relating evaluation and assessment to the early childhood principles

Having a clear framework for working with children means having principles which are borne in mind, as a backcloth against which work is set. Put simply, it is not sensible to check how well one is progressing unless one has a destination, or at least a steady direction.

Fulfilling legal requirements may be thought of as having a sense of direction, but this is pragmatic only, although the Framework for Inspection (Ofsted) support the early childhood principles. It is challenging to fit legal requirements to long established and time honoured principles, but much more rewarding and worthwhile to work in this way with children and their families because it is thoughtful, reflective and helps staff to know why some aspects are of fundamental importance (Bartholomew and Bruce, 1998, second edition).

Principle 1

In terms of evaluation and assessment, this means that what is offered must be relevant for future knowledge but also appropriate for the moment. This is sometimes called a 'developmentally appropriate curriculum' (NAEYC, 1990).

Principle 2

Records need to be kept of all aspects of the child's development. There are multi-professional implications in this. Health records are confidential, but it is of central importance for those professionals responsible for the child's education and care since these two aspects inevitably link. It is also important to bear in mind both the child's strengths and weaknesses, especially for a child with any kind of special educational need. Specialists of all kinds (medical, social workers, educational psychologists and educators) will need to share and build vital information together with the parent as required by the SEN Code of Practice (1994). Building records in a partnership can enable early diagnosis or monitoring of special needs, temporary or permanent, and indicate the level of support a child will need. This approach is particularly helpful in the field of health surveillance, and as a means of offering appropriate help in terms of preventive treatment, remediation or dealing with handicap.

Principle 3

Emphasising a broad, integrated curriculum reasserts this principle, and provides a yardstick for teacher-led evaluation and assessment of the adequacy of the curriculum. A broad context enables children to practise newly emerging thinking in a variety of settings. The child who is an emergent reader of print might also be at the early stages of reading musical notation. The child, who is beginning to tell stories, which the teacher writes down, may also choreograph a dance which the teacher helps to shape, or compose music which the teacher writes down.

Principle 4
Principle 5

Assessing whether children are able to initiate, or whether they depend on others to goad them into action, requires close observation and recording of what they choose to do, what spontaneous or planned work excites and catches their interest. These will give the adult clues about what is likely to encourage the child's intrinsic motivation to flourish. Recent empirical research (Athey, 1990; EEL Project, Pascal and Bertram, 1997; Goldsmiths PIP Project, 1996) emphasises the need to 'use' the child's initiatives and intrinsic motivation rather than cut across these. As part of this the adult needs to see if conversations, activities and group times are promoting the child's initiatives and motivations, or dominating and damaging them.

The teacher needs to observe and record how often he/she imposes control and discipline on the child; and to what extent children have self-discipline and can curb themselves. This is particularly important where a child has behavioural challenges. Recognising, appreciating and valuing children's efforts increases self-discipline, and noting progress fosters feelings of self-worth and well-being (Laevers, 1997).

Principle 6

The more the adult can establish the exact point in development and learning of the child the better. Looking at key areas of development can help (as in Principle 2, the importance of the whole child). The Piagetian schema is a useful mechanism for adding detail to this.

Principle 7

Each child is unique, and has a learning style which is part of his or her personality and character. Some children learn best through three dimensional wooden blocks, small world, pushing carts around outside, throwing bean bags and balls. Another child might learn exactly the same subject (about forces in physics) in an entirely different way, by spending the whole session at the sand and water areas and also at the graphics area. Children do not have to use pencil and paper to be learning. Adults often worry 'he/she never does drawings/paintings, never sits down'.

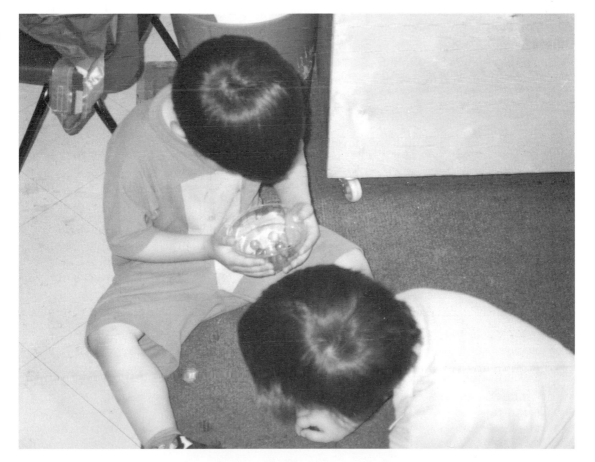

Adults need to be sensitive and know when to influence and when to hold back

Providing good narrative observation techniques are in place and formative assessment is thorough, a child's needs can be met through using a wide range of materials. Drawing at a table might not appeal to a child, but drawing with a bucket of water and a large brush on the table outside might lead to very similar learning outcomes. The key is not to make the child come to the drawing table, but to take the drawing possibilities to the child, by building on what the children can do.

Principle 8

Since the ideas the child is developing and has developed makes such a major contribution to progress in symbolic behaviour (which is central to human functioning at a higher level), it is important to develop sound strategies and techniques in assessing and evaluating these. Narrative observation notes, photography, video tapes and collecting examples of models, painting and drawings and written work, help to capture the processes and outcomes of the development of symbolic behaviour.

It is as important to plot progress in dance choreography, musical composition and performance skill with a bat and ball as it is to see development in a child's written or number work.

Principle 9

Accurate assessment of children's development is only possible if work displayed on walls and in books is their own.

> A parent at an Open Day said to Harry (aged three) 'What a lovely train. You clever boy to do that.' It was a template outline of a steam train which had prints from cotton reels on it. Harry said, 'I only did those' (meaning the cotton reel prints). The teacher had had the idea of making a train to fit a project on transport. She cut out the template and required Harry to print on it. She called this 'personalising' it.

All this illustrates is that he can follow a simple instruction – and print on an outline – which is a very low level achievement unworthy of the label 'creative'. Teacher-dominated displays, although attractive, reveal a very low level of achievement which underestimate what children can do.

In contrast, displays of work initiated and carried through by children, given adult support, demonstrate what children can do. The children's work can be beautifully mounted by adults, and where appropriate, explanatory notes about the contents or processes of the work (since the result may not be obvious, for example a blob of paint on a page is representing a ball bouncing) can be given. This method shows the adult's role as supporting and extending, what the child can do (Vygotsky's zone of potential development) then sharing this through the classroom display, which illuminates the child's work but does not take it over.

Adults who help children to extend what they can do by themselves are more useful to children long-term than adults who help them to perform through giving them easy props to lean upon in the short-term. Deep down, children know the difference, and their self-esteem is enhanced if they feel real ownership of their achievements. The reward is knowing 'this is me being able to do this'.

Principle 10

In earlier chapters it was suggested that the early childhood curriculum involves a process with three aspects:

- the child;
- the context;
- the content.

A flow chart may be useful in highlighting these. Flow charts safeguard balance and breadth as well as depth of curriculum. They allow for flexibility as staff develop a scheme of work (Pollard, 1997), and help to decide the order in which knowledge is introduced with the possibility of adding to the chart.

Some aspects can be left out if they become inappropriate or irrelevant as the work develops. In this way general plans and possibilities, carefully thought out, can emerge, but individuals can be catered for. Flow charts can be shared with parents. Some teachers pin them on the walls for parents to see.

There is a tendency to become immersed in the evaluation aspect and to ignore the assessment aspect. If flow charts are to be of use, there is a constant need to relate the child and the chart. The developing plan should become a formative assessment of the child, and a formative evaluation of what is offered. For example, the child's name may be added to the flow chart, and dated, to show when he or she became involved in an aspect of the chart. This can be cross-referenced to the child's individual record, where more detail can be given. Other forms of record keeping will emphasise assessment only.

If record-keeping is to contribute to classroom practice, teachers need to think carefully about which forms of record-keeping are most helpful.

CONCLUSION

Early childhood educators need to feel strong in the work to which they are committed. They are then in a position to develop and communicate their work. They need to see evaluation and assessment as useful instruments illuminating and highlighting the value of what they strive to do, and useful indicators of areas which need attention and re-thinking. In this way, they can identify for themselves their strengths and weaknesses.

12

THE WAY FORWARD

The aim of this book has not been to prescribe how adults should work with young children. Rather it has been to provide a framework within which to work with some confidence that the approach will be consistent and be based on established theory and recent research. Detailed methods of work must depend on the individual adult, and most importantly, on the child him/herself and the family and socio-cultural setting.

The basis of the framework is the ten principles of early childhood education, which are set out once again below, reworded since 1987 to make the language more contemporary.

They are:

1 The best way to prepare children for their adult life is to give them what they need as children.

2 Children are whole people who have feelings, ideas and relationships with others, and who need to be physically, mentally, morally and spiritually healthy.

3 Subjects such as mathematics and art cannot be separated; young children learn in an integrated way and not in neat, tidy compartments.

4 Children learn best when they are given appropriate responsibility, allowed to make errors, decisions and choices, and respected as autonomous learners.

5 Self-discipline is emphasised. Indeed, this is the only kind of discipline worth having. Reward systems are very short-term and do not work in the long-term. Children need their efforts to be valued.

6 There are times when children are especially able to learn particular things.

7 What children can do (rather than what they cannot do) is the starting point of a child's education.

8. Imagination, creativity and all kinds of symbolic behaviour (reading, writing, drawing, dancing, music, mathematical numbers, algebra, role play and talking) develop and emerge when conditions are favourable.

9. Relationships with other people (both adults and children) are of central importance in a child's life.

10. Quality education is about three things: the child; the context in which learning takes place; the knowledge and understanding which the child develops and learns.

From these principles, and taking account of prevailing practice, as well as policy pressures, the following action points are proposed.

- There needs to be more emphasis on partnership and reciprocity between adults and children. This requires better understanding of child development and of the different areas of knowledge.
- While recognising the importance of being child centred, there is a need to become more family centred.
- There is a need for better and more multi-professional exchanges between workers and services, including voluntary agencies.
- It is essential to have a better conceptual articulation of what good early childhood education is, with appropriate assessment and evaluation, which does not cut across its valuable traditions.

The past leads to the future through the present.

Heraclitis said:

> You can put your hand in the river once.
> You cannot put your hand in the same river twice.

REFERENCES AND
BIBLIOGRAPHY

Abbott, L. and Rodgers, R. (eds.) (1994) *Quality Education in the Early Years.* Buckingham/Philadelphia: Open University.

Acredelo, L. and Goodwyn, S. (1997) *Baby Signs.* London: Hodder & Stoughton.

Aitchinson, J. (1994). *Words in the Mind: An Introduction to the Mental Lexicon.* Oxford: Blackwell.

Aleksander, I. (1997) *Impossible Minds: My Neurons, My Consciousness.* London: Imperial College.

Alexander, R., Rose, J. and Woodhead, C. (1992) *Curriculum Organisation and Classroom Practice: A Discussion Paper.* London: DES.

Arnold, C. (1990) *Children Who Play Together have Similar Schemas.* (Available from Pen Green Centre for Families and Children Under Five, Corby, Northants). Project Submitted as Part of the Certificate in Post Qualifying Studies NNEB, December 1990.

Athey, C. (1990) *Extending Thought in Young Children: A Parent-Teacher Partnership.* London: Paul Chapman Publishing.

Audit Commission (1996) *National Report: Counting to Five: Education of Children Under Five.* London: HMSO.

Ball, C. (1994) *Start Right.* London: Royal Society of Arts.

Barnes, P. (ed.) (1995) *Personal, Social and Emotional Development of Children.* Oxford: Open University, Blackwell.

Bartholomew, L. and Bruce, T. (1993: 1998 second edition). *Getting to Know You: A Guide to Record-Keeping in Early Childhood Education and Care.* London: Hodder & Stoughton.

BBC, (1996, March) *Teaching Today: Staff Development. Child Development: Primary.* Available from BBC Educational Development, PO Box 50, Wetherby, W. Yorkshire LS23 7EZ.

Bedford Local Education Authority (1989) *Schema Ahead Booklet.*

Birmingham City Council Education Department joint venture with NFER/Nelson (1997) *Climbing Frames: A Framework for Learning from Birth to Five.* Windsor, Berkshire NFER/Nelson.

Blenkin, G. and Kelly, V. (1988:1996 Second edition) *Early Childhood Education: A Developmental Curriculum*. London: Paul Chapman Publishing.

Blenkin, G. M., Rose, J. and Yue, N.Y.L. (1996) *Government Policies and Early Education: Perspectives from Practitioners*. EECERAJ, 1996, vol. 4, no. 2, p.21.

Bradburn, E. (1989) *Margaret McMillan: Portrait of a Pioneer*. London: Routledge.

Bredekamp, S. (ed.) (Expanded Edition) (1987) (1992) *Developmentally Appropriate Practice in Early Childhood Programs. Serving Children from Birth Through 8*. National Association for the Education of Young Children, 1834 Connecticut Avenue, NW Washington DC.

Brennan, M. (1978) 'Talking Hands'. BBC TV 'Horizon' programme.

Brice-Heath, S. (1983) *Ways with Words*. Cambridge: Cambridge University Press.

Brown, A. (1996) *Developing Language and Literacy*. 3-8. London: Paul Chapman Publishing.

Bruce, T. (1976) 'A Comparative study of the Montessori Method, and a Piaget- based conceptualisation of the pre-school curriculum'. Unpublished MA dissertation, University of London.

Bruce, T. (1978) 'Side by side. Montessori and other educational principles'. Montessori Society AMI (UK) Third Annual Weekend Conference, February.

Bruce, T. (1984) 'A Froebelian looks at Montessori's work'. *Early Child Development and Care*, 14, vols. 1 and 2.

Bruce, T. (1991) *Time to Play in Early Childhood Education and Care*. London: Hodder & Stoughton.

Bruce, T., Findlay, A., Read, J., Scarborough, M. (1995) *Recurring Themes in Education*. London: Paul Chapman Publishing.

Bruce, T. (1996) *Helping Young Children to Play*. London: Hodder & Stoughton.

Bruce, T. and Meggitt, C. (1996) *Childcare and Education*. London: Hodder & Stoughton.

Bruce, T. *Adults and Children Developing Playing Together*. EECERAJ, Spring, 1997a.

Bruce, T. (1997b) *Tuning into Children*. A Child's World. BBC/NCB.

Bruner, J. (1960:1977 second ed). *The Process of Education*. Cambridge MA: Harvard University Press.

Bruner, J., Wood, D. and Ross, G. (1976) 'The role of tutoring in problem-solving'. *Journal of Child Psychology and Psychiatry*, 17, 89–100.

Bruner, J. (1990) *Acts of Meaning*. Cambridge M.A.: Harvard University Press.

Butler, D. (1987) *Cushla and Her Books: The Fascinating Story of the Role of Books in the Life of a Handicapped Child*. Harmondsworth: Penguin Ltd.

Butler, D. (1980) *Babies Need Books*. London: Bodley Head.

Carey, S. and Daly, L. (1996) *Schema and Schema and Schema = Working Theory of the World*. Playcentre Journal, November 1996.

Chomsky, N. (1968) *Language and Mind*. N.Y:Harcourt, Brace and World.

Clay, M. (1975) *What did I write?* London: Heinemann.

Clay, M.M. (1992) *The Detection of Reading Difficulties*. Newcastle-Upon-Tyne: Heinemann.

Clements, P. and Spinks, T. (1994: 1996 second ed). *The Equal Opportunities Guide*. London: Cogan Page Limited.

Cockerill H. *Communication through Play: Non-Directive Communication Therapy. 'Special Times'*. Cheyne Centre for Children with Cerebal Palsy. 1997 p.1-23.

Coleman , J.C. (1997) *The Parenting of Adolescents in Britian Today. Children and Society*, vol.11, no.1, April 1997. p.44-51.

Conolly, Y. (1983) Keynote Speech: A Multi-Cultural Approach in Early Education. London: OMEP Conference.

Corsaro, W. (1979) "We're friends, right?". Children's use of access rituals in a nursery school. *Language in Society*. 8, 315-36.

Covey, S.R. (1989) *The Seven Habits of Highly Effective People*. London: Sidney: NY: Tokyo: Singapore: Toronto: Simon and Schuster.

Cubey, P. *Te Whaariki - The Early Childhood Curriculum of Aotearoa - New Zealand*. Pen Green Conference, November 2 1996.

Chukovsky, K. (1963) *From Two to Five*. Berkeley, CA: University of California Press.

Curtis, A. (1986) *A Curriculum for the Pre-school Child*. Windsor: NFER Nelson.

David, T. (1990) *Under Five - Under Educated?* Milton Keynes: Open University.

David, T., Curtis, A. and Siraj Blatchford, I. (1992) *Effective Teaching in the Early Years: Fostering Children Learning in Nurseries and in Infant Classes*. Stoke on Trent: Trentham.

Davies, M. (1995) *Helping Children to Learn Through a Movement Perspective*. London: Hodder & Stoughton.

Dawkins, R. (1993) *The Extended Phenotype*. Oxford: Oxford University Press.

Dearden, R.F. (1968) *The Philosophy of Primary Education*. London: Routledge and Kegan Paul.

De Graff, J. C. *Rhythm and Order in the Classroom. Teaching and Learning* The Journal of Natural Inquiry. vol. 2, no. 2, Fall 1988.

Department of Education and Science (1975) *A Language for Life*. (The Bullock Report). London: HMSO.

DES (1978) *Special Educational Needs: Report of the Committee of Enquiry into the Education of Handicapped Children and Young People*. (The Warnock Report). London: HMSO.

DES (1991) *The Children Act. Family Support. Day Care and Educational Provision for Young Children*. Vol 2, London: HMSO.

DES (1990) *Starting with Quality: The Report of Inquiry into the Quality of the Educational Experience Offered to 3 and 4 Year Olds.* London: HMSO.

DFE (1994) *Code of Practice on the Identification and Assessment of Special Educational Needs.* London: HMSO.

DFEE (1996) *Nursery Education: Desirable Outcomes for Children's Learning on Entering Compulsory Education.* SCAA.

Desforges, C. (1989) *Teachers Perspectives on Classroom Interaction* in C. Desforges (ed) Early Childhood Education. The British Journal of Educational Psychology. Monograph Series no. 4, Scottish Academic Press.

Desforges, C. (1996) *Children as Problem Solvers.* Lecture at the Nursery World Conference 1996, 18 October.

Dombey, H. (1983) 'Learning the language of books', in Meek, M. (ed.) *Opening Moves.* Bedford Way Papers no. 17, University of London Institute of Education.

Donaldson, M. (1978) *Children's Minds.* London: Fortuna/Collins.

Dowling, M. (1995) *Starting School at Four: A Joint Endeavour.* London: Paul Chapman Publishing.

Drummond, M.J. (1993) *Assessing Children's Learning.* London: David Fulton.

Dunn, J. (1984) *Sisters and Brothers.* London: Collins/Fontana.

Dunn, J. (1988) *The Beginnings of Social Understanding.* Oxford: Blackwell.

Dunn, J. (1991) 'Young children's understanding of other people: evidence from observations within the family' in Fye, K. and Moore, C. (eds.) *Theories of Mind.* Hillsdale, N.J.: Lawrence Erlbaum.

Dunn, J. and Plomin, R. (1990) *Separate Lives: Why Siblings are so Different* N.Y: Basic Books.

Early Years Curriculum Group (1989) *The Early Childhood Curriculum and the National Curriculum.* EYCG.

Edgington, M. (see Lally).

Edmund, F. (1979) *Rudolf Steiner Education. The Waldorf Schools.* London: Rudolf Steiner Press.

Erikson, E. (1963) *Childhood and Society.* London: Routledge and Kegan Paul.

European Commission (Brussels) Equal Opportunities Unit (1996) Review of Services for Young Children in the European Union.

Ferreiro, E. and Teberosky, A. (1983) *Literacy Before Schooling.* (Translation Karen Goodman Castro). London: Heinemann.

Ferreiro, E. (1997) *Reading, Writing and Thinking about the Writing System.* Conference Lectures on Literacy: from Research to Practice. Lecture at the Institute of Education, University of London. 13/3, 1997.

Fisher, J. (1996) *Starting from the Child?* Buckingham and Philadelphia: Open University Press.

Fox, C. (1983) 'Talking like a book', in Meek, M. (ed.) Opening Moves. Bedford Way Papers no. 17, University of London Institute of Education.

Froebel, F. W. (1878) *Mother Play and Nursery Songs*. (trans. Fanny E. Dwight (songs) and Josephine Jarvis (prose)). Boston, MA: Lee and Shepard.

Froebel, F.W. (1887) *The Education of Man*. New York: Appleton.

Gardner, D. (1969) *Susan Isaacs*. London: Methuen.

Gardner, H. (1983) *Frames of Mind. The Theory of Multiple Intelligence*. New York Basic Books.

Garrard, H. (1986) *Personal Communication*.

Garvey, C. (1977) *Play*. The Developing Child series, Bruner, J., Cole, M., and Lloyd, B. (eds.). London: Collins/Fontana-Open Books.

Geekie, P. and Raban, B. (1993) *Learning to Read and Write Through Classroom Talk*. Stoke on Trent: Trentham Books.

Gerhardt, L.A. *Movement Case Study of a Five Year Old Special Needs Child with Recommendations to the Classroom Teacher*. Kindle the Fire: Proceedings of the Sixth Conference of Dance and Child International (DACI). Maquarie University, Sidney, Australia, 12-20 July 1994, p.149-158.

Gesell, A. (1954) *The First Five Years of Life*. London: Methuen.

Gleick, J. (1988) *Chaos*. London, N.Y: Heinemann.

Gleick, J. and Photographs by Porter, E. (1990) *Nature's Chaos*. Sphere Books, London: MacDonald & Co.

Goldschmied, E. and Jackson, S. (1994) *People Under Three*. London: Routledge.

Goldschmied, E. and Sellek, D. (1996) *Communication Between Babies in their First Year*. (Book and Video). London, N.C.B Enterprises.

Goldsmith's College. Quality in Diversity Project. Department of Educational Studies, Lewisham Way, London SE14. (See Hurst).

Goodman, Y. (1984) 'The development of initial literacy', in Smith, F., Goelman, H. and Oberg, A. (eds.) *Awakening to Literacy*. London: Heinemann.

Goswami, U. and Bryant, P. (1990) *Phonological Skills and Learning to Read*. Hove: Laurence Erlbaum Associates Ltd.

Graves, D. (1983) Writing: Teachers and Children at Work London: Heinemann.

Greenfield, S. (1996) *A Physical Base for Consciousness*. One of three lectures on Evolution, Consciousness and Conscious Evolution. RSA Journal, vol. CXLIV, no. 5470 June 1996, p.34-40.

Greenfield, S. (1997) Review by Susan Greenfield in RSA Journal vol. CXLV, no. 5478, April 1997, p.56-57. (See Aleksander, I.).

Griffin, P. (1986) Article in The Times Educational Supplement, 15 August.

Gura, P. (ed.) (1992) *Exploring Learning: Young Children and Blockplay*. London: Paul Chapman Publishing.

Gura, P. (1997) *Resources for Early Learning: Children, Adults and Stuff*. London: Hodder & Stoughton.

Gussin-Paley, V. (1981) *Wally's Stories*. Cambridge, M.A. London: Harvard University Press.

Gussin-Paley, V. (1986) *Mollie is Three*. Chicago, London: University of Chicago.

Gussin-Paley, V. (1990) *The Boy Who Would be a Helicopter*. Cambridge M.A London: Harvard University Press.

Hall, N., Holden-Sim, K. (eds) (1996) 'Debating Punctuation: Six Year Olds Figure It Out' In Hall, N. and Martello, J. (1996) *Listening to Children Talk: Exploring Talk in the Early Years*. London: Hodder & Stoughton.

Hannon, P., Weinberger, J. and Nutbrown, C. (1991) *A Study of Work with Parents to Promote Early Literacy Development*. Research Papers in Education, vol. 6, no. 2, pp. 77-97.

Harlen, W. (1982) *Evaluation and Assessment* In Richards, C. (ed) New Directions in Primary Education. London: Falmer Press.

Harrison, C. (1996) *Family Literacy: Evaluation, Ownership and Ambiguity*. RSA Journal, vol. CXLIV, no. 5474, November 1996, p.25-28.

Hazareesingh, S., Simms, K., Anderson, P. (1989) *Educating the Whole Child. Holistic Approach to Education in the Early Years*. London: Building Blocks Education, Save The Children.

Hedley, A. A Schema Story. *Beyond Desirable Outcomes*. Pen Green Conference Paper, November 1996.

Holdaway, D. (1979) *The Foundations of Literacy*. Gosford, NSW, Australia: Ashton Skelastic.

Honig, A. (1984) 'Working in partnership with parents of handicapped infants'. *Early Child Development and Care*, 14, 1-2, 13-36.

Hughes, M., Wikeley, F. and Nash, T. (1994) *Parents and their Children's Schools*. Oxford: Blackwell.

Hurst, V. (1991) *Planning for Early Learning: Education in the First Five Years*. London: Paul Chapman Publishing.

Hurst, V., Burgess-Macey, C. and Ouvry, M. (1997) *Quality in Diversity Project*. Department of Educational Studies, Goldsmiths College, Lewisham Way, London SE14.

Isaacs, S. (1968) *The Nursery Years*. London: Routledge and Kegan Paul.

James, C. (1993) *Play: The Key to Young Children's Learning*. London: BAECE.

Kaplan, L. (1978) *Oneness and Separateness: From Infant to Individual*. New York: Simon and Schuster. Quoted in Honig, A., Kellmer Pringle, M. (1974; 1980, 2nd edition) *The Needs of Children*. London: Hutchinson.

Katz, L.G and Chard, S.C. (1989) *Engaging Children's Minds: A Project Approach.* Ablex Publishing Corporation, Norwood: New Jersey.

Kegl, J. (1997) *Silent Children....New Language.* BBC: Horizon, 3rd April 1997.

Kellmer-Pringle, N. (1974: 1980 second edition) *The Needs of Children.* London: Hutchinson.

Kilpatrick, W. (1915) *Montessori Examined.* London: Constable and Co.

Kitzinger, C. (1997) *Born to be Good? What Motivates us to be Good, Bad or Indifferent Towards Others?* New Internationalist. April 1997, p.15–17.

Kohn, A. (1993) *Punished by Rewards: The Trouble with Gold Stars Incentive Plans, A's, Praise and Other Bribes.* Boston, N.Y: Houghton Mifflin.

Krashen, S. (1981) *First Language Acquisition and Second Language Learning.* London: Pergamon.

Kumar, V. (1993) *Poverty and Inequality in the UK: The Effects on Children.* London: NCB Enterprises.

Laevers, F. (1994) *The Innovative Project: Experiential Education 1976-1995.* Research Centre for Early Childhood and Primary Education. Katholieke Universiteit, Leuven, Belgium.

Lally, N. (1991) *The Nursery Teacher in Action.* London: Paul Chapman Publishing.

Lane, Harlen (1977) *The Wild Boy of Aveyron.* London: Allen and Unwin.

Leat, D. (1977) *Towards a Definition of Volunteer Involvement.* Berkhamsted: The Volunteer Centre.

Lee, V. and Das Gupta, P. (1995) *Children's Cognitive and Language Development.* Oxford: Blackwell, Open University.

Liebschner, J. (1985) *Children Learning Through Each Other.* Early Childhood Development and Care, vol. 21, 1-3, p.121-135.

Liebschner, J. (1991) *Foundations of Progressive Education: The History of the National Froebel Society.* Butterworth Press, Cambridge.

Liebschner, J. (1992) *A Child's World: Freedom and Guidance in Froebel's Theory and Practice.* Cambridge: Butterworth Press.

Lindon, J. (1996) (Third ed.) *Working with Young Children.* London: Hodder & Stoughton.

Macauley, D. (1988) *The Way Things Work.* London: Dorling, Kindersley.

Mairs, K. and Staff and Pen Green (1995) *A Schema Booklet for Parents and Carers.* Pen Green, Corby, Northants.

Mansfield, M. (1997) *Working with Parents.* Pen Green Conference, February 1997.

Maslow, A. (1962) *Towards a Psychology of Being.* Princeton: Van Nostrand.

Matthews, J. (1994) *Helping Children to Draw and Paint in Early Childhood: Children and Visual Representation.* London: Hodder & Stoughton.

McKellar, P. (1957) *Imagination and Thinking.* London: Cohen and West.

Meade, A. with Cubey, P. (1995) *Thinking Children*. New Zealand Council for Educational Research, PO Box 3237, Wellington, New Zealand. (British Distributor Community Insight, Cheney Manor, Swindon).

Meek, M. (1985) 'Play and Paradoxes. Some Considerations for Imagination and Language. In Wells, G. and Nicholls, J. (eds.) *Language and Learning: An Interactional Perspective*. London: Falmer Press.

Miller, L. (1996) *Towards Reading: Literacy Development in the Pre-school Years*. Buckingham and Philadelphia: Open University Press.

Miller, L. (1997) *A Vision for the Early Years Curriculum in UK*. The International Journal of Early Childhood Education: OMEP, vol. 29, 1997, no. 1, p.34-42.

Minns, H. (1990) *Read it to me now*. London: Virago Education with the University of London Institute of Education.

Montessori, M. (1912) *The Montessori Method*. London: Heinemann.

Montessori, M. (1949) *The Absorbent Mind*. Adyar, Madras, India: Theosophical Publishing House.

Montessori, M. (1975) *The Child in the Family*. (trans. Nancy Rockmore Cirillo). London: Pan.

Moss, P. and Pence, A. (eds) (1994) *Valuing Quality in Early Childhood Services*. London: Paul Chapman Publishing.

Mouatt, K. (1997) 'In the Balance: Child Nutrition'. *Nursery World*, vol. 97, no. 3558, May 1997, p.14.

Moyles, J. (ed.) (1994) *The Excellence of Play*. Buckingham, Philadelphia: Open University.

Nash, J. N. 'Fertile Minds'. *Time*, 3 February 1997, p.35-42.

National Children's Homes (1990) *Children in Danger*. London: NCH.

The National Commission on Education. A Report (1993) *Learning to Succeed*. London: Heinemann.

National Heart Forum (1996) *Eat Your Words: Helping Children to Choose Food Wisely*.

Nelson, K. (1986) *Event Knowledge: Structure and Function in Development*. Hillsdale, N.J.: Lawrence Erlbaum Associates.

Newell, P. (1991) *The UN Convention and Children's Rights in the UK*. London: National Children's Bureau.

Newson, E. (1972) 'Towards an understanding of the parental role', in *The Parental Role*. (Papers from annual conference). London: National Children's Bureau.

New Zealand Ministry of Education. (1996) *Te Whaariki: Guidelines for Developmentally Appropriate Programmes in Early Childhood Services*. Wellington: Ministry of Education.

Nicholls, R. (ed.) (1986) *Rumpus Schema Extra*. Cleveland Teachers, Nursery Nurses and Parents. Based on lectures by Chris Athey.

Nielsen, L. (1992) *Space and Self: Active Learning by Means of the Little Room.* Sikon (available from RNIB).

Nutbrown, C. (1994) *Threads of Learning.* London: Paul Chapman Publishing.

Nutbrown, C. (ed.) (1996) *Respectful Educators- Capable Learners. Children's Rights and Early Education.* London: Paul Chapman Publishing.

Oates, J. (ed.) (1995) *The Foundations of Child Development.* Oxford: Open University Blackwell.

Ockleford, A. (1996) *All Join In: A Framework for Making Music with Children and Young People Who are Visually Impaired and have Learning Difficulties.* RNIB.

OFSTED Handbook: Guidance on the Inspection of Nursery and Primary Schools 1997. London: OFSTED/HMSO.

Open University, Community Education Pack. *Confident Parents, Confident Children.* 1997, Open University.

Orr, R. (1993) *Play Schemas: Play Materials.* Proceedings of the Conference in Potsdam: Equal and Exceptional. International Association for the Education of the Deaf/Blind. 1993, p.257–261. Published Oberlin Haus, P.O Box 900, 248, 14438 Germany.

Papert, S. (1980) *Mind Storms: Children, Computers and Powerful Ideas.* Brighton: Harvester Press.

Pascal, C. and Bertram, T. (eds.) (1997) *Effective Early Learning.* London: Hodder & Stoughton.

Pen Green Staff (1995) *A Schema Booklet for Parents and Carers.* Pen Green Centre for Under Fives and Their Families, Corby, Northamptonshire.

Penn, H. (1995) *Seminars on Early Years Issues.* Institute of Education, University of London.

Piaget, J. (1962) *Play, Dreams and Imitation in Childhood.* London: Routledge and Kegan Paul.

Piaget, J. (1968) *Six Psychological Studies.* London: University of London Press.

Piaget, J. and Inhelder, B. (1969) *The Psychology of the Child.* London: Routledge and Kegan Paul.

Pollard, A. (1997 third ed) *Reflective Teaching in the Primary School.* London: Cassell.

Pollard, A. with Filer, A. (1996) *The Social World of Chlildren's Learning: Case Studies of Pupils from Four to Seven.* London: Cassell.

Pugh, G. and De'Ath, E. (1984) *The Needs of Parents.* London: Macmillan.

Pugh, G. (ed.) (1996) (Second ed.) *Contemporary Issues in the Early Years: Working Collaboratively for the Children.* London: Paul Chapman Publishing.

Rice, S. (1996) *An Investigation of Schemas as a way of Supporting and Extending Young Children's Learning.* Unpublished M.ed. Thesis, University of West England.

Riley, J. (1996) *The Teaching of Reading: The Development of Literacy in the Early Years of School.* London: Paul Chapman Publishing.

RNIB (1995) *Play it My Way*. London: HMSO.

Roberts, R. (1995) *Self-esteem and Successful Early Learning*. London: Hodder & Stoughton.

Robson, S. and Smedley, S. (eds) (1996) *Education in Early Childhood: First Things First*. London: David Fulton in association with Roehampton Institute.

Rogoff, B., Mistry, J., Goncu, A. and Mosier, C. (1993) *Guided Participation in Cultural Activity by Toddlers and Care Givers*. Monographs of the Society for Research in Child Development, 58 (8, serial no. 236).

Rousseau, J.J. (1762; 1963) *Emile* (trans. Barbara Foxley). London: Dent.

Rubin, Z. (1983) 'The skills of friendship', in Donaldson, M., Grieve, R., and Pratt, C. (eds.) *Early Childhood Development and Education*. Oxford: Blackwell.

Rouse-Selleck, D. (1991) *Babies and Toddlers, Carers and Educators. Quality for the Under Threes*. London: National Children's Bureau.

Schaffer, H. (1996) *Social Development*. Blackwell: Oxford.

Sharp, A. (1986) *The Learning and Development of Three to Five Year Olds.: Schema*. City of Sheffield Education Department.

Siraj-Blachford, I. (1994) *The Early Years: Laying the Foundations for Racial Equality*. Stoke on Trent: Trentham Books.

Smilansky, S. (1968) *The Effects of Socio-dramatic Play on Disadvantaged Pre- school Children*. New York: John Wiley.

Smith, F. (1983) *Essays into Literacy*. London: Heinemann.

Somerset Education Services (Early Years) (1997) *Nursery Education Curriculum for Four Year Olds*.

Southwark Council: Education and Leisure Services Department (Early Years) (1996) *Record of Achievement: Children 3-5 Years Old*.

Steedman, C. (1986) 'The mother made conscious. The historical development of a primary school pedagogy'. *History Workshop Journal* 20.

Steiner, R. (1926) *The Essentials of Education*. London: Anthroposophical Publishing Co.

Steiner, R. (1965) *The Education of the Child*. London: Rudolf Steiner Press.

Strathern, P. (1996) *Kant 1724-1804 in 90 Minutes*. London: Constable.

Strathern, P. (1996) *Locke 1632-1704 in 90 Minutes*. London: Constable.

Strauss, M. (1978) *Understanding Children's Drawings*. London: Rudolf Steiner Press.

Sylva, K. (1994) *The Impact of Early Learning on Children's Later Development*. Appendix C. In Ball, C. (1994). Start Right. London: Royal Society of Arts. The Importance of Early Learning.

Taylor, D. (1983) *Family Literacy*. London: Heinemann.

Trevarthen, C. (1993). *Playing into Reality: Conversations with the Infant Communicator*. In *Winnicott Stories*, Spring, 7, pp.67-84.

Trevarthen, C. (1993) 'The function of emotions on early infant communication and development'. In Nadel, J. and Camaioni, L. (eds.). *New Perspectives in Early Communicative Development*. London: Routledge.

Trevarthen, C. (1996) November. Lecture for TACTYC Conference, Greenwich.

Trevarthen, C. *Brain Development*. In Gregory, R..L (ed) (1987). The Oxford Companion to the Mind. Oxford, N.Y: Oxford University Press, p.101-110.

Tumin, S. (July, 1994) *Inspecting Prisons*. One of a series of lectures by distinguished speakers sponsored by The Sunday Times Newspaper at the Royal Geographical Society, Kensington, London.

Turiel, E. and Weston, D. (1983) 'Act-rule relation: Children's concepts of social rules', in Donaldson, M., Grieve, R. and Pratt, C. (eds.) *Early Childhood Development and Care*. Oxford: Blackwell.

Vygotsky, L. (1978) *Mind in Society*. Cambridge, M.A: Harvard University Press.

Weinberger, J. (1996) *Literacy Goes to School: The Parents' Role in Young Children's Literacy Learning*. London: Paul Chapman Publishing.

Wells, G. (1987) *The Meaning Makers*. London: Hodder & Stoughton.

Westminster (City of) (1993) *Great Expectations: A Curriculum for the Under Fives*.

Whalley, E. 'Patterns in Play' The use of schemas theory by teachers and parents'. In *Primary Life* 3, 2, Autumn 1994, published for the National Primary Centre by Oxford: Blackwell.

Whalley, M. (1994) *Learning to be Strong: Integrating Education and Care in Early Childhood*. London: Hodder & Stoughton.

Whalley, M. (1996) *Parents Commitment to their Child's Learning*. Paper presented at the EECERA 6th European Conference. Lisbon September 1996.

Whalley, M.(cd) and the Pen Green Centre Team (1997) *Working with Parents* London: Hodder & Stoughton.

Whalley, M. (1997) See Open University Confident Parents Pack.

Whalley, M. (1997) *Parents Involvement in Their Children's Learning: Integrating Schemas into Quality Practice*. Pen Green Conference, Saturday 12th April 1997.

Whalley, M. and Arnold, C. (1997, Autumn). *Parents and Staff Working Together. Teacher Practitioner Research Project*. Teaching Training Agency (TTA)

Whitehead, M. (1996) *The Development of Language and Literacy in the Early Years*. London: Hodder & Stoughton.

Whiting, B. and Edwards, C.P. (1992) *Children in Different Worlds: The Formation of Social Behaviour*. Cambridge M.A: Harvard University Press.

Wilkinson, R. (1980) *Questions and Answers on Rudolf Steiner Education*. East Grinstead: Henry Goulden.

Wilkinson, R.G. (1994) *Unfair Shares*. London: Barnados Publishing.

Winnicott, D.W. (1974) *Playing and Reality*. Harmondsworth: Penguin

Wood, E. and Attfield, J. (1990) *Play, Learning and the Early Childhood Curriculum*. London: Paul Chapman Publishing.

Wylie, C. (1994) *What Research on Early Childhood Education/Care Outcomes Can and Can't Tell Policy Makers*. New Zealand Council for Educational Research.

Young, S. (1989) *The Mini Explorers of Middle Earth*. New Scientist 1989, p.38–41.

INDEX